MAKING IT ON
BROKEN PROMISES

MAKING IT ON BROKEN PROMISES

Leading African American Male Scholars
Confront the Culture of Higher Education

Edited by *Lee Jones*

FOREWORD BY
Cornel West

STERLING, VIRGINIA

Stylus Publishing, LLC
22883 Quicksilver Drive
Sterling, Virginia 20166

Library of Congress Cataloging-in-Publication Data

Making it on broken promises: African American male scholars confront the culture of higher education / edited by Lee Jones; with a foreword by Cornel West.—1st ed.
   p. cm.
Includes bibliographical references and index.
  ISBN 1-57922-050-9 (hard: alk. paper)
1. African American men—Education (Higher) 2. African American men—Social conditions. 3. African American college students.
4. College integration—United States. I. Jones, Lee, 1965–
  LC2781 .M15 2002
  378.1'982996'073—dc21   2002001126

Printed in the United States of America

All first editions printed on acid free paper

First edition, 2002
10 9 8 7 6 5 4 3 2 1

*First giving full honor to God, who serves as my
strength and help . . . This book is dedicated to
the millions of African people who died so that
we might have a seat at the table to ensure that
we will fully participate in our social, political,
economic, moral, and educational pursuits.
I dedicate this book to my dad and mom, the
late Levi and Carrie Jones, without whom
I would not be the person I am and will become.
Every positive step I take is guided by their
wisdom and unyielding sacrifices they made
on my behalf. I can only pray that every step
I take is ordered by God!*

CONTENTS

Cornel West

Dr. Cornel West was born in Tulsa, Oklahoma, a place once envisioned as a homeland for Native Americans displaced by European colonization, and for African Americans acting on the idea of freedom promised by emancipation.

West thrived at Harvard, consuming the work of the black intellectual tradition, including that of W.E.B. DuBois and St. Claire Drake, as well as European philosophers such as Max Weber, Karl Marx, and Friedrich Nietzsche. At the core of West's developing self as a scholar lay the belief in integrating a religious faith with both a political engagement and an intellectually rigorous course of study. "For me there was always a vital spiritual dimension to politics," West has explained. "Issues of death, disease, and despair have always been the fundamental issues of being human, and you didn't get too much talk about these issues in political circles."

After three years at Harvard, West graduated magna cum laude in 1973 and chose to pursue graduate studies in philosophy at Princeton. In 1977 he began teaching at Union Theological Seminary in New York. His doctoral dissertation, completed in 1980, was later revised and republished as the *Ethical Dimensions of Marxist Thought* (1991).

Other universities were also eager to have West join their faculty. When Henry Louis Gates Jr. took leadership of Harvard University's Department of Afro-American Studies in 1991, he immediately began to strategize how to lure to Harvard the man he called "the preeminent African American intellectual of our generation." Excited by the possibilities of a group of scholars working across disciplines in the field of African American studies, West joined Harvard in 1993. In 1998 he was appointed to a prestigious university professorship at Harvard, becoming the first Alphonse Fletcher Jr. University Professor.

West's scholarly writing pursues philosophical inquiry into the realm of the political, exploring the existential dimension within the moral, spiritual, and political space. A mesmerizing speaker, West draws upon an African American tradition of rhetoric and improvisational public speaking. He has collected some of his many talks and essays in a four-volume work *Beyond Eurocentrism and Multiculturalism* (1993). After publishing several books and articles addressed primarily to an academic audience, West turned to a broader readership with *Race Matters* (1993). His most well known work, *Race Matters* reads like a sermon and unflinchingly confronts one of the most sensitive issues at the heart of American society: race. Yet West does not offer a specific program in this book.

FOREWORD

Cornel West

The history of the Academy in America—much like that of the professions of golf and tennis—is part of the larger story of White supremacy in the "enlightened" transatlantic societies and cultures. The gallant efforts of talented Black men to gain access to the American Academy are inseparable from the larger story of the struggle for Black freedom here and abroad. This precious book— the brainchild of the visionary Professor Lee Jones—provides an occasion to examine the complex conjuncture between the White supremacist realities of the American Academy and the often threatening presence of brilliant Black men in the Academy. This challenging book also should serve as an inspiration for a new generation of Black men deeply devoted to the life of the mind in or outside of the Academy.

The plights and predicaments of Black men in the American Academy are multifarious. On the one hand, their very presence reveals the racist stereotype of Black male persons far removed from or less capable of intellectual work to be a blatant lie. On the other hand, their very presence often constitutes a threat to those colleagues still (more or less) captive to the spell of this lie. Therefore "success" in the Academy for Black men is not simply a relative affair—it also is a fragile and contingent matter. To be a Black man in America is to be at risk; to be a Black man in the American Academy is to be subject to unexpected (and usually unwarranted) disrespect. Hence, highly "successful" Black men in the Academy who refuse to be mere displays of the American dream readily admit to the dis-ease they create among some of their colleagues. And, so-called less "successful" Black men in the American Academy often see through the relative arbitrariness of their colleagues' "success."

In short, any perspective of the Academy—including those that highlight Black men's presence—from the vantage point of "success" makes a mockery of serious intellectual life and constitutes an insult to the struggle for Black freedom.

Genuine intellectual work flows from a profound vocation that takes the form of intense discipline, high energy, and a loving cultivation of talent. This work and vocation may possibly take place inside the Academy, but the Academy has no monopoly on them. In fact the worst of academic professionalism can be foes against this work and vocation, just as the best of the Academy can enhance and enrich one's genuine intellectual work and vocation. In this sense, "success" in the Academy may have little to do with engaging in one's serious work or authentic vocation. Similarly, intellectual contributions to the struggle for Black freedom rarely constitute a crucial part of the criteria for "success" in the American Academy. As with giants like W.E.B. Du Bois and C.L.R. James or geniuses such as James Baldwin and Lorraine Hansberry, to use such "success" as a measure of Black intellectual greatness is an insult to such people and their (our) cause. Yet this same "success" can be a weapon in this cause if we do our work well and remain true to our vocation.

We need a new generation of Black men who have a deep love of learning and are on fire for justice. Only by downplaying our wounded egos and overcoming our narrow quests for professional status can we truly become bold and free Black men of self-confidence and self-respect who do not ask for permission from anyone to pursue our projects, yet do solicit criticism from others to ensure the high quality of our work. The key is to preserve our integrity and sustain our solidarity—in the name of the elders who came before and the unborn who will come after us.

PREFACE

Lee Jones

As I reflect on what caused me to develop a passion to dedicate my life to higher education, I am reminded of the countless people—seen and unseen, heard and unheard—who have impacted my life. As I tell my students of all races, you should be very careful in selecting your careers because there will be times when you will question your sanity with regards to why you chose your professions. I also tell them that you should never work in an environment if you do not feel good about getting out of bed and coming to work. This is a creed that I decided to live by twenty years ago. One of the things that I did not understand when I decided to live by this creed was that the Academy is a plethora of contradictions. On the one hand "it" espouses to be one of the most liberal and democratic organizational enterprises that exist. On the other hand it has never been challenged to the point of looking at its practices and seeing the constant injustices African Americans and other underrepresented groups have to face.

This book, *Making It on Broken Promises: Leading African American Male Scholars Confront the Culture of Higher Education,* attempts to address some of the foundational and root causes of the injustices we face in the Academy. I am positive that there will be some in the Academy who will, just from the very title of this book, reject the opportunity to think critically about what is postulated in this book. This blatant disregard for critically dealing with inequality in the Academy is at the base of why this book was developed by senior African American male scholars in the Academy. Further, the public debate that many of us have followed in the media surrounding our elder, mentor, scholar, and statesman, Dr. Cornel West, gives us reason to pause and reflect upon just how far we have not come in the Academy. Whether one agrees with the ideology of Cornel West or not, the mere fact that he has been challenged by the establishment to not only examine how he spends his time, but also to acquiesce to the status quo is mind boggling and extremely discouraging. It is mind boggling because Cornel West represents the true essence of a scholar in that his research and what he postulates is sound and truly represents opportunity for critical dialogue for "scholars" in the myriad of fields his work crosses. Additionally, his work has consistently been well regarded and has been critically analyzed by some of the greatest minds in higher education. The Cornel West debate as I respectfully call it, is very discouraging because if West's work can be attacked by those who refuse to not only see their own arrogance, but who refuse to open their lens to broaden our definition of scholarship, it leaves little hope for developing scholars like myself to find a place in this monolithic culture of higher education.

As I travel this country, I am often asked by many African American and Latino students, why should I choose to pursue a terminal degree and teach at the collegiate level when one is not free to teach and produce scholarship that reflect one's own experiences. While I have very few answers to this question, my response is always fraught with hope that one day our persistent efforts to transform higher education into a "true" community of scholars will be realized! I would be remiss if I did not acknowledge the diligence and hard work of scholars, both Black and White, who have gotten us to this point. I really believe that we have made significant progress in opening the doors to higher education. Institutions like my own, Florida State University, and others have been on the forefront of transforming higher education. I hasten to say, however, that we have come far but yet have far to go. It would be nice to work in a profession like higher education where one's day is consumed only with activities like teaching, research, and service like our White counterparts. The truth of the matter is that regardless of whether African Americans choose to ignore the challenges, or roll up their sleeves and actively participate in helping to change the culture, we have—and from the looks of it, will have to continue— to serve multiple roles, including that of serving as a mentor for many African American students and an "experiential" group for many White students who, through their own isolation, have never been taught by an African American professor. So, not only are African Americans asked to participate in an academic setting whose ethos we have not assisted in developing, but we are also asked to be the constant experts on African American issues. This plethora of contradiction first manifests itself when one is told subtly and blatantly that one's research interests (passion) are slanted toward "minority issues," and therefore do not fit this predetermined narrow view of "authentic" scholarship. Not only is one forced to re-evaluate a research agenda, but one is also forced to deal with philosophical, spiritual, and psychological internal debates. The issues that confront African American men in the Academy are not unlike issues that women and many underrepresented groups confront. What makes African American male issues more pronounced are the very low numbers of Black male Ph.D.s and what Dr. Na'im Akbar, a noted international scholar, calls the "stimulus value" placed upon us.

Making it on broken promises is not a new phenomenon. Throughout our storied past, Black men have always carried the heaviest torch, stepped over the most hurdles, climbed the highest mountains, and overcome the insurmountable barriers that have been placed before and upon us.

Content

Making It on Broken Promises is yet another response to the consistent and persistent conditions that many African Americans and other underrepresented groups find themselves addressing everyday. The significance of this books is that its contributors are some of the most thought-provoking, enlightening, brilliant scholars in higher education, and, particularly, in the African American community. The book intentionally focuses on African American men in the Academy. The African American male focus is extremely relevant in light of the diminishing numbers of African American men achieving graduate degrees. I chose specific scholars in the Academy to contribute to this book because in many ways they represent the highest level of thinking in their perspective fields. It should be obvious to any informed reader that the contributors to this book represent only a small number of brilliant African American male scholars in our society. By no means do we suggest that the scholars who were chosen to participate in this book make up the voice of the African American community. In fact, the beauty of the African American community is that we are not monolithic.

Cornel West, current Harvard Professor of Religion, writes the foreword. He speaks to the historic struggles that African American men have faced in education as well as in society. His foreword gives you a quick dose of reality. While I in no way view myself as a seasoned scholar, Chapter 1 provides a broad overview of many issues African American males face as they attempt to find their place in society. The goal of this chapter is to set the tone for the book by outlining some of the conditions and dilemmas that have caused a persistent perpetuation of Black male "genocide" in America.

Bill Harvey's Chapter 2 provides us with the sobering reality of some staggering statistics that cause us to wonder why, after over 400 years on the shores of America, African Americans continue to be underrepresented in almost every field of human endeavor. While some may see this as a gross overstatement, when the data speak there is no rest for the weary. Perhaps one of the most dominating forces that African American men in the Academy face is the social, moral, educational, political, and economic impact of blatant and subtle isolation. Internationally known psychologist Na'im Akbar takes us on a journey of self-exploration. He talks critically about the I.I.L.s of the Academy—Identity, Ideology, and Legitimacy. He asks the question, "Who am I?" While this may appear to be a quick answer for many in the Academy, the dominant ideology that tends to assume and consume many African American male scholars is examined and explored in this chapter.

Asa Hilliard's chapter, "One By One, or One: Africans and the Academy," provides a thorough account of some of the modern day issues that affect African American men in the Academy. He speaks eloquently of the two periods to keep in mind as one attempts to comprehend the African American experience: (1) pre-colonial and (2) pre-slavery. In Chapter 5, Cyrus Ellis, an emerging scholar in the field of Counselor Education, outlines the hidden dangers African American men must avoid in higher education. He suggests that African American men confront and consistently deal with a plethora of conflicting external and internal forces. These forces are both destructive and pervasive.

Charles Rankin, who has been at the "grass roots" of the African American struggle since his career began, helps us in his chapter to understand the culture and ask the question, "Is There Room for African American Male Ph.D.s?" He speaks succinctly to the quasi evolution of culture in the Academy that underlies this important question.

We were extremely fortunate to provide our readers with an exclusive interview with Dr. Joseph White, renowned psychologist and professor emeritus at the University of California at Irvine. Dr. White's interview is thought-provoking and animated. He addresses the issues of racism in education, racial identity development, and the role of the Black professorate.

Ideologically shaped by the militant racial politics of the 50s and 60s, Dr. Bill Watkin's chapter speaks fluently to the socialization process of the Academy. He views higher education as a hallowed training ground for the intellectual elite based on an individualistic and theological ideology rooted in the Protestant Reformation. He helps us all to understand the socialization process for African American men in the Academy.

Perhaps one of the least talked about areas in post-secondary education is the important role of Community Colleges in increasing the numbers of African American men through the pipeline to the Ph.D. ranks. Dr. Irving McPhail, one of the most brilliant and outspoken community college presidents in America takes us on a journey to better understand the culture, style, and cognition of African American learners in community colleges. This chapter is extremely significant to the mission of this book because higher education espouses and re-enforces a theoretical frame of "one size fits all." Dr. McPhail challenges and confronts the culture of the Academy by presenting research, theory, and practice that indicate different cultures have different cognitive styles, ways of processing information, knowledge, and experience. He further expands the notion that those culturally diverse students become successful learners when these differences are taken into account in the classroom. A powerful and a must read chapter!

Nathan McCall took time from his peripatetic schedule to provide an exclusive straight talk interview about his views on the role of the Black college in educating African American males. His candid thoughts about America's most precious enterprise give us great insights.

Respectfully known as the father of Afrocentricity, Dr. Molefi Asante's chapter, "Afrocentricity and the African American Male in College," is a scholarly piece of work which goes to the core of our conversation in higher education. He first defines Afrocentricity as "African centered ideology that centers African people within a historical context, but also allows us to be agents within our own sphere." He further speaks to the critical importance for African American men on college campuses of learning the story of how "our" barbaric treatment began; of how the African's dignity was stolen; how cultures were destroyed; and how death swam next to the ships on the dreaded middle passage.

Clarence "Skip" Ellis, the first African American man to receive a Ph.D. in computer science provides a reflective chapter on "Affective Computing: The Reverse Digital Divide." He offers his personal history and observations as a Black computer scientist.

Known as a prolific orator and scholar, Dr. Frank Hale Jr. reminds us of the ways and means of expanding opportunities for access and success in higher education. There are many reasons why Dr. Hale's insights are useful and tangible results for the Academy. He recounts how he led Ohio State University's Diversity Initiatives by developing the Graduate and Professional School Visitation Day where over 80% of all minority graduate students who went through this program received a terminal degree. He offers important insights for any policy maker whose goal is to increase the number of underrepresented Ph.D.s.

Dr. Wade Nobles helps to balance the significance of this book with his chapter, "From Na Ezaleli to the Jegnoch: The Force of the African Family for Black Men in Higher Education." He ties many of the chapters together as he explains the key crises and challenges in African American cultural actualization. He talks about the need to rebuild the Black family structure and the elder brothers' duty to consciously claim the responsibility for seeing the world and ourselves as African people.

Finally, Dr. Charlie Nelms, two time university president and esteemed researcher and administrator, concludes the book with his chapter, "The Prerequisites for Academic Leadership." This chapter highlights and provides sound guidance in preparing African Americans to not only strive for scholarship, but simultaneously to prepare for academic administrative positions. He suggests several prerequisites for succeeding as an academic leader in higher education.

After reading this book, many will agree that this book leaves no stone unturned as we "Make It On Broken Promises" while we "Confront the Culture of Higher Education." So, make yourself comfortable and join us in transforming the academic culture to become a more equitable and ideologically diverse place to exist.

Acknowledgments

We in the academy do not become researchers, teachers, service providers, and facilitators of knowledge alone. Thinking about who to acknowledge is always an easy task! There are so many people to thank for the development of this book. First, honor is bestowed upon God who gave me the energy to bring these outstanding scholars together and to edit and coordinate this book. I pay humble homage to my mother and father, the late Carrie and Levi Jones. They have always taught me to dream the impossible dream and to never give up, no matter how daunting the task. My siblings have always been there in ways they will never know. I appreciate their patience with my hectic travel schedule. To my future wife, wherever she is in the world. Please know that reading through and editing the chapters of this book have helped me to become a better man for you! This book simply would not be possible without the humble spirits and scholarly contributions of those who submitted chapters. People all across this country have asked, "How did you get 15 of the brightest minds together in one book?" My response is simple, (1) God's divine order and (2) elders who are seriously committed to the cause. Mere words cannot begin to express full appreciation to: Na'im Akbar, Cornel West, William Harvey, Asa Hilliard, Cyrus Ellis, Charles Rankin, Joseph White, William Watkins, Irving McPhail, Nathan McCall, Molefi Asante, Clarence "Skip" Ellis, Frank Hale Jr., Wade Nobles, and Charlie Nelms. Asante Sana (Thank You)! I send a special "shout out" to two of my graduate students, Tony Anderson and Kamau Siwatu, both of whom had a once-in-a-lifetime opportunity to interview Nathan McCall and Joseph White, respectfully.

To my excellent staff, without whom I could not have completed this monumental task. Thank you for your competence and allowing me to macro-manage/lead you. To Marsha Strickland, my administrative assistant, I am sure she had no idea what she got herself into as she took on the task of keeping me administratively focused. Thank you for the wonderful conversation and your efficient work ethic! To the entire membership of the Brothers of the Academy (BOTA), you have reaffirmed my belief in African people coming together to accomplish a common agenda. The BOTA leadership team is by far the most impressive group of scholars and professionals I have ever worked with. To the Sisters of the Academy. Wow! You are such a joy and an inspiration to work with. All of you will play a major role in holding the Academy to the values they (we) espouse. To my boss, Dean Richard Kunkel, for he has brought true meaning to the word teamwork. I honor and very much appreciate our working relationship and look forward to enjoying many more years of mentoring from you. To Marvelena Hughes, President of California State University at Stanualis, Betty Sigel, President of Kennesaw State University, Lou Castenel, Dean of Education at the University of Georgia, and Dr. Jack Miller, Chancellor of the University of Wisconsin, thank you for taking time from your busy schedules to talk with me and for your belief in me and this project. I will be forever grateful to you. To Dr. James Scott King, Chair of the Department of English at Delaware State University, thank you for the many long telephone conversations and for keeping my feet on the ground and head to the sky as I live my passion. Neither time nor space will allow me to list the hundreds of my students who constantly reinforce the reasons I chose higher education as a profession. Suffice it to say that you know who you are and I thank all of you around the country.

Finally, What can I say to John and Robin von Knorring, owners of Stylus Publishing Company? Rarely do I use the word *friendship* loosely. Over the last three years they have not only been true soldiers in our quest to bring a balanced voice(s) to the Academy, but they have been true friends to me personally! I am honored and humbled to work with them both! I look for many more books in the future!

Get ready! Get ready! Get ready for *Making It on Broken Promises: Leading African American Male Scholars Confront the Culture of Higher Education!*

Lee Jones

Dr. Lee Jones currently serves as the associate dean for academic affairs and instruction in the College of Education and associate professor in Educational Leadership at Florida State University. He is a member of the dean's administrative team. Dr. Jones is responsible for coordinating many functions within the College of Education, including the offices of Clinical Education, Academic Services, and Student Access, Recruitment, and Retention. In addition to all his academic and administrative responsibilities, Dr. Jones produces and hosts a television talk show that reaches over 1 million viewers throughout the state of Florida and parts of southern Alabama and Georgia.

Dr. Jones has received over 175 awards and citations including the Alumnus of the year award from Delaware State University, and the Graduate School Leadership award from Ohio State University. He holds a bachelor of arts degree from Delaware State University, in Drama, Speech, Communication, and Theater. He has a master of arts degree in Higher Education Administration, a master of arts degree in Business and Administration, and a Ph.D. in Organizational Development from Ohio State University. Dr. Jones completed his high school education in Newark, New Jersey's Barringer High School, which is the third oldest high school in the country.

Known as a prolific orator, Dr. Jones has been in great demand as a speaker throughout the country. He has also been invited to speak in England, Canada, and Puerto Rico. His speeches have received rave reviews and he is consistently requested to appear for repeat engagements. He is a member of Kappa Alpha Psi Fraternity Inc., National Association for Equal Opportunity, American Association for the Study of Higher Education, American Association for Higher Education, Academy of Human Resource Development, Association for Quality Control, member of the Board of Trustees at Keystone College, and a host of other civic and professional organizations. His motto is "The bottom line is results and anything else is rhetoric."

I

A MESSAGE
FROM OUR ELDERS

Lee Jones

America's Black males may be the forgotten people of modern times. Since the arrival of Black males on the shores of America, sociologists, economists, and social scientists have been documenting the critical situation of Black males in America (First World Magazine, 1990). African American males have historically been at risk since being brought as human chattel to what is now the United States. They were at risk from the time of their recorded presence in 1619, and, unfortunately, are still in a vulnerable state over 350 years later. What is made clear by all of the statements from Ward, Wilson, Glasgow, and Hill (1990) is that young black men who are poor, who are not educated, and who are without skills, are finding themselves either in jail or involved in crime to a significant extent. And more than that, they, along with others in this group, are becoming more and more isolated from the general society. As a result there has been no concentrated body of knowledge on the status of the African American male, especially males who matriculate through college. Hilliard, Asante, Ben et al. (1997) have documented the conditions that led to this so-called "at risk" label. Most of the early research was directed toward trying to question or validate stereotypical personality characteristics assigned to Black men (Parham & McDavis, 1987; Green, 1977). Inquiries did not support the premise that the Black male is "endangered," "disadvantaged," or "forgotten." These studies have made the case that the larger society has seemed insensitive to the interest of the Black male and have shown little willingness to promote his welfare (Parham & McDavis, 1987; Green, 1977).

Addressing the problem facing America as it relates to the plight of Black males, former Howard University President Franklyn G. Jenifer states, "So many African American males today find themselves caught between the proverbial rock and hard place. They are caught between the rock of educational attainment and the hard place of job qualification." This proverbial hard place has forged a distressing plight for young Black males in America and has also had an indelible impact on our ability to attract, retain, and ultimately graduate large numbers of African American males from terminal degree programs. Its circumstances have pushed Black males into a negative social context predicting impending doom. The result of this negative trend is reflected in various aspects of the lives of Black males. These aspects are reflected in prison statistics, homicide rates, suicide rates, and educational consequences.

For example more than 30 percent of all Black men in the United States between the ages of twenty and twenty-nine are either in prison, on parole or on probation, many for drug offenses (Edelman, 1995). Other statistics quoted by Edelman indicate that, according to the most recent data available from the Sentencing Project, there are 306,319 Black men in prison, 351,368 on probation, and 130,005 on parole. The percentage of Black men aged twenty to twenty-nine years old in jail or prison or on probation or parole has grown by almost half since 1989 (The Sentencing Project, 1990).

Statistics coming from the states on this issue are also alarming. For example figures from the Florida State Board of Community Colleges indicate that Black males represent 6 percent of the United States population, only 3 percent of college enrollment, and 47 percent of America's prisoners. A Black male in the United States is seven times more likely to end up in prison than a Black male in South Africa; overwhelming facts and statistics such as these have caused and are causing grave concern among politicians, community leaders, and educators (Miller, 1992). A second factor reflecting the negative context is the homicide rate among Black males. Homicide is the leading cause of death for Black males between the ages of fifteen and twenty-four (Jenifer, 1992). More young Black males died from homicide in one year (1977) than died in ten years in the Vietnam War. Black men are six times as likely as White men to be murder victims. Murder is the fourth leading cause of death among Black males from ages twenty to twenty-nine.

Another alarming fact regarding Black males is the growing number of suicides. Wilson (1990) indicates that the trend is for young Blacks to grow old in some aspects of life while still young chronologically. Wilson (1990) states, "Black men kill themselves when their futures are ahead of them and White men kill themselves when their futures are behind them." (Wilson,

1990). Suicide, when combined with other dire consequences impacting young Black males, continues to make the plight of Black males even more overwhelming.

It has become quite apparent that educational deficits are at the root of observed social consequences (Richardson and Evans, 1992). Black underachievement constitutes a crisis of legitimization because it throws into question the credibility of the educational system and the professional competence of educators and policy makers (Kincheloe and Steinberg, 1992). Teachers and educators are being bombarded with new and contradictory demands. They are being asked to generate an ethos of harmony and equality at the same time that they are having to respond to increasing governmental pressure to foster competitive individualism and "excellence" in schools. In many ways, federal policies of cutting back on financial support for the higher education of low-income students within the past decade have sent out a message that has been highly destructive for the education of minorities. In a period when rewards and resources are becoming scarce, the gap between winners and losers is widening. Black youth have fallen victim to a system that says: "You are not a priority . . . you do not really matter" (Wright, 1992 p. 15).

This pattern of severe Black disadvantage is also reflected in the statistical information now available on racial inequality in schooling in the United States. Hann, Danzberger, and Lefkowitz (1987), the authors of *Dropouts in America,* contend that in 1996 40 percent of Hispanic and 26 percent of Black students had dropped out of school compared with 13 percent of White high school youth. Today there are fewer black high school graduates entering colleges than there were in 1976. In the decades since 1976 the proportion of Black high school graduates who go to college has declined from 33.5 percent to 26.1 percent. And of those Black students who make it to college, only 42 percent of them continue through to graduation (Sadarkasa, 1988). The statistic of those who actually go on to receive terminal degrees is even more frightening.

Teacher Expectations of Black Males

Numerous studies have shown that a student's academic performance often parallels teacher expectations. When teachers encourage students, students learn, and when teachers don't think students can learn, they don't (Kunjufu, 1990). Often teachers make judgments on very mundane criteria, such as family background, the way a child dresses, or, unfortunately, skin color. The impact of these expectations is manifested in poor academic performance, which often yields placement in special education classes. Unfortunately, African American males are found to be there more than twice as often as non-Black males (Hood, 1994 p. 29).

Kunjufu (1990) states that many of the classrooms today are battle zones between students and teachers. These battles are, more often than not, fought between male students and teachers. Interestingly enough, though macho behavior is considered a preferential characteristic among males in America, when such behavior is expressed by Black male youth they are labeled delinquent or deviant and are subject to severe discipline. If a classroom teacher's expectations of such behavior in young Black males are validated, their own worst fears have then been realized. Their only resort, in many instances, seems to be such extreme forms of discipline as suspension or expulsion (Wright, 1991). According to Dent (1989), African American males are twice as likely to receive corporal punishment and to be suspended as their White counterparts. Data collected shows African American males' perception of their high rate of punishment is that they have no place in the academic world.

Kunjufu (1983) states that what happens to boys in school by the age of nine to thirteen will determine whether they go to college or jail and how much income they will earn in years to come. Garibaldi (1991) surveyed teachers in the New Orleans Public Schools and found that sixty percent of the teachers polled did not expect their Black male students to go to college. Sixty percent of the respondents were elementary teachers, 70 percent had ten or more years of teaching experience, and 65 percent of the teachers were Black.

From their many studies at the Institutes for Independent Education, Ratteray, et al. (1989) found that African American students do not need to be surrounded by White students and high-income families in order to experience academic success. In a survey of several magnet schools where the enrollment was predominately African American with large numbers from low-income families, it was found that high expectations on the part of the teachers—that is, believing that the students' were capable of high achievement—played a pivotal role in the student' success (Green, 1990; McKenzie, 1991).

Cultural Discontinuity

James P. Comer (1988), Professor of Child Psychiatry at Yale University, dismissed what he believes are uninformed and unfair comparisons between the historical experiences of Blacks and that of White and Asian immigrants. "Immigrant communities, although they had hardships, also had cultural continuity," he explained. "They often came from the same place in the old country and so were able to adjust, assimilate, and become part of the mainstream" (pp. 265–267).

This cultural continuity strengthened the social cohesion among the immigrants, Comer noted, and along with the vote helped them to secure political, economic, and social power—all within a generation. Indeed, opportunities in the society triggered a kind of push/pull process. That is, mainstream opportunities pulled on families to function well and train their children to take advantage of the opportunities. This, in turn, created a push within the families for development and good functioning.

This cultural discontinuity, on the other hand, devastated the lives of Blacks wrenched from West Africa's protective and direction-giving governmental and political institutions (McAdoo, 1988).

Many believe, and it is perpetuated by those in the educational system, that African Americans have inherited no culture of their own, primarily because it did not take the same form as the written history of European Americans (Ratteray, 1989). In some instances, such as during "Black History Month," educators try to provide some type of cultural diversity in the schools; however, the cultures of Asian, African, Hispanic, and Native Americans are seldom treated equally in the curriculum, on the classroom walls, or in the hallways (Locust, 1990, p 6).

For example in Twinsburg, Ohio, during Black History Month, the school board decided not to recognize the observance, but replaced it with "Multi Cultural Awareness Month." The principal activity for the school district's Multicultural Month was simply the offering of different kinds of food. This illustration is quite typical of the kind of attention given to social and cultural diversity, whereby these central issues are treated as add-on to social studies or history lessons or as peripheral cultural events. This sends a message to a child that people of color have not contributed anything of meaning, that their contributions are not worthy of "real learning," and that "real knowledge" is largely the domain and legacy of Euro Americans (Locust, 1990, p. 6; Nichols, 1991).

Institutional Life Conditions
Corporal Punishment
A sense of dignity is essential in building self-esteem and self-respect. Corporal punishment is dehumanizing, humiliating, and damages personal worth. One of the most logical reasons against its use is that it is inflicted more often on Black pupils, in particular Black males (Radin, 1988).

The National Association for the Advancement of Colored People (NAACP) is but one of many national organizations that has opposed corporal punishment on the grounds that it is racially biased and counterproductive to building positive self-concept (PTAVE, 1990).

Corporal punishment is an old and deep-rooted method of discipline in American public schools. This practice is administered disproportionately upon minority school children, especially upon young Black male students from impoverished homes. Its use is discriminatory; race, sex, age, and socio-economic status, rather than the student's misbehavior, generally determine the degree of its administration. Young African American males are twice as likely to be paddled and suspended than their Caucasian peers are (Radin, 1988). These forms of punishment convey negative and dangerous messages to many Black boys: that they are inferior and cannot excel in academic endeavors. Their self-concept is in danger of being destroyed, and an attitude of learned helplessness often creates learning problems and eventual withdrawal from education. Most children start school eager to learn, but negative experiences replace that eagerness with opposition and defiant behaviors. By the fourth grade or by nine years of age these students are potential "drop-outs" (Harry and Anderson, 1994, p. 603).

Suspensions

African American males face multidimensional problems in school (Agada, 1994). In Detroit, to cite a representative example, studies regarding school discipline and African American youngsters showed that although Black and White students are tardy for class at practically the same rate, African American students are disproportionately referred to the principal's office for punishment (Dent, 1989). These results are replicate of the findings of the analyses of many academic records of Black males in the elementary school systems (Dent, 1989).

All over the nation, one of the key factors to this problem is the lack of uniform discipline procedures, combined with liberal suspension policies that leave teachers with too much discretionary authority in the administration of discipline. Further African American males are disproportionately the victims of corporal punishment and suspension. For example in a study conducted in Milwaukee African American males account for 50 percent of all suspensions, even though they make up 27 percent of the school system's population. (Whitaker, 1991; Dent, 1989; Kunjufu, 1986).

Poor Achievement

In a study of Black males in the New Orleans Public Schools there was a disproportionate number represented in almost all categories of academic failure. While Black males represented 43 percent of the New Orleans' public school population in 1986–87, they accounted for 58 percent of the non-promotions, 65 percent of the suspensions, 80 percent of the expulsions, and 45 percent of the dropouts (Garibaldi, 1989). In addition African American males and other non-Asian minorities are being placed in special education classes more often than members of majority groups are. They are disproportionately misclassified and placed in classes for the mentally retarded or are tracked into slow learning classes with the possibility of never being main-streamed (Harry and Anderson, 1994). Yet all the while, children from majority groups are being placed in academic areas such as advanced science and math course that prepare them for college placement in competitive institutions (Kunjufu, 1986, Dent, 1989).

With regard to academic achievement, numerous studies have shown that the African American male achieves at significantly lower levels than other groups. For example in Milwaukee 80 percent of the city's Black male earn less than "C" average in high school (Collision, 1991; Whitaker, 1991).

Staff members at Benjamin Tasker Middle School in Bowie, Maryland were surveyed regarding the achievement level of the school's seventh and eighth grade African American males. Results indicated that the majority of African American males at Benjamin Tasker lagged behind other male students in the areas of math, English, and reading. Although they attended classes, many did not participate in class activities, complete assignments, or take part in tutorial programs because of feelings of hopelessness, previous failures, and low self-confidence.

The majority of the teachers surveyed believed African American males would not excel because they had no interest in school, no goals, and no opportunity to break though barriers (Hood, 1994, p. 29).

The traditional educational model in which the teacher lectures and the children respond seems to be extremely inefficient in working with Black male children. Boys are generally more active than girls. These behaviors, coupled with an academic curriculum that is often seen as totally irrelevant to their daily lives, may well be the explanation behind the high dropout rates experienced by Black males today (Hare and Hare, 1991).

J. P. Comer and his colleagues at Yale University's Child Study Center conducted a study at two inner-city schools in New Haven, Connecticut in 1968. They worked with teachers and administrators to foster their ideas about learning. Teachers were encouraged to believe that the children could learn and to treat them with respect. They concluded, "the way to academic achievement is to promote psychological development in students, which encourages bonding to the school" (Comer, 1988). At the end of their study, four years later, the school had raised its rating from twenty-five out of thirty-three schools in the district to number three!

Comer further explains that by the age of eight, kids begin to recognize how other families differ from their own in income, education, and sometimes race and style. Many are unable to achieve in school and subsequently see academic success as unattainable. They, therefore, decide that school is unimportant. With education no longer an option, they turn to other ways to seek a sense of adequacy, belonging, and self-affirmation in non-mainstream groups that do not value academic achievement, i.e., dropout, teen pregnancy, drug abuse, and crime. Psychologists, social workers, and guidance counselors today believe that because of the lack of historical facts describing the contributions Blacks have made to American history, many children, Black and White, male and female, have a distorted view of black people. Additionally, since most elementary school teachers are female, thereby providing few male role models in the schools, theorists are beginning to support the notion of special schools for Black males and curricula replete with an Afrocentric theme.

Winkler (1991) defines Afrocentrism as the heritage and accomplishments of Black people. Proponents of an Afrocentric curriculum believe that by including facts about African Americans into the daily curricula, minorities are able to have their story told. Critics claim that these programs sometimes violate historical accuracy with overblown claims, such as that most philosophy and civilization originated in Africa, and that they breed racial divisiveness with depiction of Whites as oppressors. One such critic is Arthur Schlesinger, Jr., a Pulitzer Prize winning historian who says, "Afrocentrism in the school is a symptom of a growing fragmentation that is threatening our society," (Winkler, 1991).

James Turner (1971) believes that traditional American education is nothing more than "White studies" and that it does nothing but teach children, Black and White, to accept and value the morals and beliefs of White society.

Marian White-Hood (1994), Principal at Kettering Middle School, Upper Marlboro, Maryland states "Pride, heritage and self-worth are the keys to African American male achievement (p. 27)." She further states that the role models of young African American males are those in the entertainment and sports arenas. Few see themselves as scholars, contributing to a common good. They have not been exposed to the more scholarly contributions of African American men, and they don't believe they, themselves, can make those kinds of contributions. There are a myraid of other reasons why we find ourselves in the conditions we are in today on the status of African American men in our society. Suffice it to say we need to find answers and solutions fast.

Summary

Today, Black males are truly an "endangered species." Data show that while money is being put into our educational system (Dropout Prevention, Chapter I

Funds, etc.), the Black male has been lost to crime, joblessness, and hopelessness. Presenting the research is not enough; educators, politicians, community leaders, and other influential groups need to choose to deal with and acknowledge symptoms of the Black male life conditions, but not the cause.

The literature indicates that there are social, economic, and psychological factors that collectively have put Black males at-risk and impeded their success. Interventions must address the life history of at-risk black males and, in turn, be designed specifically to alter the undesirable behavior.

Interventions must be early, long-term, and supported. Our nation must provide opportunity, guidance, finances, and support in this much needed effort. The goal is to maintain our diligence and hold all those accountable for the current conditions of African American men.

References

Asante, M. (1991). Multiculturalism: An exchange. *The American Scholar, 60,* 267–272.

Beatty, L., Gary, L., and Price, M. (1983). Stable Black families, final report. Institute for Urban Affairs and Research, Howard University.

Blackburn, R., & Mann, M. (1979). *The working class in the labor market.* London: MacMillan.

Boykin, A.W. (1983). The academic performance of Afro-American children. *Achievement Motives.* San Francisco: W. Freeman.

Bradley, S.A. (1994). *Breaking the spirit of the American Black male.* African Word Press.

Carmichael, & Hamilton, C. (1967). *Black power.* New York: Vintage.

Clark, J. (1988). *Critical issues of teenage pregnancy and parenthood in Florida.* Paper presented at the meeting of the House Committee on youth. Tallahassee, Florida.

Coggins, P. (1980). Status of crime among Black American men: Casual factors, prevention and treatment strategies. *Journal of Research on Minority Affairs, 1,* 77–81.

Collision, M. (1991). Black male schools. Yes. *Black Enterprise, 12,* 118.

Comer, J.P. (1988). Meeting the needs of Black children in public schools: A school reform challenge—the education of African Americans. Educating poor minority children. *Science American, 259,* 42–40.

Conciatore, J. (1989). Prisons devouring multitude of young Black males: High incarceration rate partly blamed for dwindling college enrollment. *Black Issues in Higher Education, 6*(12), 12–15.

Crichlow, W. (1985). Urban crisis, schooling and Black youth unemployment: A case study. Unpublished manuscript.

Dent, D.J. (Nov. 1989). Readin', ritin', and rage. How schools are destroying Black boys. *Essence, XX,* 54–57.

Dunn, J.R. (1988). The shortage of Black male students in the college classroom: Consequences and causes. *Western Journal of Black Studies, 12*(12), 73–76.

Edelman, M.W. (1995). To save the man one must start with the Boy. *Zebra Magazine, 3*(14), 12.

Ellwood, D.T., & David T. Rodda (March 1991). The hazards of work and marriage: The influence of male employment on marriage rates. Working Paper #H-90-5 (Cambridge, MA). Center for Social Policy Kennedy School of Government, Harvard University.

First World Magazine (February 1990), 23–25.

Garibaldi, A.M. (1989, 1991). Black school pushouts and dropouts: Strategies for reduction. *Urban League Review, 11,* 227–35.

Gary, L.E. (1983). *Black men.* Beverly Hills, CA: Sage Publishing.

Green, R.L. (1991). *African-American males: Education or incarceration.* 34–41.

Green, R.L. (1991). *African-American Males: A Demographic Study and Analysis,* 67. ERIC Document Reproduction Service, No. Ed. 346-184.

Hale-Benson, J.E. (1982). *Black children: The roots, culture and learning styles* (Rev. Ed.). Baltimore: The John Hopkins University.

Hann, A., Danzenberger, J., and Lefkowitz, B. (1987). Dropouts in America: Enough is known for action. A report for policymakers and grant makers. Washington, DC: Institute for Educational Leadership.

Hare, J., & Hare, N. (1992). *Bringing the Black boys to manhood: The passage,* pp. 18–19.

Hill (1986). Kellogg Foundation.

Holland, S. (1987). Positive primary Baker education for young Black males. *The Education Digest, 53,* 56–58.

Hooks, B. (1990). Director of the NAACP.

Inroads/Wisconsin. (1990). Investing in our nation—A link to economic prosperity: The African American male. Inroad/Wisconsin Youth Leadership Academy: A Status Report. Milwaukee: Author.

Jaynes, G.D. (1989). Williams, Robin M. Sr. Editors. *A common destiny: Blacks and American Society.* Washington, DC: National Academy Press.

Johnson, S., Prom, J., & Wallace, M. (1988). Home environment, talented minority youth and school achievement. *Journal of Negro Education, 57,* 111–21.

Jones, K. (1986). *The Black male in jeopardy. The Crisis, 93*(3).

Locust, C. (1990). Wounding the spirit. In N. Hildalgo, C. McCowell, & E. Siddle (Eds.). Facing racism in America. *Harvard Educational Review* (Reprint No. 21), 103–117.

Mann, H. (1841). Fourth annual report of the Board of Education. Boston, Dutlon & Wentworth, State Printers.

Marable, M. (1985). Toward Black American empowerment. *African Commentary, X,* 16–21.

McCarthy, C. (1990). *Race and curriculum.* London: Falmer Press.

McKenzie, R.B. (1991). *Competing visions: The political conflict over America's economic future.* Washington, DC: Cato Institute.

Milling, T.J. (October 22, 1991). Buddy, can you spare the rod? *Houston Chronicle,* 21A.

Myers, S. (1986). Black unemployment and its link to crime. *Urban League Review, 10*(1), 98–105.

Naipaul, V.S. (1989). *A turn in the South.* New York: Vintage.

Nichols, J. (1991). Students miss Black History month, *Plain Dealer, II.*

Nisbet, J., Ruble, V.E., & Schurr, K.T. (1982). Predictors of academic success with high risk students. *Journal of College Student Personnel, 23,* 227–35.

Ogbu, J.U., & Matute-Bianchi, M.E. (1986). Understanding sociocultural factors in education: Knowledge, identity, and adjustment. In *Beyond Language: Sociocultural Factors.* Los Angeles: Evaluation, Dissemination, and Assessment Center, California State University.

Ogbu, J.U., & Bianchi, M. (1986). The consequences of the American cast system: The school achievement of minority children. *New Perspectives.*

Parham, T., & McDavis, R. (1987). Black man: An endangered species: Who's really pulling the trigger? *Journal of Counseling and Development, 66,* 24–27.

Perry, I. (1990). A Black student's reflection of public and private schools.

Prince, T.J. (1990). Community service projects at Morehouse College Targeted to at-risk youth. Draft summaries. Atlanta, GA: Morehouse College Counseling Center.

Prom, J., Johnson, S., & Wallace, J. (1987). *Journal of Negro Education, 56,* 111–121.

Radin, N.A. (1989). Alternative to suspension and corporal punishment. *Urban Education 22*(4), 476–494.

Ratterag, J.D. (1989). African-American achievement. A Research Agenda Emphasizing Independent Schools. Ink.

Slate, J.R., Perez, E., Waldrop, P.B., & Justen, J.E. (1991). Corporal punishment: Used in a discriminatory Manner? *The Clearing House, 64*(6), 372–364.

Staples, R. (1985). Black masculinity: The Black males' role in American Society. San Francisco: The Black Scholar Press.

Stedman, J.J. (1989). Achievement in alternative high school. *Adolescence, 24,* 623–30.

Sudarkasa, N. (1988). Black enrollment in higher education. The unfulfilled promise of equality in National Urban League (Eds). *The State of Black America,* 1988, pp. 7–22. New York: National Urban League.

Taborn, T. (1998). Publisher of *U.S. Black Engineer.*

Taylor, R.L. (1990). Black youth: The endangered generation. *Youth and Society, 22,* 4–11.

The Task Force for High Education (1990). The urban review in schooling, language and minority students. California State Department of Education. Los Angeles: Education Dissemination and Assessment Center, California State University, 71–143.

Thomas, J. (1965, winter). Romantic reform in america, 1815–1865. *American Quarterly, VII*(4), 656–681.

Tribble, I. (1992). Making their mark: Educating African-American children, a bold new plan for educational reform. Silver Springs, MD: Becham House Publishing.

Troyna, B. (1984). Multicultural education: Emancipation or containment? In Barton, L. and Walker, S. (Eds.). *Social crisis and educational research* (pp. 75–97). London: Crown Helm.

Turner, J. (1971). *Black studies and a Black philosophy of education. Inman,* Aug./Sept., 12–17.

Whitaker, C. (March 1991). Do Blacks need special schools? *Ebony Magazine,* 46, 17–11.

Wilson, W.S. (1969, 1987). *The truly disadvantaged: The inner city: the underclass and public policy.* Chicago: Chicago University Press.

Winkler, K.J. (1991). Organization of American historians backs teaching of non-Western culture and diversity in Schools. *The Chronicle of Higher Education, 21* Feb. 6, 1991, 5–7.

Wright, D.L. (1991). *African-American males: A demographic study and analysis,* 67.

Wright, W.J. (1991). The Endangered Black male child. *Educational Leadership, 49* (4), 14–16.

Wright, W.J.I. (May 1981). The Black child: A threatened resource. Early childhood education. *Principal, 70*(5).

William B. Harvey

William B. Harvey is a thirty-year veteran of postsecondary education experience. As vice president and director of American Council on Education's Office of Minorities in Higher Education (OMHE), Harvey coordinates the Commission on Minorities in Higher Education, lends technical assistance to diversity issues at colleges and universities, and monitors the formulation of federal policies, regulations, and programs that affect minorities in higher education. Before assuming his position in July 2000, Harvey was dean of the School of Education and deputy chancellor for education partnerships at the University of Wisconsin-Milwaukee. He has served in faculty as well as administrative positions. Harvey has written and spoken on topics dealing with diversity in higher education, including tolerance, racism and race relations on campus, and obstacles facing African American and Hispanic scholars and students. Harvey's publications include *Grass Roots and Glass Ceilings: African American Administrators in Predominately White Colleges and Universities,* 1999; *New Directions for Community Colleges: Creating and Maintaining a Diverse Faculty,* 1994; and *Affirmative Rhetoric, Negative Action: African American and Hispanic Faculty at Predominately White Universities,* 1989. Harvey received a doctorate of education in anthropology and a master's in education from Rutgers University. He received a bachelor's degree in English from West Chester University (PA).

2

THE DATA SPEAK

No Rest for the Weary

William B. Harvey

Several years ago I was attending a major academic conference where a highly regarded, nationally known researcher was providing his analysis of the status of African American students in colleges and universities. He presented a litany of his concerns, ranging from lack of participation in campus extracurricular activities, to "self-segregation" in campus housing, to low graduation rates. As the session proceeded into the question and answer period, he prefaced many of his responses to questions by saying, "Well, the data clearly speak for themselves," but then proceeded to elaborate with what could easily have been interpreted as a "blaming-the-victim" perspective.

The respondent to the speaker was Dr. Walter Allen, Professor of Sociology at UCLA, one of America's preeminent social scientists and someone who was considerably more knowledgeable than the featured speaker regarding the shortcomings and the successes of African American students. In his usual soft spoken manner, Professor Allen opened his remarks by saying that the data do indeed speak for themselves, but he quickly added that how we interpret what they say can make a big difference in the conclusions that we reach, and consequently in the recommendations that we make. His statement was one of those insightful comments—simple, yet profound—that makes you sit up and say, "Oh, wow!"

The participation and success level of African American students, particularly males, in postsecondary education environments certainly manifest themselves at a lower level than their White and Asian counterparts. There is no argument there—the data make this point loudly and clearly. But the presumption that is often posited along with this observation is that the blame for this situation lies exclusively with the students, and that it can be resolved in a satisfactory manner if, and only if, they change their attitudes, habits, and practices. The prospect of implementing substantive institutional changes that would benefit all students, such as the utilization of multicultural curricula, the presence of a racially diverse faculty, and the creation of genuinely welcoming, supportive environments are seldom given serious consideration.

The nation's colleges and universities exist as a part of, not apart from, the interconnected matrix of organizations and institutions, economic and political forces, values and attitudes that comprise the larger sociocultural environment. While they have often presented themselves in such a way as to suggest that they functioned with a greater sense of humanitarianism and at a more cerebral level than the general public, where matters of race have been concerned, institutions of higher education have historically manifested discriminatory and prejudicial practices and policies. It was not an internal spirit of concern about justice and fairness within these academic environments, but the civil rights movement and the consequent passage of federal legislation, that finally led to the desegregation of America's postsecondary institutions.

The historical record documents that not until the 1970s did most predominantly White colleges and universities, whether they were located in the south or in other regions of the country, begin to even attempt to enroll African American students in substantial numbers. Now, as we move into the twenty-first century, these institutions loudly proclaim their commitment to diversity and stress their active recruitment of African American students. The most recent data available indicate, however, that among the nation's universe of higher education institutions, it is a subset of the Historically Black Colleges and Universities (HBCUs) that continue to lead the way both in enrolling and in granting baccalaureate degrees to African American males. (See Table 1.)

Entrance and Exit Patterns

Even after three decades of affirmative action and race-targeted admissions policies, few predominantly White colleges and universities have demonstrated success in enrolling and graduating significant numbers of African American males, which brings a host of questions to mind. What does one interpret from the realization that, in terms of numbers of African American male undergraduates, only eight of the top twenty-five four-year colleges and universities are predominantly White? How can that number be increased? Are there

Table 1   Enrollment Numbers

Top 100 Black Male Undergraduate Enrollments
Fall 1999 Preliminary

Rank	Institution	State	Total Men	Black Men	% Black
1	Florida A&M University	FL	4,539	4,176	92
2	Southern University and A&M College	LA	3,320	3,183	96
3	Morehouse College	GA	3,012	2,972	99
4	North Carolina A&T St Univ	NC	3,195	2,833	89
5	CUNY New York City Technical College	NY	5,456	2,439	45
6	Tennessee State University	TN	2,686	2,223	83
7	Morgan State University	MD	2,357	2,221	94
8	Norfolk State University	VA	2,376	2,118	89
9	Jackson State University	MS	2,173	2,103	97
10	Prairie View A&M University	TX	2,270	2,085	92
11	Alabama State University	AL	2,073	1,938	93
12	Alabama A&M University	AL	2,117	1,857	88
13	Hampton University	VA	1,981	1,801	91
14	Grambling State University	LA	1,862	1,782	96
15	Texas Southern University	TX	2,007	1,732	86
16	Howard University	DC	2,211	1,689	76
17	Wayne State University	MI	7,257	1,639	23
18	South Carolina State University	SC	1,701	1,602	94
19	University of Memphis	TN	6,417	1,554	24
20	Temple University	PA	7,563	1,553	21
21	Georgia State University	GA	6,347	1,498	24
22	University of the District of Columbia	DC	2,006	1,489	74
23	University of Maryland-College Park	MD	12,704	1,463	12
24	Georgia Southern University	GA	5,984	1,438	24
25	Virginia State University	VA	1,491	1,400	94
26	Florida International University	FL	11,427	1,380	12
27	Benedict College	SC	1,360	1,358	100
28	University of Houston-University Park	TX	11,478	1,323	12
29	North Carolina Central University	NC	1,484	1,322	89
30	Chicago State University	IL	1,496	1,304	87
31	University of Arkansas at Pine Bluff	AR	1,347	1,258	93
32	CUNY City College	NY	4,028	1,241	31
33	DeVry Institute of Technology	GA	1,691	1,193	71
34	Southern Illinois University-Carbondale	IL	10,181	1,189	12
35	Florida State University	FL	11,564	1,174	10
36	University of Cincinnati-Main Campus	OH	10,557	1,157	11
37	Fayetteville State University	NC	1,478	1,122	76
38	NC State University at Raleigh	NC	12,804	1,104	9
39	Clark Atlanta University	GA	1,105	1,101	100

continued

Table 1 Enrollment Numbers—*Continued*

Top 100 Black Male Undergraduate Enrollments
Fall 1999 Preliminary

Rank	Institution	State	Total Men	Black Men	% Black
40	Eastern Michigan University	MI	7,194	1,083	15
41	Ohio State University-Main Campus	OH	18,703	1,079	6
42	University of Maryland-University College	MD	4,991	1,077	22
43	University of South Carolina at Columbia	SC	6,987	1,059	15
44	Michigan State University	MI	15,853	1,058	7
45	Bowie State University	MD	1,199	1,054	88
46	Tuskegee University	AL	1,062	1,038	98
47	Virginia Commonwealth University	VA	6,443	1,030	16
48	Bethune Cookman College	FL	1,122	1,027	92
49	Fort Valley State University	GA	1,043	988	95
50	Old Dominion University	VA	5,775	976	17
51	University of Louisiana at Lafayette	LA	6,515	969	15
52	Southern University at New Orleans	LA	1,079	959	89
53	CUNY Bernard M Baruch College	NY	5,466	954	17
54	University of South Florida	FL	11,063	950	9
55	Alcorn State University	MS	968	945	98
56	CUNY Brooklyn College	NY	3,927	945	24
57	Albany State University	GA	981	934	95
58	Mississippi State University	MS	7,146	931	13
59	University of Akron Main Campus	OH	8,021	898	11
60	University of Maryland-Eastern Shore	MD	1,168	894	77

specific elements of the experience offered in the HBCUs that can be reproduced in other institutions so that they become more successful in enrolling African American males? Why does the list of the top sixty institutions include so few private colleges and universities?

With regard to the granting of baccalaureate degrees to African American males, what does it mean that one-third of the top twenty-five institutions are predominantly White colleges and universities? Are there activities or approaches being used in those institutions that should be replicated in other colleges and universities, including those HBCUs where the numbers of African American males graduating are smaller? For those persons who successfully earned their degrees, what data are available regarding such variables as their standardized exam scores, the major fields of study selected, the length of time needed to complete the academic requirements, and the amount of financial indebtedness incurred? How many of them go on to graduate or

Table 1   Graduation Rates—*Continued*

Black Male Baccalaureate Degrees in all Disciplines

Rank	Institution	State	No. of Degrees
1	Florida A&M University	FL	489
2	Morehouse College	GA	482
3	North Carolina A&T State University	NC	350
4	Southern University and A&M College	LA	347
5	Howard University	DC	290
6	Grambling State University	LA	275
7	Southern Illinois University-Carbondale	IL	273
8	Hampton University	VA	260
9	Tennessee State University	TN	252
10	Norfolk State University	FL	250
11	South Carolina State University	SC	240
12	University of Maryland-College Park	MD	224
13	Praine View A&M University	TX	224
14	Jackson State University	MS	216
15	Morgan State University	MD	211
16	Alabama State University	AL	191
17	Alabama A&M University	AL	190
18	North Carolina Central University	NC	190
19	Florida International University	FL	188
20	University of Maryland-University College	MD	184
21	University of Florida	FL	180
22	Chicago State University	IL	179
23	Georgia State University	GA	177
24	Florida State University	FL	176
25	University of South Carolina at Columbia	SC	170
26	Virginia State University	VA	170
27	Alcorn State University	MS	168
28	Wayland Baptist University	TX	168
29	Saint Leo University	FL	167
30	Bowie State University	MD	167
31	Temple University	PA	165
32	University of Michigan-Ann Arbor	MI	156
33	Fayette State University	NC	154
34	Michigan State University	MI	153
35	Rutgers University-New Brunswick	NJ	148
36	Texas Southern University	TX	148
37	Georgia Southern University	GA	147
38	University of Maryland-Eastern Shore	MD	146
39	North Carolina State University at Raleigh	NC	146

continued

Table 1   Graduation Rates—*Continued*

Black Male Baccalaureate Degrees in all Disciplines

Rank	Institution	State	No. of Degrees
40	Park University	MO	144
41	CUNY City College	NY	144
42	Tuskegee University	AL	142
43	DeVry Institute of Technology-Decatur	GA	141
44	CUNY Bernard M Baruch College	NY	141
45	CUNY York College	NY	141
46	University of Memphis	TN	141
47	CUNY John Jay College Criminal Justice	NY	137
48	Ohio State University-Main Campus	OH	136
49	Clark Atlanta University	GA	135
50	University of Southern Mississippi	MS	135
51	University of North Carolina at Charlotte	NC	130
52	University of Phoenix-So California Campus	CA	130
53	Mississippi Valley State University	MS	129
54	University of California-Los Angeles	CA	128
55	University of Central Florida	FL	126
56	CUNY Brooklyn College	NY	125
57	Virgina Commonwealth University	VA	125
58	University of Virginia-Main Campus	VA	125
59	University of Illinois at Urbana-Champaign	IL	121
60	Delaware State University	DE	118

Source: *Black Issues in Higher Education,* May 10, 2001.

professional school? How many of those who sought employment following graduation were able to secure it? What level of compensation did they receive?

These are examples of the kinds of research questions that need to be explored in greater depth so that a substantive data base can be developed that will allow for the critical analysis of issues that are pertinent to African American male participation in postsecondary education.

Struggle and Progress

Even with the variety of social and institutional obstacles that they must confront and overcome, African American males have been able to realize steady increases in the numbers of persons who earn baccalaureate degrees. (See

Table 2.) Receiving the bachelor's degree is not only an important accomplishment in terms of being a demonstration of personal growth and intellectual enrichment, but also in terms of the increased earning power and enhanced social standing that comes along with it. Of course earning the baccalaureate is also the first step for individuals who wish to proceed on for additional graduate or professional education.

The rate of growth in the number of African American male bachelor's degree holders slowed noticeably toward the end of the 1990s compared to what it had been earlier in the decade. Increasing the numbers of students who enroll in and graduate from postsecondary institutions is a widely supported societal goal, and the trend line for African American males continues to move in the right direction. The rate of success that African American males experience in earning bachelors degrees, however, is substantially smaller than that of their African American female counterparts. In 1989, 22,370 African American men were awarded bachelor's degrees compared to 35,708 African American women, but in 1998 the numbers were 34,469 degrees earned by men, and 63,663 by women, and the gap between these groups continues to expand.

This situation raises concern because it creates a pronounced imbalance between the numbers of college educated men and women, which may affect the dynamics and relationships between members of the two groups. Assuming that these female college graduates will, at some time in the future, seek partners and mates, with a preference for individuals who have similar educational backgrounds, this gap has the possibility of altering the social dynamics of the African American community.

Half Full, Half Empty

A record of consistent progress can also be seen among African American males in the acquisition of master's and first professional degrees during the period from 1989 to 1998. (See Tables 3 and 4.) The number of degrees awarded to African American males increased in both categories during each successive year. At the master's degree level, the increase was 86.1 percent, and for first professional degrees, the increase was 42.3 percent. In both categories, record breaking numbers of African American males were degree recipients in 1998. These encouraging figures clearly demonstrate the competence and dedication of African American male students.

But, although this record of progress is certainly heartening, it pales beside a comparative analysis of the gains that were made by African American females. In both the master's and first professional degrees category, African

Table 2   Bachelor's Degrees by Race/Ethnicity and Sex for Selected Years: 1989 to 1998

	1989 Total	1989 %	1994 Total	1994 %	1996 Total	1996 %
TOTAL	1,016,350	100.0	1,165,973	100.0	1,163,036	100.0
Men	481,946	47.4	530,804	45.5	521,439	44.8
Women	534,404	52.6	635,169	54.5	641,597	55.2
WHITE	859,703	84.6	936,227	80.3	904,709	77.9
Men	407,154	84.5	429,121	80.8	408,829	78.4
Women	452,549	84.7	507,106	79.8	495,880	77.3
MINORITY	129,621	12.8	195,666	16.8	220,783	19.0
Men	57,310	11.9	82,009	15.4	91,361	17.5
Women	72,311	13.5	113,657	17.9	129,422	20.2
AFRICAN AMERICAN	58,078	5.7	83,576	7.2	91,166	7.8
Men	22,370	4.6	30,648	5.8	32,852	6.3
Women	35,708	6.7	52,928	8.3	58,314	9.1
HISPANIC	29,918	2.9	50,241	4.3	58,288	5.0
Men	13,950	1.4	21,807	4.1	24,994	4.8
Women	15,968	3.0	28,434	4.5	33,294	5.2
ASIAN AMERICAN	37,674	3.7	55,660	4.8	64,359	5.5
Men	19,260	4.0	26,938	5.1	30,630	5.9
Women	18,414	3.4	28,722	4.5	33,729	5.3
AMERICAN INDIAN	3,951	0.4	6,189	0.5	6,970	0.6
Men	1,730	0.4	2,616	0.5	2,885	0.6
Women	2,221	0.4	3,573	0.6	4,085	0.6
NONRESIDENT ALIEN	27,026	2.7	34,080	2.9	37,544	3.2
Men	17,482	3.6	19,674	3.7	21,249	4.1
Women	9,544	1.8	14,406	2.3	16,295	2.5

American women more than doubled in the number of degree recipients from 1989 to 1998. A cross-racial analysis reveals that women earned more master's degrees than men among all racial and ethnic groups, but that only among African Americans did women also earn more professional degrees than men.

African American males also realized substantial growth in the number of doctoral degrees earned from 1988 to 1998, with the figures increasing from 321 degrees awarded at the beginning of the period to 520 at its end, an increase of 59 percent. In 1996 a record high number of 535 degrees were

Table 2   Bachelor's Degrees by Race/Ethnicity and Sex for Selected Years: 1989 to 1998—*Continued*

1997 Total	1997 %	1998 Total	1998 %	% Change 1989–98	% Change 1994–98	% Change 1997–98
1,168,023	100.0	1,183,033	100.0	16.4	1.5	1.3
517,901	44.3	519,360	43.9	7.8	–2.2	0.3
650,122	55.7	663,673	56.1	24.2	4.5	2.1
898,224	76.9	900,317	76.1	4.7	–3.8	0.2
401,878	77.6	399,105	76.8	–2.0	–7.0	–0.7
496,346	76.3	501,212	75.5	10.8	–1.2	1.0
231,372	19.8	243,555	20.6	87.9	24.5	5.3
94,615	18.3	98,670	19.0	72.2	20.3	4.3
136,757	21.0	144,885	21.8	100.4	27.5	5.9
94,053	8.1	98,132	8.3	69.0	17.4	4.3
33,509	6.5	34,469	6.6	54.1	12.5	2.9
60,544	9.3	63,663	9.6	78.3	20.3	5.2
61,941	5.3	65,937	5.6	120.4	31.2	6.5
26,007	5.0	27,648	5.3	98.2	26.8	6.3
35,934	5.5	38,289	5.8	139.8	34.7	6.6
67,969	5.8	71,592	6.1	90.0	28.6	5.3
32,111	6.2	33,405	6.4	73.4	24.0	4.0
35,858	5.5	38,187	5.8	107.4	33.0	6.5
7,409	0.6	7,894	0.7	99.8	27.5	6.5
2,988	0.6	3,148	0.6	82.0	20.3	5.4
4,421	0.7	4,746	0.7	113.7	32.8	7.4
38,427	3.3	39,161	3.3	44.9	14.9	1.9
21,408	4.1	21,585	4.2	23.5	9.7	0.8
17,019	2.6	17,576	2.6	84.2	22.0	3.3

Source: Harvey, William. *Minorities in Higher Education Status Report*, 2000–2001, American Council on Education, Washington, D.C., p. 63.

awarded. (See Table 5.) The growth for African American females in this category was even higher, with a 91.7 percent increase over the ten-year period. The 947 doctoral degrees awarded in 1998 is a record high figure, and so is the single-year increase of 135 degrees awarded from 1997 to 1998. African Americans were the only racial group in which women earned more doctorates than men in each of the ten years. During two years in this period American Indian women and men were tied in the number of degrees earned, and in one other year American Indian females earned more doctoral degrees than their male counterparts.

Table 3   Master's Degrees by Race/Ethnicity and Sex for Selected Years: 1989 to 1998

	1989 Total	1989 %	1994 Total	1994 %	1996 Total	1996 %
TOTAL	309,770	100.0	385,419	100.0	405,521	100.0
Men	148,872	48.1	175,355	45.5	178,661	44.1
Women	160,898	51.9	210,064	54.5	226,860	55.9
WHITE	242,764	78.4	288,288	74.8	297,558	73.4
Men	109,715	73.7	123,854	70.6	124,514	65.7
Women	133,049	82.7	164,434	78.3	173,044	76.3
MINORITY	32,793	10.6	50,814	13.2	59,952	14.8
Men	15,024	10.1	21,442	12.2	24,352	13.6
Women	17,769	11.0	29,372	14.0	35,801	15.8
AFRICAN AMERICAN	14,095	4.6	21,937	5.7	25,601	6.4
Men	5,175	3.5	7,413	4.2	8,442	4.7
Women	8,920	5.5	14,524	6.9	17,359	7.7
HISPANIC	7,277	2.3	11,913	3.1	14,412	3.6
Men	3,325	2.2	5,113	2.9	5,833	3.3
Women	3,952	2.5	6,800	3.2	8,579	3.6
ASIAN AMERICAN	10,335	3.3	15,267	4.0	18,161	4.5
Men	6,048	4.1	8,225	4.7	9,373	5.2
Women	4,287	2.7	7,042	3.4	8,789	3.9
AMERICAN INDIAN	1,086	0.4	1,697	0.4	1,778	0.4
Men	476	0.3	691	0.4	704	0.4
Women	610	0.4	1,006	0.5	1,074	0.5
NONRESIDENT ALIEN	34,213	11.0	46,317	12.0	47,811	11.9
Men	24,133	16.2	30,059	17.1	29,796	16.7
Women	10,080	6.3	16,258	7.7	18,016	7.9

Looking to the Future

The forward movement and educational advancement that has taken place within the African American community must be acknowledged. At the same time, the gaps between the African American and White communities that continue to exist and, in some instances, that are actually widening can neither be overlooked nor minimized. Raising the level of educational attainment for all African Americans must be a goal to which the society is committed, both in policy and in practice. Unless African Americans who operate from within

Table 3   Master's Degrees by Race/Ethnicity and Sex
for Selected Years: 1989 to 1998—*Continued*

1997 Total	1997 %	1998 Total	1998 %	% Change 1989–98	% Change 1994–98	% Change 1997–98
414,882	100.0	429,296	100.0	38.6	11.4	3.5
178,165	42.9	183,982	42.9	23.6	4.9	3.3
236,717	57.1	245,314	57.1	52.5	16.8	3.6
302,541	72.9	307,587	71.6	26.7	6.7	1.7
124,060	69.6	125,343	68.1	14.2	1.2	1.0
178,481	75.4	182,244	74.3	37.0	10.8	2.1
63,812	15.4	69,449	16.2	111.8	36.7	8.8
24,594	13.8	27,149	14.8	80.7	26.6	10.4
39,218	16.6	42,300	17.2	138.1	44.0	7.9
28,224	6.8	30,097	7.0	113.5	37.2	6.6
8,871	5.0	9,631	5.2	86.1	29.9	8.6
19,353	8.2	20,466	8.3	129.4	40.9	5.8
15,187	3.7	16,215	3.8	122.8	36.1	6.8
6,115	3.4	6,499	3.5	95.5	27.1	6.3
9,072	3.8	9,716	4.0	145.9	42.9	7.1
18,477	4.5	21,088	4.9	104.0	38.1	14.1
8,879	5.0	10,239	5.6	69.3	24.5	15.3
9,598	4.1	10,849	4.4	153.1	54.1	13.0
1,924	0.5	2,049	0.5	88.7	20.7	6.5
729	0.4	780	0.4	63.9	12.9	7.0
1,195	0.5	1,269	0.5	108.0	26.1	6.2
48,529	11.7	52,260	12.2	52.7	12.8	7.7
29,511	16.6	31,490	17.1	30.5	4.8	6.7
19,018	8.0	20,770	8.5	106.1	27.8	9.2

Source: *Status Report,* p. 64.

the academic environs continue to challenge their institutions to find more creative and effective ways to operationalize this goal than they have demonstrated in the past, it is unlikely to be realized.

It is then imperative that an intentional focus be maintained on the continuing, relative under-representation of African American males in those categorical areas that demonstrate advancement and social progress. A more complete understanding of the issues and situations encountered by African American males will be facilitated and enhanced by the development and

Table 4 First Professional Degrees by Race/Ethnicity and Sex for Selected Years: 1989 to 1998

	1989 Total	1989 %	1994 Total	1994 %	1996 Total	1996 %
TOTAL	70,856	100.0	75,418	100.0	76,641	100.0
Men	45,046	63.6	44,707	59.3	44,679	58.3
Women	25,810	36.4	30,711	40.7	31,962	41.7
WHITE	61,214	86.4	60,140	79.7	59,456	77.6
Men	39,399	87.5	36,573	81.8	35,732	80.0
Women	21,815	84.5	23,567	76.7	23,724	74.2
MINORITY	8,657	12.2	13,841	18.4	15,572	20.3
Men	4,959	11.0	7,119	15.9	7,843	17.6
Women	3,698	14.3	6,722	21.9	7,729	24.2
AFRICAN AMERICAN	3,148	4.4	4,444	5.9	5,016	6.5
Men	1,618	3.6	1,902	4.3	2,107	4.7
Women	1,530	5.9	2,542	8.3	2,909	9.1
HISPANIC	2,269	3.2	3,134	4.2	3,476	4.5
Men	1,374	3.1	1,781	4.0	1,947	4.4
Women	895	3.5	1,353	4.4	1,529	4.8
ASIAN AMERICAN	2,976	4.2	5,892	7.8	6,617	8.6
Men	1,819	4.0	3,214	7.2	3,533	7.9
Women	1,157	4.5	2,678	8.7	3,084	9.6
AMERICAN INDIAN	264	0.4	371	0.5	463	0.6
Men	148	0.3	222	0.5	256	0.5
Women	116	0.4	149	0.5	207	0.6
NONRESIDENT ALIEN	985	1.4	1,437	1.9	1,613	2.1
Men	688	1.5	1,015	2.3	1,104	2.5
Women	297	1.2	422	1.4	509	1.6

analysis of culturally sensitive research, which will connect the circumstances of the members of this cohort to a larger set of political, social, and economic issues that are controlled by others. Additional research needs to be, if not conducted by, then at least monitored by, those of us who have the most at stake. As noted at the beginning of this paper however, the data that will be collected will also need to be interpreted. We must make certain that the interpretations are accurate representations of the communities that we represent.

Table 4   First Professional Degrees by Race/Ethnicity and Sex
for Selected Years: 1989 to 1998—*Continued*

1997 Total	1997 %	1998 Total	1998 %	% Change 1989–98	% Change 1994–98	% Change 1997–98
77,815	100.0	78,353	100.0	10.6	3.9	0.7
45,067	57.9	44,769	57.1	–0.6	0.1	–0.7
32,748	42.1	33,584	42.9	30.1	9.4	2.6
59,852	76.9	59,273	75.6	–3.2	–1.4	–1.0
35,749	79.3	35,069	78.3	–11.0	–4.1	–1.9
24,103	73.6	24,204	72.1	11.0	2.7	0.4
16,352	21.0	17,303	22.1	99.9	25.0	5.8
8,216	18.2	8,558	19.1	72.6	20.2	4.2
8,136	24.8	8,745	26.0	136.5	30.1	7.5
5,251	6.7	5,483	7.0	74.2	23.4	4.4
2,178	4.8	2,303	5.1	42.3	21.1	5.7
3,073	9.4	3,180	9.5	107.8	25.1	3.5
3,553	4.6	3,547	4.5	56.3	13.2	–0.2
1,951	4.3	1,971	4.4	43.4	10.7	1.0
1,602	4.9	1,576	4.7	76.1	16.5	–1.6
7,037	9.0	7,712	9.8	159.1	30.9	9.6
3,798	8.4	3,993	8.9	119.5	24.2	5.1
3,239	9.9	3,719	11.1	221.4	38.9	14.8
511	0.7	561	0.7	112.5	51.2	9.8
289	0.6	291	0.7	96.6	31.1	0.7
222	0.7	270	0.8	132.8	81.2	21.6
1,611	2.1	1,777	2.3	80.4	23.7	10.3
1,102	2.4	1,142	2.6	66.0	12.5	3.6
509	1.6	635	1.9	113.8	50.5	24.8

Source: *Status Report*, p. 65.

References

Allen, W. R. (1992). The color of success: African American college student outcomes at predominantly White and historically Black colleges. *Harvard Educational Review, 62*(1), 26–44.

Brown, M. C. (1999). The quest to define college desegregation: Black colleges, Title VI compliance, and post-Adams litigation. Westport, CT: Bergin and Garvey.

Table 5   Doctoral Degrees by U.S. Citizenship by Race/Ethnicity
and Sex, 1989 to 1998

	1989	1990	1991	1992	1993	1994
TOTAL DOCTORATES[a]	34,326	36,067	37,522	38,856	39,771	41,017
Men	21,813	22,962	23,652	24,436	24,658	25,211
Women	12,513	13,105	13,870	14,420	15,113	15,806
U.S. CITIZENS[b]	23,400	24,905	25,543	25,975	26,408	27,129
Men	13,395	14,166	14,366	14,500	14,493	14,730
Women	10,005	10,739	11,177	11,475	11,915	12,399
WHITE	20,894	22,172	22,419	22,885	23,237	23,805
Men	11,987	12,690	12,679	12,828	12,852	13,052
Women	8,907	9,482	9,740	10,057	10,385	10,753
MINORITY	2,130	2,359	2,654	2,741	2,951	3,070
Men	1,129	1,210	1,344	1,416	1,473	1,509
Women	1,001	1,149	1,310	1,325	1,478	1,561
AFRICAN AMERICAN	821	900	1,004	968	1,108	1,095
Men	327	351	417	394	439	409
Women	494	549	587	574	669	686
HISPANIC	582	721	731	778	834	884
Men	307	380	370	410	423	438
Women	275	341	361	368	411	446
ASIAN AMERICAN	633	641	789	846	889	949
Men	446	427	483	530	551	591
Women	187	214	306	316	338	358
AMERICAN INDIAN	94	97	130	149	120	142
Men	49	52	74	82	60	71
Women	45	45	56	67	60	71
NON-U.S. CITIZENS	8,274	9,791	11,169	11,932	12,189	13,154
Men	6,583	7,822	8,742	9,255	9,332	9,968
Women	1,691	1,969	2,427	2,677	2,857	3,186

Davis, R. B. (1991). Social support networks and undergraduate student academic success related outcomes: A comparison of Black students on Black and White campuses. In W. R. Allen, E. Epps, and N. Hanniff (Eds.), *College in Black and White: African American students in predominantly white and in historically Black universities* (pp. 143–157). Albany, NY: State University of New York Press.

Fleming, J. (1984). *Blacks in college: A comparative study students' success in Black and in white institutions.* San Francisco: Jossey Bass.

Table 5   Doctoral Degrees by U.S. Citizenship by Race/Ethnicity and Sex, 1989 to 1998—*Continued*

1995	1996	1997	1998	% Change 1989–98	% Change 1997–98
41,743	42,415	42,555	42,683	24.3	0.3
25,158	25,267	24,944	24,653	13.0	−1.2
16,414	16,945	17,251	17,856	42.7	3.5
27,740	27,741	27,934	28,218	20.6	1.0
14,965	14,700	14,915	14,750	10.1	−1.1
12,773	13,041	12,990	13,452	34.5	3.6
23,920	23,856	23,035	23,338	11.7	1.3
13,052	12,744	12,447	12,369	3.2	−0.6
10,868	11,112	10,586	10,968	23.1	3.6
3,517	3,542	3,844	4,012	88.4	4.4
1,702	1,729	1,876	1,873	65.9	−0.2
1,815	1,813	1,968	2,139	113.7	8.7
1,309	1,315	1,336	1,467	78.7	9.8
490	535	524	520	59.0	−0.8
819	780	812	947	91.7	16.6
919	950	1,047	1,190	104.5	13.7
460	478	535	606	97.4	13.3
459	472	512	583	112.0	13.9
1,140	1,091	1,296	1,168	84.5	−9.9
670	614	740	643	44.2	−13.1
470	477	555	524	180.2	−5.6
149	186	166	189	101.1	13.9
82	102	77	104	112.2	35.1
67	84	89	85	88.9	−4.5
13,129	13,375	11,406	11,338	37.0	−0.6
9,748	9,867	8,285	8,080	22.7	−2.5
3,362	3,497	3,111	3,230	91.0	3.8

[a]Includes doctorates earned by persons with unknown citizenship status and unknown race/ethnicity
[b]Includes doctorates earned by persons with unknown race/ethnicity
Source: *Status Report*, p. 76.

Freeman, K. (1997). Increasing African Americans' participation in higher education. *Journal of Higher Education*, 5(68), 523–548.

Harvey, W. B. (2001). *Minorities in higher education, 2000–2001: Eighteenth annual status report*. American Council on Education, Washington, DC.

Roach, R. (2001). The Black male research agenda. *Black Issues in Higher Education*, May 10, 2001.

Na'im Akbar

Dr. Akbar is professor of psychology at Florida State University and president and founder of Mind Production in Tallahassee, Florida. He was born and received his early education in the South prior to the desegregation of public and educational facilities. In his late adolescence, he left this exclusively African American social environment to become a college student at the University of Michigan. He remained at the Ann Arbor campus of the University of Michigan for the completion of his B.A., M.A., and Ph.D. degrees in psychology.

On completion of his Ph.D. he was invited to join the psychology faculty at prestigious Morehouse College in Atlanta, Georgia. He rapidly progressed from an assistant professor to the position of department chair within two years and remained at Morehouse as a model teacher and administrator for five years. In 1975 he left Morehouse College to become the director of the Office of Human Development for the (then) Nation of Islam in Chicago and gained international prominence for his publications. He subsequently served on the faculty of Norfolk State University and eventually joined the psychology faculty of Florida State University where he has remained since 1979.

Dr. Akbar is a life member and has remained active in the Association of Black Psychologists. He has served on its board of directors for numerous terms and was elected president of the organization in 1987. This international organization, which is the largest Black mental health professional association in the world, has bestowed all of its prestigious honors on this distinguished psychologist and scholar.

3

THE PSYCHOLOGICAL DILEMMA OF AFRICAN AMERICAN ACADEMICIANS

Na'im Akbar

> One ever feels his two-ness,—an American, a Negro; two souls, two
> thoughts, two unreconciled strivings; two warring ideals in one dark
> body, whose dogged strength alone keeps it from being torn asunder.
> —W.E.B. DuBois, *The Souls of Black Folk* (1903)

Every African American who has ever entered an educational Academy of the
Western world (an institution that is invariably a fortress for European American hegemony) has faced some profound dilemmas. Whether the entrant to
the Academy was a student in pursuit of an enlightened future or, even more
perplexing, as a scholar committed to determining the future, these dilemmas
have greeted the non-European person at the threshold of the western cathe-
drals of learning. At one and the same time the matriculation into these hallowed halls was a promise of long-sought liberation; it was also the sealing of
the tombs of allegiance to an alien mentality. The reconciliation of these par-
adoxical "strivings" was destined to be the duel of every hopeful young
scholar who took on this challenge. Many young and enthusiastic scholars
have found this dilemma to be so wrenching that they handled the pain by a
process of denial and simply pretended that the struggle did not exist, but at
the sacrifice of their wholeness and integrity as a human being. Others have
managed the duel with a head-on and persisting confrontation that came to

consume the totality of their intellectual and emotional energy. Yet others have found a balance of partial reconciliation that has permitted them to use their creative energy similar to the inimitable scholar Dr. W.E.B. DuBois whose quote above opens this discussion and whose life serves as a model for mastering the dilemma. His life and career certainly demonstrates the devotion of one's intellect and creativity to mastering the dilemma and serving as a lantern on the road for one's contemporary generation and progeny.

Dr. DuBois addresses this dilemma in one of his most memorable treatises delivered in an address at Fisk University in 1933. In this address he describes the education of youth as a "preparation not for one common national life but for the life of a particular class or group; and yet the tendency is to regard as real national education only the training for that group which assumes to represent the nation because of its power and privilege, and despite the fact it is usually a small numerical minority in the nation." He continues:

> Manifestly in such cases if a member of one of the suppressed groups receives the national education in such a land, he must become a member of the privileged aristocracy or be educated for a life which he cannot follow and be compelled to live a life which he does not like or which he deeply despises. This is the problem of education with which the world is most familiar, and it tends to two ends: it makes the mass of men dissatisfied with life and it makes the university a system of culture for the cultured (1933).

This statement clearly describes the nature of the contradictory choices offered by the "national university" or the European American university to the non-European student and scholar.

As we prepare for lives in the European American Academy it is important for the African American scholar to have a good understanding of the dilemma that he faces. This dilemma is manifested with several psychological factors that must be reckoned with in order to achieve mastery. These factors are *identity, ideology,* and *legitimacy*.

Identity

The answer to the question of "who am I?" is certainly one of the most important questions of human existence. It is a question that all human beings must confront or suffer the consequences of having an answer imposed by a dictatorial authority that defines one's existence and then limits one's human possibility within the confines of that definition. All free people must, at least, seek an answer to this question of identity as a prerequisite for human freedom and self-determination. This question is particularly problematic for the initiate and devotee of the pursuits of the Academy of higher education. Without some satisfactory answer to the question, the Academician lives a life of adolescent indecision, drifting back and forth between dependency on the despotic rulings of others or forging a comfortable self-definition. Of course the academy has an array of prearranged definitions available. Definitions such as, professor, researcher, scientist, philosopher, historian, teacher, educator, or scholar abound in the Academy. There are numerous mantles that one might adorn oneself with that carry complex and elaborate procedures for initiation. By selecting one of these prefabricated identities, one becomes a part of a select society whose values one is taught and whose rules for admission and maintenance are strictly enforced. The degrees of qualification for acceptance into these select societies are legendary, and in order to even enter the halls of the academy one must be subjected to the rituals of passage and demonstrate the internalization of certain basic rules and values.

Most importantly one must accept a certain way of thinking and processing knowledge. With the satisfactory completion of these rituals under the tutelage of recognized elders of these elite societies in certain elite Academies, one is permitted to claim a title that is also available as a recognized and acclaimed identity. One can comfortably live one's life as a "political scientist, economist, psychologist, historian, professor, researcher, etc." These are not simply titles of vocation; they are clearly articulated identities, and most people willingly embrace these titles as their identity and devote their lives to acquiring the full recognition that is accorded to these titles.

The African American entering the European American structured and defined Academy does not have the luxury of simply stepping into the prefabricated identities that their higher education preparation has authorized them to accept. The rigors of higher education (particularly pursuit of terminal degrees) can so effectively ravage the self esteem of the candidate that to impulsively assume one of these premade titles becomes a salvage operation for what's left of his ego. A part of the role of graduate education is to reduce the candidate to nothingness and to convince him that his worth as a human being is dependent upon his favorable evaluation by his deified professors sitting on high and his ultimate acceptance into the circle of the elite. The assumption of the academic title restores the person's self worth and gives him a comfortable identity that comes with considerable relief after so much humiliation.

Unfortunately ethnic membership in a suppressed group creates an inescapable destiny. That destiny requires that one always consider race as a part of whatever identity is selected. A society that is irremediably entrenched with racial designation and appropriation does not afford the luxury of ignoring race as significant. It can be done, but at the peril of the person who chooses the path of denial. Identity should be a reality-based definition of a person's place in the world. It does not require one to accept the definitions imposed by the sometimes woefully distorted and unnatural "real world," but it does require a mentally functional person to take account of it. Otherwise there is myopia to some very essential elements of the real world that determine life, death, prosperity, success, or failure. There are a variety of ways to incorporate this important dimension of race into one's identity, but to deny its existence places one at the mercy of a merciless society that never fails to calculate race into its treatment of our humanity. One is actually psychologically handicapped if one chooses to ignore this reality that history has verified and each generation of African Americans has been forced to rediscover.

What does the integration of race into the academician's identity mean? Again, Dr. DuBois (1903) helps us with this important question. He says:

> The history of the American Negro is the history of this strife—this longing to attain self-conscious manhood, to merge his double self (Negro and American) into a better and truer self. In this merging he wishes neither of the other selves to be lost. He would not Africanize America, for America has too much to teach the world and Africa. He would not bleach his Negro soul in a flood of white Americanism, for he knows that Negro blood has a message for the world.

The awareness that both sides exist permits the African American in the Academy to accurately assess who we are and determine what are the behavioral imperatives that must be considered in our actions and what should be our expectations in realizing who we are. We need not wear our racial identity as a badge of honor nor degradation, but it should be a factor of constancy in affirming who we are. There is an ancestral responsibility to remember the penetration of these barriers that were intended to be permanent. There is a responsibility to future generations to hold the gates ajar despite the recurring tendency for the gates to be sealed and the barriers restored. Despite whatever auxiliary identity that one assumes in the Academy as researcher, professor, scholar, etc., one must ever acknowledge the adjectival prefix of one's racial identity. This ethnic designation becomes a recurring aide memoire of the context that we are required to operate within and of the responsibility that we have.

Ideology

The dilemma of being an African American academician creates difficulties in choosing an ideological framework within which to engage in one's work. Whether the work is within the rigors of science or the latitude of the arts, the ideological position of the scholar determines how he will approach his craft. Ideology is intended to identify the broader context of how we conceptualize the world and our place in it. It is not intended to suggest that there is an existing political ideology that must be chosen in order to be consistent with the identity issues that we have discussed above. It does suggest that there are broad cosmological issues that must be included in one's approach to being in the Academy that is consistent with the identity resolutions of who we are as African American scholars. We made reference above to the fact that we had a responsibility to both our progenitors and our progeny. The ideology that defines us as one with our history and our community assumes such values of responsibility to those who opened doors for us and our obligation to open doors for others. This ideological inference is quite different from an ideology that gives priority to individual responsibility in preference to anyone or anything else. The African-centered ideology sees people as interconnected with a built-in commitment to preserve and cultivate those ties. This value of mutual and generational responsibility would supersede any individualistic imperatives. This would mean that one's work as a scholar, researcher, scientist, even technician would require those activities to be evaluated within an ideological context of mutuality or service to others. It implies that one's responsibility is always to the "us" and not limited to considerations for the "I."

Ideology also determines what we consider to be the essence of reality. The European American academic ideology assumes "materiality" to be the essence of reality. Those things that are not observable by the senses and, ultimately, measurable are not considered real. Conclusions that cannot be validated by reference to such observable reality are rejected. This certainly precludes the possibility that the essence of things may be in fact unobservable and of a spiritual form. Such speculation is inadmissible in the Academy because of its fundamentally materialistic perspective. However, most of the civilized world, while not invalidating materiality as real, would not conclude that the essence of all things is seen in the material form. Nor would they conclude that causation can only be attributed to logical positivism that sees any material effect must only be caused by something that is temporally and spatially connected to that effect. The facts of causation from other higher planes of reality are relegated to philosophical, or maybe religious, speculation that is considered to be irrational and nonscientific. Within the Western ideology, the ultimate indictment of the invalidity of an idea is to classify it as "unscientific." If African American scholars dismiss the relevance of the spiritual dimension, then they dismiss the most likely cause of African survival in America when confronted by the horrendous and dreadful material conditions that should have logically rendered us extinct. There is little if any evidence to suggest that a reliance on material factors could explain the fact that the African captives were able to survive conditions that were clearly structured to destroy us as a people. The implicit capacity of Africans to transcend their conditions and draw from a higher moral and energy plane permitted an endurance and mastery of conditions that would have destroyed a people who saw only the material plane of existence. Regardless of which spiritual system (religion) the captives were permitted to practice, an implicit worldview that they brought to the captor's den gave them the power of survival. Economic factors, political factors, even biological issues affecting health and nutrition, cannot account for the incredible resilience of this people who were relegated to the condition of chattel property for nearly three centuries under materially impossible conditions for ordinary survival. Within only a few years of acquiring some modicum of freedom and gradually acquiring opportunities, the former slaves have excelled in any arena into which we have succeeded in gaining entrance.

This demonstrates the crucial importance of ideology in the successful use of the Academy. It is vital that the ideological substratum of the academy should be critiqued, and the African American scholar must select those elements that advance the understanding of the human experience from the perspective of the African's unique experience. Imagine how much we miss by failing to grasp the significance of a scholar's perception of essence in effecting access to information. Ideology provides an effective mindset that permits the African American scholar to move towards mastery of the dilemma of the Academy. Even more importantly, ideology offers a map towards the critical acquisition of self-knowledge, which is the ultimate source of empowerment for any people (Akbar, 1999; Hilliard, 1997; and Woodson, 1933).

Legitimacy

The dilemma of the Black academician probably reaches its most critical expression around the issue of *legitimacy*. Legitimacy has to do with the issue of who is the audience for your academic enterprise and who can authenticate your work. Of course the academic institution that pays your salary has a somewhat unfair advantage over anyone else claiming the right to authenticate your scholarship. Contract renewal, tenure, promotions, and merit raises are all contingent on the standards that the institution has established for deter-mining if you still have a legitimate role in that setting. The criteria of what scholarship, published where, evaluated by whom, and accepted by what audi-ence will all determine whether you will be able to remain in that institution or not. Because of the practical survival issues of being able to maintain gain-ful employment, the conflicted scholar often succumbs to the legitimacy demands of the institution. Without a doubt this is a realistic choice despite the fact that it may cause one some consternation at the idea that so much of his creative and scholarly energy must be expended in living up to the stan-dards that permit him to remain legitimate in the institution. Again the choices are not as dichotomous as they may appear because there are options that per-mit him to maintain sufficient legitimacy to maintain his survival in the aca-demic institution that pays his salary and simultaneously speak to his special audience and secure legitimacy there as well.

One of the options for achieving this dual legitimacy is the choice of insti-tution where you choose to work. Most academic institutions differ in the degree to which they emphasize research and empirically-based publications as their criteria for legitimacy, and there are teaching institutions that have a broader criteria for acceptable publications and scholarship. The difficulty is that one must sacrifice certain kinds of prestige and rewards depending upon the choice that one makes. The institutions that emphasize teaching tend to be primarily undergraduate institutions, often with less prestige and definitely fewer resources than their research-oriented counterparts. In simple language, one makes less money and, in the broader European American ideological con-text, one will have lower status. One is likely to have a much larger teaching load and much greater personal involvement with less advanced students; in return one will gain greater flexibility in utilizing one's creative and scholarly energies and a greater opportunity to cultivate other arenas outside of the Academy where you would like to secure legitimacy. Along the same lines of selecting alternative institutions, it is important to remember that the Histori-cally Black Institutions usually offer similar flexibility to that which you get in the less research-based institutions. In order to survive in recent years, how-ever, the HBCUs (especially the state sponsored institutions) are placing greater emphasis on "traditional" scholarly research as a major requirement to legitimize their faculty. If one's intention is to cultivate legitimacy as a Black scholar, then the Historically Black Institution is much more likely to offer a supportive environment with colleagues of similar interests and a much closer contact with the African American community. Of course one must make these choices on the basis of the kind of identity and ideology that the academician is formulating for himself.

Of course the other option in securing this dual legitimacy of being a traditional scholar and a kind of activist scholar seeking authentication by one's indigenous community is in the kind of scholarship that is chosen. There are many topics that can be phrased in the kind of empirical mode that will permit acceptance to the European American academic audience. This same topic can have currency within the scholar's African American community. The topic selected must have relevance to the issues confronting our communities and can be translated into an understandable language that will make sense to a predominately nonacademic audience. Such schizoid intellectual gymnastics requires a great deal of the academician, and this probably explains why so many African American academicians choose legitimacy from one audience or the other rather than the complicated process of trying to straddle these two often contradictory worlds.

Many of our most exemplary scholars, such as Dr. DuBois, have managed this daunting task quite effectively. It is not for the faint of heart however, because of the kind of biculturalism and bilingualism that is required. Once one has resolved the issues of identity and ideology, decisions about legitimacy are probably somewhat predetermined. If one has identified oneself as an African American scholar with an ideology committed to the liberation of oppressed people (especially African American people) and their cultural authenticity, then one is obligated to gain legitimacy with that community and this must be, at least, an audience that authenticates one. Of course the vast majority of African American scholars (even those who resolve an identity that places their ethnicity as a standard part of their academic entitlement) choose to legitimize themselves only through the traditional academic institution. As indicated above, the tangible rewards that come from these institutions are often too lucrative to resist, and it is often much easier to play the game rather than to live in the "double-consciousness." There is a much greater sense of internal consistency if the African American academician is successful in forging the kind of compromise that permits him to be whom he is. If he can abide by a self-affirming ideology and simultaneously achieve the standards that permit him to obtain the financial and social legitimacy that allows comfortable and acceptable survival in the European American social setting, then there is inner peace, personal efficacy, and political clout in the alien social environment. The African American scholar who has endured the test of higher education and emerged with a tenable Black identity intact, then, is already prepared to continue along the same path as he constructs a legitimate and gainful career for himself.

Conclusion

The psychological dilemmas faced by the African American academician are challenging to say the least. The challenge is as basic as determining whom one is in the affirmation of an identity within the academy and within the broader society. This issue of determining whom we are serves as the foundation for whatever else we might do. It determines whom our associates are, what our political leanings are, how we engage in economic enterprise, what our values are, and basically every dimension of how we engage in the complex process of living. Identity is the very foundation of our being. We have suggested in this discussion that, though identity contains many crucial elements about what we are, what we believe, and how we approach life and other people, the ingredient of race remains a critical variable in the complex of identity. Ethnic or racial identity is an essential ingredient for all people in a society that utilizes race and ethnicity as a means of identifying, judging, and treating people. For members of the dominant society, such racial classification does not have to be explicit because it is such an implicit part of the culture, one's education, and ultimately one's self-definition. The content and the structure of education and culture is screened through the mesh of racial ethnic identity. It is not accidental that the referent point for time, history, and reality is the experience of the European-originated racial group. For example, America's history has its genesis with the landing and discovery by the European sailor, Christopher Columbus. Both time and history begin with the appearance of the European. Any activity prior to that occurrence is viewed as something from the irrelevant past. Certainly the lives and history of the people who inhabited this land for thousands of years before the coming of the Europeans is dismissed and occupies no essential place in the concept of American culture and history. So to study American history is implicitly to study the European invasion of the land of its indigenous inhabitants. One need not state that this study is a study of White European history because it is implicit in one's definition of what America is. The same is true in every arena of human knowledge, and the conspicuous absence or marginalization of other people affirms that there is selectivity in facts of reality that inform the White European American identity.

The issue of identity must be made explicit for the excluded or marginalized, otherwise they run the risk of defining themselves within the context of other people's definition of them or how they are seen by the outside group. Therefore the African American academician must affirm and articulate the parameters of his identity or he accepts a fraudulent identity. We have clearly suggested that race should not be the totality of the African American's identity, as it should not be for any group of human beings, but whatever the other elements that one chooses to define identity, this dimension must be critical.

From the foundation of identity, the African American academician must select the ideological parameters that guide his scholarship and academic presence. We have defined ideology as the broad cosmological perspective that identifies the context of one's work and expression. Examples are offered of how the African-based ideology sees reality as much broader than the empirical and material focus and limitation of the European ideology. The collective self-definition that transcends the individualistic focus of European scholarship is offered as a contrast to how the African-based ideology is guided by service, and reciprocity. These are only two broad examples of how the ideological selection creates yet another critical dilemma for the African American academician. The resolution of this dilemma becomes another aspect of resolving the double-consciousness that is described so succinctly in the observations of Dr. W.E.B. Dubois.

Finally, this discussion identifies "legitimacy" as the final component of the psychological dilemma of the African American academician. Legitimacy has to do with the selected audience that the scholar selects to address his work and to whom he looks for the legitimacy of his work. The determination that is made in this aspect of the academician's dilemma is to a great extent shaped by the answers he has reached for the components of "identity," and "ideology." We discussed the inevitable conflicts of the source of rewards and status as very influential determinants in this aspect of the dilemma. Certainly those who control the Academies and our material survival exercise a considerable influence on this selection. Even though it should be guided by identity and ideology, the outcome can be confounded by the absence of institutions that function for the express affirmation and articulation of African life. The limited control of resources to insure the material survival of proponents of our own advancement as a people makes a selection committed to the ultimate ascendancy of African people a very risky selection. In order to avoid being "torn asunder," it takes "dogged strength" and conviction to carefully identify one's audience and legitimization in such a way that survival is not compromised. In the same light, however, if the academician has successfully resolved the questions of his identity and his ideology, then neither can he compromise these definitions by legitimizing himself totally with alien audiences.

Perhaps this is the challenge of the next generations: to construct institutions that draw upon the unique contribution of the double-consciousness that the African American brings to the academic table and to dispense the appropriate rewards and legitimacy to those committed to the advancement and affirmation of Black life on this planet.

References

Akbar, N. (1999). *Know Thyself.* Tallahassee, FL: Mind Productions and Associates.

DuBois, W.E.B. (1903). *Souls of Black Folk.* New York: Penguin Books, 1989. (First published by A.C. McClurg & Co., 1903.)

DuBois, W.E.B. (1933). The field and function of the Negro college. In Aptheker, H. (1973) (Ed.). *The Education of Black People: Ten Critiques 1906–1960 by W.E.B. DuBois.* New York: Monthly Review Press, pp. 83–102.

Hilliard III, A.G. (1997). *SBA: The Reawakening of the African Mind.* Gainesville, FL: Makare Publishing.

Woodson, C.G. (1933). *The Miseducation of the Negro.* Trenton, NJ: Africa World Press, Inc. (1990). (First published by the Associated Publishers, Washington, DC, 1933.)

Asa G. Hilliard III

Dr. Asa G. Hilliard III is the Fuller E. Callaway Professor of Urban Education at Georgia State University, with joint appointments in the Department of Educational Policy Studies and the Department of Educational Psychology and Special Education. A teacher, psychologist, and historian, he began his career in the Denver Public Schools. He earned a B.A. in educational psychology, an M.A. in counseling, and an Ed.D. in educational psychology from the University of Denver, where he also taught in the College of Education and in the Philosophy colloquium of the Centennial Scholars Honors Program.

Dr. Hilliard served on the faculty at San Francisco State University for eighteen years. During that time he was a department chair for two years, dean of education for eight years, and was consultant to the Peace Corps and superintendent of schools in Monrovia, Liberia, for two years.

He has participated in the development of several national assessment systems, such as proficiency assessment for professional educators, and developmental assessments of young children and infants. He has been active in forensic psychology, serving as an expert witness in several landmark federal cases on test validity and bias.

Dr. Hilliard is a founding member of the Association for the Study of Classical African Civilizations and serves as its first vice president. He is the co-developer of a popular educational television series, *Free Your Mind, Return to the Source: African Origins,* and has produced videotapes and educational materials on African history through his production company, Waset Education Productions.

Dr. Hilliard has written numerous technical papers, articles, and books on testing, Ancient African History, teaching strategies, public policy, cultural styles, and child growth and development. In addition, he has consulted with many of the leading school districts, universities, government agencies, and private corporations on valid assessment, curriculum equity, and teacher training. Several of his programs in pluralistic curriculum, assessment, and valid teaching have become national models. He has also been the recipient of numerous honors and awards.

4

ONE BY ONE, OR ONE

AFRICANS AND THE ACADEMY

Asa G. Hilliard III

Falsification

Encyclopedia
"When we classify a man by color, the only one of the primary
races . . . which has not made a creative contribution to any of our
twenty-one civilizations is the Black race."
—Arnold Toynbee, *Study of History*

Some of the biggest lies
Ever told
Have been bound with leather
Printed with gold
Careful Black child
What you read
Books are bags
Full of seeds
Waiting for the place
And time
To sprout inside
A fertile mind
Vigilant eyes
Will pierce the scheme
To deify
The European
—Listervelt Middleton (1985). *Southern Winds African Breezes.*

The Alien Center

"We have been handed down a vision of a slave man roaming in the desert sand—a perfect image of our hollowed chiefs today. Language he had not, not ours, and not his own. It had been voided out of him, his tongue cut out from his mouth. He pointed to the gaping cavity. Thinking he still had a soul, even mutilated, we imagined he was after sympathy. We were mistaken—he was pointing to the hole with pride. They who had destroyed his tongue, they had put pieces of brass in there to separate the lower from the upper jaw. The slave thought the brass a gift. Its presence made sweet to him the absence of his tongue. He communicated his haughty pride to us, indicating in the sand with precise remembrance when he had achieved each piece of brass, what amazing things he had been made to do in order to be given them."
—Ayi Kwei Armah (1979). *Two Thousand Seasons.*

Research, "Knowledge," Production, and Domination

"The whole process of colonization can be viewed as a stripping away of *mana* (our standing in our own eyes), and an undermining of *rangatiratabga* (our ability and right to determine our destinies)." Research is an important part of the colonization process because it is concerned with defining legitimate knowledge. In Maori communities today, there is a deep distrust and suspicion of research. This suspicion is not just of nonindigenous researchers, but of the whole philosophy of research and the different sets of beliefs which underlie the research process. Even in very recent studies this hostility or negative attitude to research in general has been noted. Research methodology is based on the skill of matching the problem with an 'appropriate' set of investigative strategies. It is concerned with ensuring that information is accessed in such a way as to guarantee validity and reliability. This requires having a theoretical understanding, either explicitly or implicitly, of the world, the problem, and the method. When studying how to go about doing research, it is very easy to overlook the realm of common sense, the basic beliefs that not only help people identify research problems that are relevant and worthy, but also accompany them throughout the research process.

Researchers must go further than simply recognizing personal beliefs and assumptions and the effect they have when interacting with people. In a cross-cultural context, the questions that need to be asked are ones such as:

Who defined the research problem?
For whom is this study worthy and relevant? Who says so?

What knowledge will the community gain from this study?
What knowledge will the researcher gain from this study?
What are some likely positive outcomes from this study?
What are some possible negative outcomes?
How can the negative outcomes be eliminated?
To whom is the researcher accountable?
What processes are in place to support the research, the researched, and the researcher?

—Linda Tuhiwai Smith (1999), p. 173.

Classic Statement on Miseducation

"It may be of no importance to the race to be able to boast today of many times as many 'educated' members as it had in 1865. If they are of the wrong kind the increase in numbers will be a disadvantage rather than an advantage. The only question which concerns us here is whether these 'educated' persons are actually equipped to face the ordeal before them or unconsciously contribute to their own undoing by perpetuating the regime of the oppressor."

. . . " 'Highly Educated' Negroes denounce persons who advocate for the Negro as a sort of education different in some respects from that now given the white man. Negroes who have been so long inconvenienced and denied opportunities for development are naturally afraid of anything that sounds like discrimination. They are anxious to have everything the white man has even if it is harmful. The possibility of originality in the Negro, therefore, is discounted one hundred percent to maintain a nominal equality. If the whites decide to take up Mormonism the Negroes must follow their lead. If the whites neglect such a study, then the Negroes must do likewise. The author, however, does not have such an attitude. He considers the educational system as it has developed both in Europe and America an antiquated process which does not hit the mark even in the case of the needs of the white man himself. If the white man wants to hold on to it, let him do so; but the Negro, so far as he is able, should develop and carry out a program of his own."

"In this untoward situation the Negro finds himself at the close of the third generation from Emancipation. He has been educated in the sense that persons directed a certain way are more easily controlled, or as Ovid remarked, 'in the time bull is brought to bear the yoke.' The Negro in this state continues as a child. He is restricted in his sphere to small things, and with these he becomes satisfied. His ambition does not rise any higher than to plunge into the competition with his fellow for these trifles. At the same time those who have given the

race such false ideals are busy in the higher spheres from which Negroes
by their mis-education and racial guidance have been disbarred."
—Carter Goodwin Woodson, *Miseducation of the Negro.*

Ancient African Wisdom and the Purpose of Education, "Good Speech"

"Do not be proud and arrogant with your knowledge. Consult and con-
verse with the ignorant and the wise, for the limits of art are not reached.
No artist ever possesses that perfection to which he should aspire.

  Good Speech is more hidden than greenstone (emeralds), yet it may
be found among maids at the grindstone."
—Ptahhotep, 2350 B.C.E.

Who are we and why are we here? What is "higher education" and "the Academy?" How do we see our place in "the Academy?" Unless there is something
special about us, there is no need to write about us. There are already thousands of books about going to school. However there is something very powerful and special about African people and higher education. As shown in the
last quotation above from the oldest text and the oldest professor to stand out
in world history, African traditions in deep thought in higher education go
back for thousands of years.

For virtually everyone today, higher education is full of both intrinsic and
utilitarian value. It is also a gateway and a hurdle. It is supposed to prepare us
for the world of work. It certifies us and grants to us a measure of legitimacy.
It is a key that opens some doors. It anoints us and gives us status in the eyes
of the broader community. It may even yield some personal satisfaction.

However, from an African perspective, and in keeping with our ancient
and modern traditions, it ought to be far more than that. It ought to be a profound spiritual, intellectual, social, and physical *transformation* process. It
ought to "Afrient" us, and neither "occident" nor "orient" us. We have thousands of years of our own powerful traditions to tap, though many of us have
little or no knowledge of this important rich legacy.

I know that it may be strange to many Brothers of the Academy, many of
us mis-educated and mis-socialized, to say that we ought to have our own
community expectations of higher education, rooted in our own ancient traditions, and in our own cultural values and world views. Present education
/socialization practice for the masses of us, even the part that we control,
draws an iron curtain between us and our traditions and our people, and
clouds our minds. This prevents us from making critical analyses of our cur-

rent conditions, of which European Western hegemonic "higher education" is a central part.

Much of this essay is critical of current and recent past conditions caused by European hegemony over Africans. *However, I want to be very clear, while oppression has been and still is a major problem for us, opposition to oppression in no way constitutes the most important part of our concerns. Understanding our essense as a people and understanding our purposes, content, and methods of achieving excellence in higher education/socialization throughout the millennia must be the base from which we attack our current problems and determine our future course.*

Let's get the record straight; there is no "universal" higher education. All higher education today is embedded in an ethnic or cultural and socio-economic-political matrix. The powerful control others by trying to define reality for everyone, and to get everyone to accept their particular ethnic-cultural version of reality as their own. As Wade Nobles says so often, "True power is the ability to define reality and to get others to respond to your definition as if it were their own." Frantz Fanon has also clarified the behavior of colonizers who always make a "unilateral declaration of the normative value" of their own culture. Further, cultural genocide is practiced on dominated peoples, following that notion.

Ultimately ideas control behavior. Therefore it should come as no surprise that the *primary instruments of domination is the control of education-socialization and media.* European-centered institutions of higher education and media tend most often to be those that have served a domination agenda—to establish their international hegemony, in keeping with their nationalist's agendas. The central active role of higher education in serving the agendas of slavers, colonizers, segregationists, and White supremacists is so well documented that it should require little comment (Carruthers, 1995e; Chase, 1977; Deloria, 1997; Guthrie, 1998; Hilliard, 1997; King; 1971; Hodge, Struckman, and Trost, 1975; Sheldon, 1991; Skutnall-Kangas, 2000; Spivey, 1978; Tucker, 1994; Weinreich, 1946; Wilson, 1998; Young, 1990). The brothers of the Academy cannot be ignorant of this Academy history. True, withering counterattacks to this hegemonic tradition have also come from within the Academy. The point is, however, that we cannot take anything at face value, especially those who claim objectivity and scientific validity for their work. We certainly cannot accept willingly any false and hegemonic uses of the Academy, surrendering African people's interests to cultural genocide.

As a result of the fact that most of us have little knowledge of our ancient higher education traditions and have not experienced the finest of our diaspora higher education in some of our best Historically Black Colleges and

Universities (HCBUs), we approach higher education with a severe handicap, a tunnel vision, a case of severe cultural amnesia, and worse, a hunger for validation, by anyone other than by our own people.

We do not know what we should expect or demand from the Academy. We do not know how, why, or even that we have been deprived of our cultural birthright, nor what that birthright is. Some of us may even feel that we do not really belong in the academy. We may simply approach higher education, accepting it wholesale, without a critical awareness. By approaching it uninformed about our awesome record in the Academy, including the development of the oldest recorded Academy, (Hilliard, 1998) the most that we can get from even the best of the most "elite" higher education institutions is "partial fulfillment," on someone else's terms.

One might think that under ordinary circumstances the ideal would be for a student to move through a seamless education and socialization process from the preschool through postdoctoral studies. However, for African people *all over the world* our circumstances have been anything but ordinary. Over the past 400 years in particular, and even now, we have been and still are alienated from our greatest traditions. We have been socialized and "educated" in hegemonic systems that are most often blatantly anti-African. The negative aspects of those system have yet to be dismantled. It is very difficult for us to grasp the nature and magnitude of our plight and the consequences of it (Watkins, 2001; King, 1971; Chinweizu, 1987; Wilson, 1998; Cabral, 1973).

The publication of *Brothers of the Academy* (Jones, 2000) deservedly has been very well received. It surfaced many deep and abiding issues about higher education experiences of African men. For many readers this book helped greatly to clarify their felt experiences, some for the first time. Obviously major needs were met by the carefully selected set of insightful chapters, therefore, there should be no surprise that there is a demand for more.

At the outset, I must raise a simple but fundamental question. Do we come to the Academy "one by one" or as "one?" In other words, do we come as *individuals* or as members of a *family* and *community,* as members of an ethnic community? I have no message whatsoever for the "lone rangers," those who are clear that they are *individuals*. I cannot even imagine why they would be interested in a book such as this. "Brothers" of the academy implies *family* unity to me. I proceed on that assumption.

Many of us are acquainted with the enormous special challenges that are faced by Africans in institutions over which we have limited control at best, even in our "private" institutions, our Historically Black Colleges and Universities, HBCUs. There are many valuable and truly heroic individual survival stories to tell.

Why are we in the Academy, and whose interests will we serve? It matters greatly where the emphasis is placed. My own mission here is to examine the question of "Brothers in the Academy," from the point of view of the *global African family* in its struggle to survive and thrive. Because of that I find it necessary to situate questions about the experiences of Africans in the Academy in the context of African people's higher education experience as we have marched through history in Africa and in the African diaspora. There is connection and continuity here that we allow to be broken at our peril.

It is extremely important for us to understand that the story of our experience as African people in higher education does not begin with our relatively recent struggle from the fifteenth century to the present, to overcome European slavery, colonization, apartheid, and white Supremacy ideology. Our ancient Academies, from the Nile to the Niger, were destroyed systematically. Our ancient culture and our bonded relationships, which were rooted in our culture and tied to our Academies, were primary targets of oppressors. This pattern has never stopped anywhere in the African world. There have been and there continues to be a systematic and pervasive cultural genocide, beginning with enslavement, colonization, apartheid, and White supremacy ideology (ben Jochannan,1972; Cabral, 1973).

A deep understanding of what came before this *maafa* (a Kiswhahi term meaning unimaginable horror and terror, [Ani, 1994]) is essential to understanding what happened next, what is happening now, and what will happen in the future. These are the things that the Academy does not tell us. These are the things that our community has forgotten.

I use the term *African* as the family name of people of African ancestry, worldwide, although I sometimes use the popular term *Black*. I am referring to the *cultural* deep structure that we still share and that makes us one. It is our ethnic identity more that our "racial" identity that our oppressors have sought to crush. They have tried to reduce us to an adjective, *Black,* to a term that refers only to our pigment, an aspect of our phenotype, our physical makeup, in order to keep us from a focus on our shared culture and creativities. If we know our culture, we not only have a source of unity, we also have the information that protects us from defamation and White supremacy ideology, given the global impact of our genius. Those who seek to dominate us want to keep us from our culture at all costs!

Elsewhere I have dealt in detail with the history, rationale, and analysis of the European construction of "racial" identity to place the identity matter into its political and historical perspective. We are certainly phenotypically a "Black" people. Culture had always been the basis for *core fundamental identities* for everyone in the world until European domination of Africans began with a vengeance (Hilliard, 2001). The old rules for identity determination were changed from culture to the fabricated construct "race." Then, as a part of the effort to dehumanize us, the attempt was made to alienate us from our history and culture and to rank the "races" with Africans at the bottom. Again, this strategy is still in operation, centered in the Academy.

Who are we? The matter of our ethnic identity is fundamental or else there really is no *we.* I have no message at all for anyone of African descent who does not see himself or herself as a part of the African ethnic *family,* but rather acts as one who has no ethnic ties. I wish all such "individuals" well. Any confusion over family identity is a guarantee of defeat for our people. Likewise clarity regarding family identity is a prerequisite for self-determination and direction.

In general, students, faculty, administrators, and policy makers do not come to higher education with a neutral identity, even though they may not be conscious of their identity until there is a crisis. Everyone expects their involvement in the Academy to be beneficial to them *and to their communities.* Traditionally for Africans we expect benefits from higher education for ourselves and for mankind as a whole, however, some of us have lost consciousness and now seek to be rescued by others, and by their vision of the world.

To review, the African experience with hegemony, over the past 400 years in particular, has been one where European oppressors created a conceptual master stroke, *cleverly shifting the focus of identity determination for African people and others from the traditional global criterion of shared culture and civilization to aspects of phenotype, using the fabricated construct of "race."* One critical consequence of this devious and deliberate shift from culture to phenotype is that it facilitated the *devastating alienation of Africans from our ancient and modern unique cultural systems.* The explicit intent of oppressors was *dehumanization,* not merely physical containment. Since *culture is the essence of humanity,* the brunt of the attack on us was directed there. The iron curtain was drawn between Africans and traditional African culture worldwide. An attempt was made to offer a falsified history and culture in place of the authentic one. That mis-education process continues today. Any concern with African culture at all was for purpose of economic, ideological, or military exploitation, not African liberation.

While phenotype is related to ethnicity, a divide-and-conquer focus on the *individual "Black"* person's current political and economic struggle is quite insufficient to deal with matters that are of utmost importance to Africans. *It is our people's collective, self-determined welfare and destiny that must be at the center of our thoughts and actions!* This consciousness and self-determination is the very thing that oppressors oppose, violently if necessary.

Our *condition*, oppression, or political-economic powerlessness is not our identity. Our identity is not "the poor," "the disadvantaged," "the oppressed," "the at risk." Like all other successful ethnic groups, our *identity is a function of our shared cultural creativities and traditions and in our shared destiny.* With this in mind anyone should be able to decode the attempts by power brokers to select people of African descent to function as individuals who are then *appointed* as our "leaders," "spokespersons," and "role models," with no confirmation by members of the African community.

We must never forget that the critical issues facing Africans in "the Academy" are global. We make a grave error by using the relatively recent American experience with slavery, segregation, and White supremacy ideology as the exclusive basis for a fundamental analysis of our situation. We existed as a highly developed and civilized people long before there was a Europe as a concept. Yet the African continental experience with oppression is virtually the same as the African experience in America and the rest of the diaspora as well. There is no place today where African people are free of European economic, political, and ideological domination. Virtually all our people who receive a "higher education" do so in institutions that are under the direct or indirect control of philanthropists or governments, virtually none of which are controlled by Africans, even on the African continent.

The character of the system of hegemony is the same everywhere. Its use of higher education and scholarship as power tools in the system of domination has been central and is thoroughly documented. We are faced, therefore, with a problem of awesome proportions. We may have no choice except to be "educated" in systems of higher education that still do not have our interests at the center, and indeed in many cases have been designed explicitly to destroy us as a people. On that the record is crystal clear. That is not rhetoric. That is history (Chase, 1977; Guthrie, 1998; Ani, 1994; Chinweizu, 1987a, 1987b; Wilson, 1998; Shujaa, 1995; King, 1971; Watkins, Lewis, and Chou, 2001; Hilliard, 2001; Watkins, 2001).

The African Intellectual Tradition

Any brother in the Academy must start with awareness of the African excellence tradition, ancient and modern, in higher education, which *predates slavery, colonization apartheid,* and *White supremacy ideology.* Many African students have, as a function of mis-education, come to expect global experiences in higher education as something that is owned and legitimized solely by non-African people. In fact, some Africans in the Academy believe that access to higher education is a favor or a privilege given, rather than an inalienable right and a continuity of African heritage as well as the heritage of others. They may even feel that they do not belong in the Academy. As will be shown, nothing could be further from the truth.

Africans developed towering intellectual institutions long before Europe existed as a concept, and independent of Europe, even after its rise to power in recent centuries. KMT (Egypt) developed independent of and in most cases prior to Europe's existence, prior even to ancient Greece (Diop, 1991; Chinweizu, 1987a; Hilliard, 1998; Asante & Abbary, 1996; Van Sertima, 1994; Finch, 1998; Carruthers, 1995a). Ancient Greek records claim an African priority and influence on Greece's development of science, philosophy, religion, the arts and architecture, etc. One thing is certain, there is a robust record of African intellectual excellence thousands of years before the "Greek miracle."

Those Greek claims of African anteriority and influence are confirmed by independent documentation of the antiquity of African civilization and by the relationship of these older forms to later European borrowings. This includes higher education itself. For example there is no earlier recorded surviving university, with actual structures and texts, than those found at Waset, KMT (Luxor, Egypt), specifically at the University of Ipt Ast (Karnak-Luxor temple complex). The Pyramid Texts, Coffin Texts, and numerous papyri and temple and monumental inscriptions attest to advanced medicine, architecture, philosophy, astronomy, engineering, mathematics, etc., long before 4000 years ago (Van Sertima, 1994; Diop, 1991; Obenga, 1992)! Brothers of the Academy need to become familiar with the records. It is likely that this will have to be done on one's own initiative. The Academy in general seems to have no knowledge to offer here.

Brothers of the Academy must also be familiar with the Niger valley and environs in West Africa in such locations as Jenne, Timbuktu, and Gao, as well as the more distant Sokoto in Nigeria. In addition we have yet to master an understanding of the rich traditional secret higher education of the Dogon in Mali, the Lemba in the Congo, and other similar complex systems of higher education. We did not come to the Western hemisphere ignorant and empty handed (Saad, 1983; Thompson, 1981).

The fact that these towering achievement are so little known, even within the community of African people, paves the way for common views of African traditions as "illiterate," "non-intellectual," "savage," "pagan," etc. Many Africans choose not to look back beyond the curtain that is drawn at 1492 on the history. Some fear being shamed. Some fear that remembering is a waste of time. Some see no connection to themselves. Yet it is clear to any one who knows these things that African people can walk, heads held high, into any— including the most elite—institutions of higher education with a full sense of entitlement.

Two things in particular must be kept in mind when trying to comprehend the African experience; that is the pre-colonial and pre-slavery African experience in higher education. One is the aim or purpose of higher education. The other is the content/process for teaching and learning. Africans have set the pace here (Carruthers, 1995a; Obenga, 1992).

It is absolutely essential that African people and the world understand that the current low condition of African people is due directly to European *cultural wars* on Africans that began in earnest nearly 2000 years ago with the Romans, specifically initiated by Emperor Constantine. The culture war was continued by Roman emperors who followed, such as Justininan and Theodosius. These culture wars included hundreds of years of military campaigns up the Nile to shut down all systems of indigenous cultural transmission. Culture wars then and later, during the slavery, colonization, apartheid, and White supremacy periods meant that Africans would not only be conquered, but would be fundamentally changed to become *not African*. At least that was the intent. As John Henrik Clarke said so often, "Europeans would not only colonize the world, *they would also colonize information about the world. They would colonize scholarship. They would even colonize the image of God!*"

We must understand the massive, sophisticated, and systematic dehumanization and mis-education process. It was a two-part thrust. On the one hand oppressors acted to *prevent intergenerational cultural transmission by any means necessary.* On the other hand they shaped a crippling, falsified, and dehumanizing curriculum. Picture European slavery with its "dis"-education. *Picture gatherings of European powerbrokers meeting in secret at Lake Monhonk retreat in New York and at Capon Springs retreat in West Virginia over the course of more than two decades at the turn of the twentieth century to design the miseducation process for Africans!* This is one of the smoking guns. From these meetings came the design and implementation of a ceiling and a culturally disorienting schooling for African higher education worldwide. Africans were sentenced to a weak and disabling form of "industrial education." Kenneth King (1971), Carruthers (1999a, 1995b), and more recently William Watkins (2001) have gone into great detail to document the calculated and sophisticated structuring of hegemony and mis-education in higher education for Africans on the *continent and in the diaspora* (Anderson, 1988).

For example in the early 1900s Thomas Jesse Jones from the United States, C.T. Loram from South Africa, and E.K. Oldham from England, with the help of the Phelps Stokes Fund, worked as a committee to control nearly all of higher education for Africans on the continent and in the diaspora during the early part of the twentieth century without the advice or consent of

Africans. *This was truly the uncomprising battle for the collective mind, soul and spirit of the African,* not merely the African individual.

This mis-education process has taken many forms, from the think tanks in the woods at Lake Mohawk and Capon Springs to the contemporary think tanks that have produced newer, even more deadly and sophisticated culture wars (Bloom, 1987; Schlessinger, 1998; Lefkowitz, 1997). A whole literature is available that comes from these wars over time. The Brothers of the Academy must be familiar with that literature. The form of the uses of higher mis-education have changed but the intent remains in much of higher education today (Woodson, 1969; Aptheker, 1973; King, 1964; Watkins, 1992). Witness the publication of *The Bell Curve* supported by the Bradley Foundation, with the book's surviving author, Charles Murray, connected to the Heritage Foundation. Neither foundation has disavowed this shoddy scholarly propaganda and defamation.

In the face of European attempts to establish and to maintain mental hegemony, African intellectuals went to war (Carruthers, 1999b). That war continues. It is a war to rescue and to reconstruct the hidden traditional paths. It is a war to reinstate the process of intergenerational cultural transmission within the African family or community. It is a war for Africans to have a meaningful influence in the common higher education institution, which professes a mission to serve all, and which claims for itself the label "university."

The role call of role models for Brothers in the Academy is one that could go on forever. The role models have challenged the philosophy and structure of the Academy. The role models have had a major impact of academic disciplines. They have acted with great courage in the face of great challenges.

Hegemony Understood in Higher Education

The essence of the practice of hegemony is the *division of collective,* the destruction of the ethnic family, the elevation of the loner, and the acceptance of the propaganda of individualism. For that to happen cultural genocide is perpetrated (ben Jochanan, 1972).

History has shown that higher education is essential to hegemony, since in the final analysis ideas are the most potent of all weapons. A massive literature documents the uses of higher education institutions, the scholarship that defines and legitimates reality as the engine of domination (Schmidt, 2000; Carruthers, 1995b; King, 1971; Shujaa, 1995; Wilson, 1998).

"The Academy" is always an imperfect vehicle, reflecting the bias and the power agenda of the society within which it is embedded. The institutional ideals of the search for truth are not the only ideals that are present. Moreover the personnel who carry out the higher education agenda are themselves vested in their own personal interests. This statement is not based upon a naive notion of very human institutions. It is simply a challenge to the rhetorical claims for the mythical "objectivity" and "dispassionate" knowledge creation and transmission process that really serves as a sign of self-serving scholarship.

Response to Our Awaking

To assert these things is to stimulate predictable challenges to our objectivity, to our "particularism" as opposed to the desired "universalism" to validity etc. These challenges usually come from the most biased, particularistic academicians whose work may even by overtly propagandistic (Young, 1990; Schmidt, 2000; Smith, 1999).

There is overwhelming evidence of the superiority of student achievement and superiority of higher education institutional achievement, contradictory to the rumors of African inferiority. The astonishing record of Dr. Abdulalim Shabazz is something to behold. With marginal-to-good students in mathematics, his teaching at Atlanta University during the 1960s and the 1970s resulted in the production of nearly half of the Ph.D.s in mathematics ever produced in the United States! So much for their low SAT and ACT scores. Note also the awesome work of Dr. Israel Tribble with the McKnight Scholars program sponsored by the Florida Endowment in Tampa, Florida. Hundreds of Ph.D. students are in the pipeline or have already graduated in all curriculum areas, mainly science and mathematics! Note the work of Dr. Leroy Irving, who established a developmental studies program for specially admitted weak students at the University of Georgia during the 1980s. One evaluation showed that the overwhelming majority of marginal special admittees tested out of the developmental studies program in one year or less and equaled or outperformed the regular admitted students in the core academic program at the university!

The point to be made is that our genius requires nothing other than good nurturance. Our students do not lack ability. That is not the issue. The issue is what type of higher education will we receive?

We still live in a society that has failed to acknowledge the depth of the abuse inflicted upon us, especially the cultural genocide, and to atone for that oppressive treatment through centuries, aided and abetted by many in the higher education community. Worse, higher education institutional structures still have not been purged of their legacies of false, defamatory, and hegemonic scholarship.

The Task Now

Brothers of the Academy have the task of getting over hurdles, blasting through them, or requiring that the African standard of *maat* (truth, justice, righteousness, balance, order and reciprocity) be upheld. African preservation and uses of our culture are required. African critical consciousness is required. The African process of becoming *Jegnas* is required. In African terms, the *Jegna* (in Cush or Ethiopia), the *Jeli/Jelimuso* (in West Africa, also called *Griot* by French speakers), and the *Sesh* or *Sba* (in KMT or Egypt) are the deep thinkers and committed scholar-activists who, "at the price of their lives, protect their people, land and culture." They have uncommon courage and are tried in battle. *These great African teachers strive to always speak the truth!* It is these traditional high standards toward which the Brothers of the Academy should strive.

We can chose to be in the academy one by one, or as one. This is the choice of a lifetime. May we honor our ancestors with the right choice and with "Good Speech" (Carruthers, 1995a).

References

Akbar, N. (1992). *Chains and images of psychological slavery.* New Jersey: New Mind Productions.

Anderson, J.D. (1988). *The education of the negro in the south: 1860–1935.* Chapel Hill: University of North Carolina Press.

Ani, M. (1994). *Yurugu: An African centered critique of European thought and behavior.* New York: Africa World Press.

Aptheker, H. (ed). (1973). *The education of the Negro: Ten critiques, 1906–1960 by W.E.B. DuBois.* New York: Monthly Review Press.

Armah, A.K. (1995). *Osirus rising.* Popenguine, West Africa: Per Ankh.

Armah, A.K. (1979). *Two thousand seasons.* Chicago: Third World Press.

Asante, M.K. (1987). *The Afrocentric idea.* Philadelphia: Temple University Press.

Asante, M.K., and Abarry, A.S. (eds.). (1996). *African intellectual heritage: A book of sources.* Philadelphia: Temple University Press.

ben Jochannan, Y. (1972). *Cultural genocide in the black and African Studies curriculum.* New York: Alkebulan Press.

Bloom, A.D. (1987). *The closing of the American mind.* New York: Simon and Schuster.

Cabral, A. (1973) *Return to the source: Selected speeches by Amilcar Cabral.* New York: Monthly Review Press.

Carruthers, J.C. (ed.) (1999a). *African world history project.* Los Angeles: The Association for the Study of Classical Civilizations.

Carruthers, J.C. (1999b). *Intellectual warfare.* Chicago: Third World Press.

Carruthers, J.C. (1995a). *MDW NTR: Divine Speech, a historical reflection of African deep thought from the time of the pharaohs to the present.* London: Karnak House.

Carruthers, J.C. (1995b). Science and oppression. In Daudi Azibo (ed.), *African psychology in historical perspective and related commentary.* Trenton, New Jersey: Africa World Press.

Chase, A. (1977). *The legacy of Malthus: The social costs of the new scientific racism.* New York: Alfred Knopf.

Chinweizu. (1987a). *Decolonizing African literature.* Washington, DC: Howard University Press.

Chinweizu. (1987b). *Decolonizing the African mind.* London: Pero Press.

Cruse, H. (1967). *The crisis of the Negro intellectual.* New York: William Morrow.

Davis, K.C. (1990). *Don't know much about history: Everything you need to know about American history but never learned.* New York: Avon Books.

Deloria, V. Jr. (1997). *Indians and anthropologists: Vine Deloria Jr. and the critique of anthropology.* Tuscon: The University of Arizona Press.

Diop, C.A. (1991). *Civilization or barbarism: An authentic anthropology.* Brooklyn: Lawrence Hill.

Finch, C. (1998). *Star of deep beginnings.* Decatur, Georgia: Khenti Inc.

Guthrie, R. (1998). *Even the rat was white.* New York: Harper and Row.

Hilliard, A.G. III (2001). Race, Identity, hegemony and education: what do we need to know now? In Watkins Williams, Lewis, James H., & Chou, Victoria (eds.). *Race and education: The roles of history and society in educating African American students.* Boston: Allyn Bacon.

Hilliard, A.G. III. (1998). *SBA: The reawakening of the African mind.* Gainesville, FL: Makare Publishers.

Hilliard, A.G. III. (1997). *Psychology as political science and as a double edged sword: Racism and counter racism.*

Hilliard, A.G. III. (1995). *The maroon within us: Essays on African American community socialization.* Baltimore: Black Classics Press.

Hilliard, A.G. III, Payton, S.L., and Williams, L.O. (1990). *The infusion of African and African American content in the school curriculum: First national conference proceedings, October 1989.* Chicago: Third World Press.

Hodge, J.L., Struckman, D.K., and Trost, L.D. (1975). *Cultural basis of racism and group oppression: An examination of traditonal "Western" concepts, values, and institutional structures which support racism, sexism, and elitism.* Berkeley, CA: Two Riders Press.

Karenga, M. (1982). *Introduction to Black studies.* Los Angeles: University of Sankore Press.

King, K. (1971). *Pan Africanism and education: A study of race, philanthropy and education in the southern states of America and East Africa.* Oxford: Clarendon Press.

Lefkowitz, M. (1997). *Not out of Africa: How Afrocentrism became an excuse to teach myth as history.* New York: Harper Collins.

Lowen, J.W. (1996). *Lies my teacher told me: Everything your American history text got wrong.* New York: Touchstone.

Lowen, J.W. (1995). *Lies across America: What our historic sites got wrong.* New York: Touchstone.

Ngubane, J.K. (1989). *Conflict of minds.* New York: Books in Focus.

Nobles, W. (1986). *African psychology: Towards its reclamation, reascension and revitalization.* Oakland, CA: A Black Family Institute.

Obenga, T. (1992). *Ancient Egypt and black Africa: A student handbook for study of ancient Egyptian philosophy, linguistics, and gender relations.* Chicago: Front Line International.

Ptahhotep, 2350 B.C.E., KMT (Egypt) (*Good* or Beautiful *Speech* is an ideal of true, just, right, balance, and harmony). In Asa G. Hilliard III, Larry Obadele Williams, & Nia Damali (Eds.) (1987). *The Teachings of Ptahhotep: The Oldest Book in the World.* Atlanta: Blackwood Press.

Saad, E. (1983). *The social history of Timbuktu: The role of Muslim scholars and notables, 1400 to 1900.* New York: Cambridge University Press.

Schlessinger, A. (1998). *The disuniting of America: Reflections on a multicultural society.* New York: W.W. Norton.

Schmidt, J. (2000). *Disciplined minds: A critical look at salaried professionals and the soul-battering system that shapes their lives.* New York: Rowman and Littlefield Publishers, Inc.

Sheldon, S. (1991). Selective traditions and the science curriculum: Eugenics and biology textbooks, 1914–1949. *Science Education, 75,* 493–512.

Shujaa, M. (1995). *Too much schooling, too little education: A paradox of Black life in White societies.* Trenton, NJ: Africa World Press.

Skutnall-Kangas, T. (2000). *Linguistic genocide in education: Or worldwide diversity and human rights:* Mahwah, NJ: Lawrence Erlbaum Associates Publishers.

Smith, L.T. (1999). *Decolonizing methodologies: Research and indigenous peoples.* New York: Zed Books Ltd.

Spivey, D. (1978). *Schooling for the new slavery: Black industrial education, 1868–1915.* Westport, CT: Greenwood.

Tucker, W.H. (1994). *The science and politics of racial research.* Chicago: University of Illinois Press.

Wa Thiong'o, N. (1987). *Decolonizing the mind: The politics of language in African literature.* Portsmouth, NH: Heinemann.

Watkins, W. (2001). *The White Architects of Black Education: Ideology of Power in America, 1865–1954.* New York: Teachers College Press.

Weinreich, M. (1946). *Hitler's professors: The part of scholarship in Germany's crimes against the Jewish people.* New York: Yiddish Scientific Institute.

Wilson, A.N. (1998). *Blueprint for black power: A moral, political and economic imperative for the twenty-first century.* New York: Afrikan World InfoSystems.

Woodson, C.G. (1969/1983). *Miseducation of the negro.* Washington, DC: Associated Publishers.

Wright, B.E. (1975). The psychopathic racial personality. Chicago: Institute of Positive Education.

Young, R. (1990). White mythologies: Writing History and the West. New York: Routledge.

Cyrus Marcellus Ellis

Cyrus Marcellus Ellis is currently an assistant professor of counselor education in the Department of Educational Studies at the University of Tennessee-Martin. He specializes in counselor education instruction and socioracial conditions. Dr. Ellis' professional employment history focused on clinical treatment and the re-employment of individuals suffering from chronic mental illness and substance abuse. Dr. Ellis is an active member of the American Counseling Association, the Brothers of the Academy Institute, the Association for Counselor Educators and Supervisors, and CHI SIGMA IOTA an international honor society. Dr. Ellis served in the United States Army for 16 years in both the active and reserve components.

5

EXAMINING THE PITFALLS FACING AFRICAN AMERICAN MALES

Cyrus Marcellus Ellis

". . . What from the slums
Where they have hemmed you,
What, from the tiny huts
They could not keep from you—
What reaches them
Making them ill at ease, fearful
Today they shout prohibition at you
'Thou shalt not this'
'Thou shalt not that'
'Reserved for whites only'
You laugh.

One thing they cannot prohibit—
The strong men . . . coming on
The strong men gettin' stronger
Strong men . . .
STRONGER . . ."

—Sterling A. Brown

The Civil Rights movement of the 1950s, the Black Power movement of the 1960s, and the resulting exposure of the African American experience over the last thirty years in music, cinema, and art have revealed the consciousness of a people wrestling with legitimate and illegitimate barriers to their existence.

Legitimately African American people, as well as other persons, have to contend with various biological and environmental barriers that potentially hinder their ascension to greater levels of society. African American people are not significantly different from other people in the nation who are acquainted with birth abnormalities, chemical dependency among parental units and offspring, deteriorating housing conditions, increasing inflation, greater demands on school budgets, single parenthood, and the need to work beyond retirement age (Ellis, 2000). Illegitimately African Americans experience barriers that are disparate from other groups. Judicially African American men represent 88 percent of the prison population convicted for crack cocaine (Neuner, 1999). The Sentencing Project (1995) revealed that one in three African American men in their twenties are either incarcerated in jail, in prison, or are on probation. Additionally African Americans accounted for 13 percent of drug users but constituted 35 percent of drug possession arrests, 55 percent of drug convictions and 74 percent of prison sentences. The Sentencing Project stated that if the same statistics were among Caucasian men the nation would declare a national emergency. African American people live in a nation that possesses contradictory *rules of engagement*. The term *contradictory rules of engagement* refers to the emotional, behavioral, and cognitive response sets transmitted by members of the dominant culture towards African American people regarding their perceived intelligence, overall capabilities, social/work habits, and sexuality (Samuels, 1995). While it is not a new phenomenon for African American people to wrestle with biased and prejudicial treatment, the methods employed by individuals to watch over themselves while navigating these harsh environmental forces require specific identification and articulation. In order for African Americans to withstand the inequitable response sets from the dominant culture as well as the explicit and implicit messages of our society, strict attention ought to focus on the individual at the epicenter of the dilemma. Notwithstanding the racial stigma shared between African American men and women (U.S. News and World Report, 2001), this text involves specific dimensions related to the pitfalls surrounding African American males.

Webster defines the term *pitfall* as a trap or a concealed pit in the ground designed to snare an animal. The term *pitfall* is also defined as an unexpected difficulty or hidden danger. The latter supplies the premise for the direction of the text.

The African American male confronts a plethora of external forces and conflicting internal messages (Webber, 1999). Understanding the areas that shape the self has the potential to assist an individual to avoid various hidden dangers located within our society. The focus of this commentary involves the examination of three areas possessing hidden dangers that African American men face: (a) articulating the particular items involved in developing a healthy sense of self, (b) the precarious posture of nihilism, and (c) the nature of higher education for African American men. The first two areas relate directly to the phenomenology and phenomenological responses of African American men in today's society and the third area speaks to the nature of higher education and the pitfall of an aimless collegiate existence.

Pitfall I: Understanding the Determinants of the Self

Attempting to articulate the parameters of the self is an intricate undertaking for anyone. Adding to the difficulty of determining the self is the influx of societal cues that complicate the unbiased and impartial development of self-evaluations. Ruth C. Wylie (1961) began the formal process addressing the indistinctness of defining the self. Wylie's work revealed that a universal understanding is necessary when defining the self in critical terms. Where Wylie's work began the investigation into identifying the critical nature of the self, Richard J. Shavelson, Judith J. Hubner, and George C. Stanton's (1976) work labeled the nature of the self. Richard Shavelson et al.'s work granted access to the understanding of self by eloquently stating that an individual's self-evaluation was dependent upon his discernment of himself, as well as his reactions to his circumstances. Crain and Bracken (1994) formalized the process of examining the self by combining the work of Shavelson, et al., and in so doing created a model of understanding the self by interlocking six identifiable domains (affect, social, physical, competence, academic, and family) that constitute a global self-concept. Crain and Bracken's definition of the self is systematic according to identifiable and comprehensive responses involving an individual's achievements and failures in an assortment of environments, the way in which other people choose to respond to their actions, and the approach other persons take to mirror their actions and transmit their behaviors. Consequently Crain and Bracken encapsulates the self, "as an organized response pattern that is acquired and maintained through an individual's actions upon and reactions to stimuli in various environmental contexts." (p. 497). Understanding the self through Bracken's established point of reference generates some interesting questions when applying this construct to African Americans: (a) to what extent do socioracial injustices factor into the African American male's response pattern to his environment, and (b) what are the affects on the self when African American men respond to imperceptible environmental stimuli?

Judith Porter and Robert E. Washington (1989) began the process of answering these questions by reviewing the dimensions of the self from the viewpoint of Black Americans. Porter and Washington (unlike Wylie, Shavelson, and Crain and Bracken) explored the factor of racial injustice on the African American psyche. Porter and Washington's work explored the consequences of the assumed personal insecure nature of minorities in America as well as the phenomenon known as "the mark of oppression," a psychoanalytically pretentious model suggesting the entirety of African Americans internalized negative, racial images of themselves (p. 341). Their analysis provided insight into the role socioracial injustice impact African American response patterns to their environment. Porter and Washington point out that this view dissolved with the rise of the Black militancy movement of the 1960s that infused the African American community with self-pride and positive racial images. The rise in positive black images and the promotion of pro-Black ideals changed the manner in which African American males viewed their environment. Porter and Washington concluded that the way Black people saw themselves was a combination of individual and racial awareness. Individual awareness involves the overall view of self that reflects self worth, aptitude, and self-respect. Racial awareness encompasses the progressive movement towards understanding the role of race in one's life.

Today African American men are facing a resurgence of the climate that supported the mark of oppression just a short time ago. Negative images of African American men have resurfaced into profitable endeavors, thereby recreating an environment of unfavorable but positively framed racial images broadcast by two of the farthest reaching mediums—television and radio. Located within the glamour and popularity of Black entertainment, there exists the projection of a negative, although financially rewarded, Black image. Historically African American men have faced negative images as lazy, shiftless, and simple people. Currently these images take the form of modern day gangsters and oversexed men fulfilling a multitude of hedonistic desires. What is the problem? The problem is that the African American male environment that inherently involves the display of negative images of African American men now includes socially acceptable and profitable images of negative behavior that are considered to be the construct in describing the Black male. Young Black males have been duped into believing that the lyrics broadcast and visual images displayed on television through the overabundance of rap and video shows correspond to their true nature as African American men (Matthews, 2000). The adoption of these synthetic value sets form a posture within the psyche of African American males that possesses the potential to hamper their ability to develop healthy relationships with African American women, potentially add to the overpopulation of Black males in prison (currently number-ing around one million), and decrease the college enrollment rates for African American men (Roach, 2001). Matthews conceptualizes this thought (when referring to the impact of rap music on African American men) by stating, "We all need to get serious about helping these young people discern the inevitable consequences of hipping and hopping their opportunities away. Believe me, if we don't, the unsavory pied pipers of hip-hop will lead them to a place that none of us wants to see them go."

Whether it is Crain and Bracken's (1994) notion of the self, Porter and Washington's (1989) dual vision of the self, or a contrived meaning of self, African American males must avoid the hidden snare of subscribing to artifi-cially formed determinants of Black identity created by the images of the twenty-first century. African American men must come to realize the danger of the re-institution of negative images framed by monetary reward, hedonistic pleasure, and status as a detriment to developing healthy self-evaluations regarding themselves as African Americans.

The notion that African American males adopt artificially generated ideas to govern their sense of self carries with it a second hidden danger. As societal genres change, the individual who looks to societal mores for guidance must also change. If societal values conflict with individual, familial, or racial norms, the individual may find himself at the crossroads of skepticism and despondency. Many young African American males find themselves in this pre-carious position on a daily basis. They are unsure as to the direction of their lives and are additionally hesitant about choosing endeavors that are repre-sentative of foreign social and cultural beliefs. If this cloud of despair goes unrestricted, the second, and most dangerous, hidden snare will claim future generations of African American males.

Pitfall II: Nihilism

Discussing nihilism as a pitfall facing African American men is a topic that connects with countless facets of the Black man's experience in America. In every dimension of African American life there stands an eternal struggle to determine for oneself the underpinnings of one's existence. Throughout the hundreds of years that African American men have existed in America, socio-racial conditions have created an existential vacuum—a condition of empti-ness and hollowness that results from meaninglessness in life—that has fueled the fires of nihilistic living for many of our young brothers.

Nihilism, as proposed by Albert Camus (Novak, 1999), is a problem of meaninglessness for each individual. Vincent Perez (2000), writing about nihilism and cultural memory in Chicano urban narratives, describes nihilism from the perspective of a race-based and punitive society that inexorably surrounds urban youth. This is an examination of nihilism as a position unconsciously assumed by African American males to the idea that all values and beliefs are enigmatic and worthless and, consequently, existence is artificial. This does not mean to presuppose that all African Americans possess a disposition of nihilism. Rather the departure from previously held values by many African Americans is a result of nihilism. The author's experience as a Health and Human Service professional serving the poor and working class African American population located in a large urban city will provide additional information to draw out this point.

To begin, many African Americans in our community may not know nor care about the term *nihilism,* although they may have experienced it and verbalize it, somewhat, on a daily basis. Perez (2000) conceptualizes this point by examining Richard Wright's text *Native Son,* illustrating that nihilism in the mind of the urban African American is a cognizant response that manifests itself to oppose the inequitable socioracial and political conditions inherent in the urban community. African American opposition to society can take the form of gangs, cessation of educational endeavors, and involvement in the use and/or distribution of illicit substances. The nature of our society, when applied to members of particular racial and economic groups, carries with it inequitable treatment. Social structure theorists have studied the manner of our society and the manner by which society creates the feeling of nihilism in minority and low income groups. Strain theorists posit a model of understanding the resulting oppositional behavior from individuals living at lower levels of the socioeconomic ladder. It does not contend that a person's socioeconomic status nor their value set motivates the manifestation of opposing behavior **but it is** the illegitimate denial of achieving like social and financial successes that does (Siegel and Senna, 1988). The "strain" that develops in the individual is the realization that the products and pleasures of life available to other members of society are personally out of reach. Therefore individuals affected through this process develop alternative means (gangs, illegitimate enterprise, etc.) of acquiring the superfluity of American culture. The pitfall of nihilism, then, is in the period of time between the individual's recognition of strain and the chosen attitudinal and behavioral responses to that strain. At the point of recognizing the inauthenticity of societal values and the aspiration to abandon any continued adherence to them, the African American man will find himself in an extreme circumstance.

As a Health and Human Service professional, I have witnessed the emotional devastation and the resulting negative behavioral actions of African American men who have dismissed the morality of their environment because of the incongruence between explicit social messages (liberty and justice for all, fair and impartial jury, equal opportunity employer) and staunch reality.

Working with African American men and adolescents on issues ranging from recovery to interpersonal skills has revealed to me indispensable amounts of insight. I remember talking to a group of African American adolescent males ranging in age from fifteen to seventeen years of age. They were part of program designed to house young boys torn between leaving or returning to their homes. I was asked to come into the program and attempt to motivate the youngsters to return home and re-engage in a society that has already demonstrated numerous inconsistencies regarding love, education, and opportunity. I remember one young man was a few months away from his eighteenth birthday. Throughout our discussion this young man consistently denied attachment to any definable set of cultural, social, or ethnic values. He preferred to espouse his desire to participate in arbitrary local subculture rituals of hanging out late, skipping school, smoking blunts (cigars emptied of their tobacco and refilled with marijuana), drinking wine, and doing as little as possible. When asked the question, "Do you see a change coming in your life?" he replied, "No." I called to his attention his impending birthday. I asked him if he saw the significance of that day. The young man only replied that it is just another day. I answered him by saying, "For you that may be the case, but for the law it is not." I wanted him to see that his reasoning of negating the values and beliefs of his home, community, and society—thereby rendering them meaningless in his life—did not remove the consequences that his behavioral responses would bring upon him under the auspices of being socially and legally defined as an adult. It is in this state that African American men find themselves susceptible to the additional snares of our society, such as contact with the justice system, missed educational and vocational opportunities, and susceptibility to drug addiction. Where there exists nothingness, nothing matters. Whether it was my role as a social worker or as an outpatient therapist, I have personally witnessed the internal struggle that surrounds African American men caught in the snare of nothingness. The snare of nothingness creates uncertainty in the minds of African American males that unconsciously shapes their reactions to the world around them. These reactions, however justified in the mind of the Black male, encounter a dominant culture primarily disconnected and largely unresponsive to the plight of persons living along the racial divide.

Pitfall III: The Nature of Higher Education for African American Men

The nature of higher education encompasses various levels of challenges, obstacles, and rewards. The role higher education plays in society is an important one, for it facilitates the movement of the society (Hall and Rowan, 2000). My alma mater, the University of Virginia, exemplifies this belief by using the words of its founder, Thomas Jefferson, to describe the importance of higher education within a democracy. Mr. Jefferson believed that the key to a democracy was an educated citizenry. Unfortunately, early on these words were not met with equal action for all people at all institutions. Although the face of higher education has changed on the grounds of UV and other campuses, the nature of higher education for African Americans, particularly African American males, comprise a variety of hidden snares, of which Black men need to be cognizant.

Nature is defined as the physical world and its phenomena. Nature is also defined as the process and forces *producing* and *controlling* the physical world. For African American men who are successful in navigating the harsh waters of a society with contradictory rules of engagement and emerge as an individual petitioning to enter higher education, the nature of higher education can be problematic for Black men until they recognize those forces producing and controlling the academic environment they have entered. The nature of African American men on college campuses involve (a) their level of academic preparedness, and (b) facing a harsh school climate.

Large populations of African American men begin their collegiate journey at a disadvantage from their European counterparts (Hall and Rowan, 2000). Academic preparedness refers to the degree to which an individual has received educational opportunities prior to entering higher education. Smith (1999) identified academic preparedness, as well as other social tools, as a major factor in nonretention for African American male college students. Comprehensive academic coursework in high school, as well as exposure to academic opportunities beyond high school, increases the African American student's ability to set clear collegiate goals, declare a major, and complete his program. According to Smith, Black men entering college lacking a clear academic focus, a solid educational beginning, and knowledge of what they wish to study, do not persist and drop out of school.

The academic environment that receives African American male students is multifaceted and is potentially harmful to the overall success of Black male students. College campuses around our nation possess student bodies and faculty members who have disparaging views concerning African American students. African American athletes carry the stigma of the "dumb", Black, athlete only present in college because he can run, dribble, or block, and who ordinarily would not be a student. The historical connotations regarding African American men and their intellectual ability still exist in the psyche of the American public. The African American male student is confronted with the expression of this premise in higher education. These conditions contribute to feelings of isolation and the impersonality of the institution, thereby draining potential academic motivation from the student semester-to-semester.

The forces producing and controlling the environment of higher education are intertwined around administrators, faculty, support staff, geographic location, and student body to name a few. Each force shapes the culture of the institution and forms the manner by which it addresses a variety of issues. African American males entering this arena need to pay careful attention to the climate of their particular institution in order to be successful in their academic pursuits. Nikki Giovanni (1991) provides insight into specific behaviors for African American students ought to adopt to be successful on predominately White college campuses. They include: (a) go to class, no matter how you feel or how you think your professor feels about you, (b) meet with your professor and assist them in learning your name, (c) complete your assignments when directed and inform your professor of any changes, and (d) inquire about your work and seek their guidance to improve it to "A" level work. Greater insight into the ability to navigate the college campus environment can be found by following up on the programs detailed in Joan Morgan's (1996) article in *Black Issues in Higher Education*.

Conclusion

African American men face a number of environmental and internal stressors. Among the multitude of entrapments facing African American men, understanding the impact of modern Black images on developing a positive self identity, as well as the danger of abandoning all values and social norms, stand as two areas upon which to concentrate.

African American men need to closely monitor the role of socially accepted negative images affecting their personal evaluations. Careful attention needs to focus on the glorification of financially rewarded representations of Black culture that promote the establishment of negative racial images as the construct for Black identity.

Secondly, African American men need to be conscious of the strain that develops from living in an oppositional society. African American men need to educate themselves to the various illegitimate barriers present in their lives and, more importantly, monitor their reactions, cognitively and behaviorally, to the strain that results from coming into contact with an unbalanced society. Monitoring their behavioral responses to this strain allows African American men to remain connected to society. In so doing Black men avoid entering a state of meaninglessness indicative of developing unfavorable life patterns.

Lastly, African Americans in higher education face many of the same hurdles found in the American fabric. Low expectations and racial bias exist on college and university campuses across our nation. While it may be some time before concerned people can eliminate the roots of racism in our society, African American males can work to avoid the trap of becoming a dropout statistic as well as negatively reacting to a campus environment by preparing themselves for success. Careful attention to developing clear academic pursuits, developing a healthy support network, and sound academic behavior can assist African American male students in completing their academic journey in higher education, thereby contributing to society and their community (Morgan, 1996).

References

Brown, S.A. (1966). Strong men. In Abraham Chapman *Black voices* (pp. 419–420). New York: Penguin Books.

Crain, R.M. & Bracken, B.A. (1994). Age, race and gender differences in child and adolescent self-concept: Evidence from a behavioral-acquisition, context-dependent model. *School Psychology Review, 23,* 496–511

Ellis, C.M. (2001). *Racial attitudes and the counseling environment.* Paper presented at the meeting of the American Counseling Association, San Antonio, TX.

Giovanni, N. (1991). Campus racism 101; on the subject of being Black on a White college campus, professor and (poet) Nikki Giovanni offers this freshman course on how to ace it. *Essence, 22,* 71–73.

Hall, R.E., & Rowan, G.T. (2000). African American males in higher education: A descriptive/qualitative analysis. *Journal of African American Men, 5,* 3–14.

Mathews, F.L. (2000). Hipping and hopping our opportunities away. *Black Issues in Higher Education, 17,* 7.

Morgan, J. (1996). Reaching out to young black men: A dedicated and determined group of scholars offer the lure of the academy. *Black Issues in Higher Education, 13,* 16–20.

Neuner, M. (1999). The injustice of criminal justice. Available: http://www.lincolnnu.edu/~diverse/pollock/afroam/cj.htm.

Novak, M. (1999). Nihilism and experience. *Society, 36,* 60-68.

Perez, V. (2000). "Running" and resistance: Nihilism and cultural memory in chicano urban narratives. *Melus, 25*, p. 133.

Porter, J.R., & Washington, R.E. (1989). Developments in research on black identity and self-esteem: 1979–1988. *Revue Internationale de Psycholgie Sociale, 3*, 339–353.

Roach, R. (2001). Where are the black men on campus? *Black Issues in Higher Education, 18*, 18.

Samuels, H. (1995). Sexology, sexosophy, and African-American sexuality: Implications for sex therapy and sexual education. *Siecus Report, 25*, 3.

The Sentencing Project. (1995). Number of black men in judicial system on rise. *Jet, 24*, p. 59.

Shavelson, R.J., Hubner, J.J., & Stanton, G.C. (1976). Self-concept: Validation of construct interpretations. *Review of Educational Research, 46*, 407–441.

Siegel, L.J, & Senna, J. J. (1988). *Juvenile delinquency: Theory, practice, and law* (3rd ed.). St. Paul, MN: West Publishing Company.

Smith, S. (1999). Invisible men. *Black Issues in Higher Education, 16*, 14–16.

U.S. News and World Report. (2001). The great divide: Racism in America. *U.S. News and World Report, 130*, p. 14.

Webber, F. (1999). Black rage confronts the law. *Race and Class, 40*, p. 83.

Wright, R. (1998). *Native son.* New York: Harperperennial.

Wylie, R.C. (1961). *The self concept. Vol. 1, A review of methodological considerations and measuring instruments.* (rev.ed). Lincoln, NE: University of Nebraska Press.

Charles Rankin

Dr. Rankin received his doctorate in Urban Education from Kansas State University in May 1973, and formerly served as the director of the Midwest Equity Assistance Center from 1978 to 1987 and from 1990 to present with the rank of professor of Foundations and Adult Education. Prior to accepting this position he directed the Midwest Center for Equal Educational Opportunity at the University of Missouri-Columbia, for five years. Dr. Rankin has directed the Cooperative Urban Teacher Education Program and the Preparation Retraining Institute for Developing Educators in Kansas. He has been an elementary school teacher and principal. He has taught courses at Kansas State University and the University of Missouri, including Black Family, Educational Sociology, Teaching Disadvantaged Students, Multicultural Education, and Education of the Exceptional Child. Dr. Rankin has extensive national and international experience in the area of school desegregation. His experience has included conducting desegregation studies and surveys, providing expert witness testimony in several federal desegregation court decisions, and serving as a member of several regional and national school desegregation and sex equity committees. He was one of the founding members of the National Committee on School Desegregation. This organization lobbied Congress to resurrect the legislation that reestablished the Magnet School Assistance Program. He has also served as a consultant to numerous public schools and universities, race relation programs, and state departments of education.

6

EQUITY AND EXCELLENCE

Is There Room for African American Ph.D.s?

Charles Rankin

I, the man of color, want only this: That the tool never possesses the
man. That the enslavement of man by man ceases forever. That is, of
one by another. That it be possible for me to discover and to love man,
wherever he may be.
—Franz Fanon, *Blackskin, White Masks* (1956)

If history is going to be scientific, if the record of human action is
going to be set down with that accuracy and faithfulness of detail,
which will allow its use as a measuring rod and guide posts for the
future of nations, there must be set, some standards of ethics in
research and interpretation.
—William Edward Burghardt DeBois, *Black Reconstruction* (1915)

The fundamental question: Is there a place for African American Ph.D.s in the
American Society? Both DuBois and Fanon dedicated their lives and careers not
only to social criticism, but also to social action in the interest of American social
transformation. DuBois clearly warned us that African Americans should not see
this lack of reflection of African Americans as accidental, but rather as the deliberate action of one interest group determined to shape particular images of man
and maintain social control of the goods, resources, and services of American
society, indeed, as the attempt to exclude African Americans from world history.

The 1980s were an anomaly in American universities. A greater proportion of African Americans, graduated from college during the 1970s than in earlier decades, and their indicators of competence increased during this period. However, the number of African Americans in graduate school during the 1980s decreased from the number in post-college educational programs during the 1970s.

Until the midpoint of the twentieth century, the best chance for graduate professional education for African Americans was found in institutions established specifically for African Americans. In the year 1968, the year Martin Luther King, Jr., died, 80 percent of African American physicians and dentists were graduates of Meharry Medical College and Howard University, two historically African American universities. According to James Blackwell (1987) "no historically African American college offered a doctoral degree in a discipline of the Arts and Sciences before 1954." Thus the opportunity for African Americans to obtain doctoral degrees is a recent phenomenon limited largely to the second half of the twentieth century.

In 1950, before the Brown v. Topeka Board of Education decision of the Supreme Court declared segregated education to be unlawful, only 2.2 percent of African Americans over the age of twenty-five had graduated from college. Meanwhile the number of White college graduates at the midpoint of the twentieth century, 6.6 percent, was three times greater than the number of African Americans who had achieved this level of schooling. Toward the end of the twentieth century the African American percentage dramatically increased to 12 percent, while White college graduates increased to 20.9 percent, only 1.7 times greater than their African American counterparts.

In the August 8, 2001, issue of *Education Week,* a commentary by Julian Weissglass titled, "Racism and the Achievement Gap," made a compelling case for communities in the United States to face head-on how racism and class bias contribute to persistent "disparities" in school achievement between poor or racial-ethnic minority students and those who do not share those same characteristics.

By focusing on racism Weissglass argues that it is learned behavior and that it is reinforced by "institutionalized racism," lack of information and misinformation, "tenacity of belief systems," "internalization and transfer of racism," and "lack of opportunities to heal from hurt." Weissglass then seizes on the last point to propose that, in order to eradicate the achievement gap, the United States must move beyond celebration of diversity and declarations that all students will learn, to create what he calls "healing communities" in which individuals participate in an honest dialogue about racism. Through this process of caring and commitment to change, the country begins to heal.

And with emotional healing, racism will whither away and, freed from its burden, students will achieve more and more equitably.

Surely racial equality has come a long way since the turn of the twentieth century. For example, according to some surveys, 70 percent of Whites now appear to be willing to vote for an African American for president. Yet the fact remains, social policies, circumstances, and economies continue to shape stereotypes about minorities, Hispanic and African American in particular. Research by David Williams from the University of Michigan suggests that: 1) all minorities are viewed negatively by Whites in terms of potential for violence; 2) 45 percent of Whites think African Americans are lazy; 3) 29 percent think African Americans are unintelligent; 4) less than one in five think African Americans are hard working; and 5) 56 percent of Whites feel that African Americans would rather live on welfare than work.

Higher education in the United States currently exists in a state of paradox. On the one hand, U.S. institutions of higher education want to appear to be strongly egalitarian. On the other, the nation's colleges and universities have played a significant role in historically discriminating against women, African Americans, and other people of color (Altbach, 1991; Anderson, 1988; Darder, Torres and Gutierrez, 1997). These American institutions continue to struggle with how to become more liberal, inclusive, and tolerant of gender and racial/ethnic minorities. For their part, African Americans overwhelmingly consider a college degree to be an important vehicle for self-determination and upward social mobility (Anderson, 1988). African Americans have been as determined as any other racial/ethnic group to struggle through societal barriers to achieve the American dream of equal opportunity and success through education and hard work (Feagin, Vera, and Imani, 1996).

Despite this strong determination, African American students are not promised that their efforts of preparation and hard work will be realized on primarily White college campuses without having to endure a hostile racial climate. African American students often report a sense of insensitivity among Whites toward the issue of student diversity. They also indicate the belief that their racial and cultural backgrounds are invalidated by White students, faculty, administrators, and staff on traditionally White college campuses (Feagin, et al., 1996; Smith, 1998). When the campus environment is racially hostile or specifically antiAfrican American, learning for all students becomes impaired, and the overall educational process may stall or cease.

It has been argued that United States society remains stratified by race, ethnicity, and class. Being African American continues to have particularly negative connotation and consequences (Peters, 1981). Despite the academic achievement and educational gains made by African American students in recent years, an achievement gap between students of differing racial and ethnic background in the United States continues to exist (Miller, 1995).

Given such adverse social conditions, researchers have maintained that African American students especially must be guided to develop a positive sense of self and their identity in order to be successful (Boykin, 1986; Johnson, 1981). If African American students are to be sufficiently prepared to meet the challenges of the twenty-first century, they must come to see themselves as intellectually and effectively competent in both academic and social circles, and know that they are able both to enter as well as graduate from institutions of higher education.

How can African American students be prepared for the twenty-first century? Researchers and policymakers have discussed this question regularly, as if successful African American students constitute a rare and only rarely sighted species that had not yet been classified. Researchers seem to accept almost intuitively that successful African American students are somehow different from their peers and from their African American counterparts. The vast amount of research produced on the sociological factors that contribute to this presumed difference between African Americans and non-African Americans includes factors such as poor and underfunded schools, economically depressed communities, single-parent families, etc., that are all aimed at explaining the seemingly inevitable failure of large numbers of African American students. (Yet, some of these African American students do succeed. The question is, at what cost?)

There is much that African American students currently attending White institutions of higher education can learn from their predecessors of thirty and forty years ago that will help them continue to work inside the system for programs and policies that will ensure the success of the students who will follow in our footsteps. As history has demonstrated, African American college students' resolve to determine independently the type, nature, and purpose of education that they will receive has not diminished. Until White institutions of higher education demonstrate a concerted commitment to African American students and their academic and psychological survival, African American students will endeavor to create such an environment in defense of themselves.

References

Altbach, P.G. (1991). *The racial dilemma in American higher education.* Albany: State University of New York Press.

Anderson, J.D. (1988). *The education of Blacks in the South, 1860–1935.* Chapel Hill: The University of North Carolina Press.

Blackwell, James E. (1987). *Mainstreaming outsiders*. (2nd ed.). Dix Hills, NY: General Hall.

Boykin, A.W. (1986). The triple quandary and the schooling of Afro-American children. In U. Neisser, (ed.), *The Schooling Achievement of Minority Children: New perspectives*. Hillsdale, NJ: Erlbaum.

Darder, A., Torres, R.D., & Gutierrez, H. (eds.). (1997). *Latino and education*. New York: Routedge.

DuBois, W.E.B. (1915). *Black reconstruction*. New York: Holt, Rinehart and Winston.

Fanon, F. (1956). *Black skin, white masks*. New York: Grove Press.

Feagin, J.R., Vera, H., & Imani, N. (1996). *The agony of education*. New York: Routeledge.

Johnson, R. (1981). The Black family and Black community development. *Journal of Black Psychology, 8*, 35–52.

Miller, S. (1995). *An American imperative: Accelerating minority educational advancement*. New Haven, CT: Yale University Press.

Peters, M. (1981). Effects of Black student's racial identity on perceptions of White counselors varying in cultural sensitivity. *Journal of Counseling Psychology 28*, 120–157.

Smith, W.A. (1998). *Are college students pre-socialized toward racial apathy? A multicultural examination*, Manuscript submitted for publication.

Weissglass, Julian. (2001). Racism and the achievement gap. *Education Week*. August 8.

Joseph White

For the past forty years, Dr. White has enjoyed a distinguished career in the field of psychology and mental health as a teacher, mentor, administrator, clinical supervisor, writer, consultant, and practicing psychologist. He is currently Professor Emeritus of Psychology and Psychiatry at the University of California, Irvine, where he spent most of his career as a teacher, supervising psychologist, mentor, and director of ethnic studies and cross-cultural programs. Dr. White received his Ph.D. in clinical psychology from Michigan State University in 1961. Dr. White is the author of several papers and three books: *The Psychology of Blacks: An African-*

American Perspective (1990, 1984); *The Troubled Adolescent* (1989); and *Black Man Emerging: Facing the Past and Seizing a Future in America* (1998). He was a pioneer in the field of Black psychology and is affectionately referred to as the "Godfather" of Black psychology by his students, mentees, and younger colleagues. His seminal article in *Ebony* magazine in 1970, "Toward a Black Psychology," was instrumental in beginning the modern era of African American and ethnic psychology. He has served as a supervising psychologist and staff affiliate psychologist to five hospitals and three clinical practices in Southern California. He has worked as a consultant with school districts, universities, private organizations, drug prevention programs, and government agencies.

Kamau Siwatu

Kamau Oginga Siwatu is currently a doctoral student majoring in educational psychology at Florida State University. He holds a bachelor of arts degree from California State University-Dominguez Hills in psychology and Afrikani studies and a Master of Education degree from Florida State University in educational psychology with an emphasis on learning and cognition. Kamau's research interests include the Black and White Test Score Gap, academic self-regulation, and motivational patterns of Afrikan American students. Currently Kamau is engaged in research investigating the impact of the Stereotype Threat on test performance.

7

COME SO FAR, BUT SO FAR TO GO

Interview with Dr. Joseph White

Joseph White and Kamau Siwatu

I am reminded by a proverb that states "The first step to wisdom is silence; the second is listening." Using this proverb, it can be understood why many of us have failed to rediscover the wisdom of our elders. The inability to control the environment around us along with its external influences (i.e. television and music) has prevented many individuals from reaching the first step of wisdom, which is silence (Akbar, 1985). The inability to achieve silence may account for Western societies' repeated failure to recognize (listen to) and tap the wealth of knowledge and wisdom of one of our greatest resources: our elders.

Words of Wisdom: Straight Talk with Elders in the Academy is an interview that taps the wealth of knowledge of one whom many consider to be "The Father of Black Psychology," Dr. Joseph White. In a thought-provoking and animated conversation, Dr. White addresses the issue of racism in education, racial identity development, and the role of the Black professoriate.

Kamau: Nelly Fuller is cited in Frances Cress Welsing's book *The Isis Papers: Keys to the Colors* [Welsing, 1991] as saying "If you do not understand white supremacy (racism)—what it is and how it works—everything else you understand, will only confuse you." Welsing asserts that racism is active in nine areas of human activity, one of which is education. What is your definition of racism and how does it operate in academia?

Dr. White: Well my definition of racism is that the White folks of America want to control the decision-making process. The decision-making process in politics, higher education, the corporate structure, and in the government. It repeats itself from every generation, and periodically there will be some "token Blacks" in the decision-making roles but the final shot callers are White folks.

Kamau: Can you elaborate a little on your concept of token Blacks?

Dr. White: In President Bush's administration, Condaleeza Rice and Colin Powell have vital jobs, a great education, but I don't think you should ever confuse yourself as to who is going to make the final decisions.

At Florida State University, you have Blacks in the administrative roles, but the Board of Regents and the President at the university who makes the decisions are predominately White folks. When they wanted to change the admission standards, it was the government and his White folks that did it in Florida.

Kamau: How does the existence of racism account for the underrepresentation of Afrikan Americans[1] in higher education?

Dr. White: I'll start at where you are, with the graduate students. That is, the majority culture —white folks—decide who is going to get admitted into the doctoral programs in higher education. They decide who is going to be picked to be groomed. They decide who is going to be picked to be mentored and guided through the process. Furthermore they decide who will get the good jobs in the next generation. If you look at the flow of doctorates, especially when you move towards the sciences, the disciplines get Whiter and Whiter. Furthermore, the people inside the university who make the major decisions in academic affairs, the full professors and the academic deans are predominately white. And if you go to a conference of college administrators you will see the that a brother or sister might be vice president of student affairs, but the people who call all the academic shots regarding the curriculum, on hires, on graduate students, on young professors who get into the academy, that is almost exclusively a White club.

They will let some brothers and sisters into the club, but once you get in you have to toe the party line. For example I got out of graduate school in 1961, and I thought that I was a reasonably-well rounded first year professor and Ph.D., but when I jumped up and tried to change the university, this is when I ran into trouble. I proposed to the University that we go over to Compton and South Central (Los Angeles) and admit some Black folks on special admission when I said I wanted faculty development and ethnic studies programs. As soon as I wanted to change the way they had arranged the furniture, then they blocked it off. Kamau, let me put it this way, then I met resistance. So when you get in the club, if you are an Afrikan American you're expected to act like a Black Anglo-Saxon.

Kamau: Dr. White, so what you are saying is that it all comes down to again, control and domination?

Dr. White: Yes, most certainly, control and domination of the decision-making processes.

Kamau: Early in your career as a psychologist, you cite that one of the pitfalls of traditional psychology is that it tends to emphasize a Eurorcentric paradigm. In the classic article "Towards a Black Psychology," you discuss why it makes sense to view the world through an Afrikan-centered paradigm. In the context of education, discuss these paradigm differences in academia.

Dr. White: First of all, I wrote that article in 1968. So we are talking about the 60s and things have not changed that dramatically. I want to go back to American society, then I'll go to psychology. In the American society, there was a belief system that White folks, especially White males were superior. They were the ones that had the right stuff. They had the leadership abilities, the intelligence, the capacity to make decisions under pressure. They were kind of the chosen folks. Top of the line. That was the American belief system. Then when they created psychology in the late 1880s early 1890s, and on into the twenty-first century, they wrote psychological theories that ran parallel to the belief system. So in psychology the White male was used as the norm. Everybody that was different from him—from the way they talked, walked, and thought—were considered inferior. Women were considered inferior. Blacks were considered inferior. When the first psychology books were written, Blacks were either invisible or they were depicted as what I call the "deficit deficiency model."[2]

So you will find terms in psychology that imply that Blacks are dumb, lazy, have poor impulse control, and are unable to make major decisions. In both of the major wars, World War I and II, they said that we should not be trained for complex tasks because we (African Americans) lack the ability (intelligence). So what I am trying to say is that there were two parallel belief systems. One in the popular culture and then, when psychology was written, it paralleled the popular culture. In both belief systems we were either invisible or inferior. One of the two; take your choice. I outline that very clearly in the 1984 book *The Psychology of Blacks* [White, 1984].

White psychology is built on dichotomies and opposites. White is better than Black. Male is better than female. White is better than Chinese. They are always coming up with these either/ors. We (Black psychologists) are trying to avoid the either/or and move to synthesis rather than dichotomies. White psychology has this big claim of being logical and rational, yet it comes out with things that dehumanize other people. For example, calling folks dumb and this and that. By saying that they don't have the right stuff. Or by saying that they don't have the stuff to go to college. Or they don't have a high GPA. They are always coming up with these numbers and these rationalizations. Whereas we come in from a humanistic spiritual framework. We say all people deserve access to more options in life. If you have a state university, then all children should be able access that university some kind of way. And if they don't qualify the first year, we should put them through another year of post-high school education and then qualify them and get the students in. There are all kinds of ways to help people to become competent. But they will freeze and say, "oh no, you have to go to high school and have a GPA of 3.7. If you don't meet those requirements you can't come in here." Then if we try to give some type of solution, then they say that we are admitting inferior people. Again, notice that inferior-superior dichotomy. They'll fall back on that psychology.

What happens is that Black psychology is more spiritual. It is more spiritual, and it has a greater flavor for human concern. Black psychology also tries to avoid dichotomies. When Black psychologists see that people are different from us they try to look at the common ground. We try to find a way of resolving differences that brings both sides together. Black psychologists call this synthesis.

Kamau: Many Afrikan Americans have fallen short of meeting the requirements needed to enter graduate school. Many scholars and educators cite that the Black-White test score gap has played a significant role in the underrepresentation of Afrikan Americans in higher education. What are your feelings towards standardized tests? Better yet what are your feelings toward psychometric scientism?

Dr. White: Standardized tests prevent us from getting into the institution. We can't get into some jobs because we can't pass the standardized tests. What the Association of Black Psychologists has said about testing is that the test should be used for guidance. So if I give you a test on algebra, and you only score at the ninth grade level and you are supposed to be at the twelfth grade level, then I am supposed to ask myself, "From that test what do I need to do to get you up to that twelfth grade level?" Apparently, whoever was teaching you was not teaching you right. The White man says that the test should be used as the final judge of merit. And if you don't pass you don't get in. And we're saying, "No, if you are going to use the test," which I don't necessarily believe in, "then let's use it for guidance purposes."

Lets also figure out where the bias is in the test. When I was tested back when I was nine years old, the White boy asked me what a shilling was. I'd never been to England. I don't know a damn body in England or, for that matter, what a shilling was! Now if he would have asked me what gold dust or dust was, I would have been able to run it down to him. But he never did ask me that. So we have to get the bias out of the test. If we are going to keep using the test, which they are, then we need to use the test for guidance purposes.

We must also make sure that the test predicts what it says it does. When I admitted that first group of Blacks to med school, a number of them did not have that high score on that MCAT exam. By the time I restructured the environment, such as implementing study skills classes, supplying them with supplemental notes, and providing them with tutors, they ended up the first year doing as well as the other students. By the second year they were doing superior. So the test does not often predict what it says it is going to predict. And they claim that the test is like a ruler—that it is an absolute measurement and predicts 100 percent. Neither of which are true.

Finally, Black kids who have to struggle with inner city schools are what I call "late bloomers." So they may not begin to show their true potential until they are twenty years old. Whereas the kids that live in neighborhoods such as Irvine, California, where I live, get all kinds of tutors night and day. I'm talking about the "A" students getting tutoring. So they blossom fairly early. But brother man working down there twenty hours, attending Long Beach Poly High School, and has one child, at the same time trying to run track there, that brother there has his hands full.

Kamau: You shared with us your attempt to rearrange the furniture in the house of education, which was met by resistance. Speaking with many brothers and sisters in the Academy, it is apparent that many of them have visions for change. How do you suggest that these scholars strategically go about change?

Dr. White: Let me reinforce that statement Kamau. When you come into academia, if you are going to change anything you have to survive first. In order to survive you have to get a couple more tickets punched after you get your Ph.D., by being promoted to associate professor, full professor, a dean, whatever. The same folks who determined if you got into graduate school are those that determine whether you get promoted.

So now the first thing that you have to understand is, when you step outside of this box and begin to try to change the school (college) of education, the people running it are not going to roll over and play dead and just let you do it. So one way that they can punish you is by not giving you tenure. So if you look at higher education, every year a few new Blacks come into faculty positions, but then a few do not get tenure. So its like a revolving door.

You have to understand and be able to effectively manage the power and decision-making centers. There are two power centers in higher education that you have to be able to understand and manage effectively. The first power center exists outside the university, but yet it is attached to it. The second power center is inside the university. The three power centers outside the university include the Board of Regents/trustees, the state legislature (which funds the university), and the funding sources such as the National Science Foundation, Ford Foundation, Rockefeller, and the other philanthropic organizations. You have three powerful external forces.

Now a brother trying to do some change must figure out a way to get some influence in those three structures. For example, if you live in Florida and there are two Black members on the board of trustees, then you should know who they are and build a relationship with them. That way when someone moves on the brother, somebody can protect him and back him up. The second thing is the state legislature. The state legislature helped me tremendously. During just about my whole career, Willie Brown was a powerful influence in the California state legislature. He was speaker of the house for fourteen years, and prior to that he was in the legislature for sixteen years. One time I was trying to get some Blacks admitted into the medical school at the University of California—Irvine (UCI), and I was having all kinds of trouble until they passed the seventy-two million dollar bond issue and Willie Brown controlled the money. So Willie, in a nice way, told UCI that if they did not admit Blacks that he would take the money and send it up to University of California—Davis (UC Davis). And in a matter of hours the medical school was restructured. Otherwise, without the influence of Willie Brown I was just out there talking. So I had the back up.

Then another time I received a $500,000 grant to start a master's degree program for Urban Teacher Corps, and the college had to match it with $500,000. So I had a million dollars at my disposal. But when I had that million, a whole lot of people were interested in returning my phone calls because White folks had ex-girlfriends, wives, daughters, and granddaughters who wanted a master's degree in education. You got me?

When you have the symbols of power, people respect that. American moves on power and reciprocity. You scratch my back and I scratch yours.

A brother has to begin to understand that before he makes his move. Otherwise they will just cut him off at the pass.

Back to the power centers inside the university. Inside of the house we have to quit playing this numbers game and begin to understand that the power inside the university is in academic affairs. That's where the power is. That's were the Nobel prizewinners are. That's where the Pulitzer prize winners are. They are the full professors. They are the deans. They are the vice presidents of academic affairs. They are the ones who determine who comes in and who does not. They are the ones who determine who attends graduate school and who does not. They are the ones who determine what young professor is groomed and who gets tenure. So we have to begin to move our people up the ranks. The problem is that when a young professor comes up for promotion, all the senior professors are White. And so now we have to move our senior people in and stop playing this numbers game and get people into the full professor rank. I'm a full professor, so when a Black professor comes up for tenure, I can write a strong letter of recommendation. One time I was on the tenure board at San Francisco State University. I was the chair of the internal tenure board. There were a total of seven votes. So all I needed was four votes to do anything. So the man understood that if sometimes he did not vote with me, that I was going to block his action. So we have to move to positions of power inside the academy. It is okay for brothers and sisters to be in student affairs, but we also have to have some people in academic affairs.

Kamau: Based on your response, I'm reminded of the Ashanti proverb that states "by the time the fool has learned the rules of the game, the players have dispersed." Are you suggesting that we hurry to play their game?

Dr. White: You have to play their game to a certain extent. You don't have to "Uncle Tom," but you have to understand the power and decision-making game. If you don't understand that then you are just out there throwing stones. You can talk a lot of rhetoric, but you have to understand the power game.

Kamau: Dr. Na'im Akbar frequently reminds his students that before they can master Afrikan (Black) psychology, they must first become versed in European psychology, a process which he calls "paying the dues." What is the dues paying process that Afrikan American males in higher education must go through in order to be successful in academia? [Akbar, 2000; Kwaku, 1996].

Dr. White: You have to get your ticket punched before you can do anything in America. Credentials are big in America. Before you can make any substantive change in higher education or even outside of education, you have got to get your ticket punched. The way you get your ticket punched is going through undergraduate and graduate school, and the people who control the ticket punching are White folks.

Kamau: Students at predominately White institutions (PWIs) are in dire need of Afrikan American faculty members. As a result of this high demand, many professors have to play multiple roles. Discuss the multiple roles that Afrikan American faculty members must play in academia.

Dr. White: You start off with the teaching, which you have been hired to do. Then you have to do your research that you have been hired to do as well. You may get into trouble with that because you may want to do research on Black topics, and the White man, like in psychology, may want you to run numbers and rats. All professors then have some committee work (i.e., committee on education, committee on certification). You have to do your committee work. Then, because there are so few Black professors, every time something happens to some Black students on the campus they want you on that committee. They want you on the admissions committee. They want you on the ethnic studies committee. They want you on the graduation ceremony committee. Then after they finish with that, the people in the community want you working with them as well. For example when I first moved to Long Beach (California) a boy got hit by a car, which resulted in the people demanding a stop light at the intersection. I had to go downtown to get that. Then I had to go get a building because they wanted Headstart and Job Corp programs. So I had to go and do all that. Soon I was doing everything but that which I was hired to do. Yet when I came up for promotion, the man asked me, "Well what have you been doing with your time?" So on the one hand, the man wants you all over doing these Black things, but when it comes time for promotion, then he asks you, "Let me see how much research you've been doing." But usually they burn out these young professors by scattering them among so many things.

Kamau: Does the type of research matter?

Dr. White: Yes the type of research would matter, because if you are an ethnic person in my discipline you are probably going to be doing some Black psychology research. At UCI I am the only Black psychologist in the school of social science. The school of social science has seventy-five faculty members. Now who is going to evaluate my research? They don't know what I am doing.

Kamau: So how do we work around this dilemma and begin to manage all of these extracurricular roles?

Dr. White: One way you work around being stretched out on all these committees is that you sit down with the man ahead of time and you tell him, "Look here, you are going to have to give me some release time. If you want me on all these committees, rather than teaching three courses, I am only going to teach two so that I will have time to do my research and do my regular work plus all this other stuff that you want me to do." You try to get that settled up front. Now that is very difficult to do. But now if you have some Black folk in the senior faculty ranks, or at the senior administrative ranks, well then they can take care of that. The way I got around doing this is that the students threatened to tear up the college, and then the man needed me to go over there and work with them. The man gave me all the time I wanted.

Kamau: What year was this?

Dr. White: 1967–1968, right after the Watts riots. Some people from the state legislature called him up and said that they wanted me to do this and that. The people of Sacramento called the president of the college. That's why I told you about that power and decision-making business.

Kamau: So is there a certain responsibility on the professor to effectively manage his/her time?

Dr. White: Yes there is certainly a responsibility for time management. But it is hard to manage your time when you are one of a few Black professors. There was a student outside my door all the time. Not just during office hours. Black people want to see you when they want to see you. So you can't tell them, "Look here I can't do that today because I am organizing my time." As a matter a fact it used to take me an hour just to walk across campus. With Black people you can't say, "well I am in a hurry to a meeting." You have to stop and talk to them. That means that I have to leave a hour early just to get across campus or some sister will be running back to the building saying, "I saw Professor White, and he would not even talk to me. He sure is uppity lately. I saw him talking to some White girl, but he would not talk to me." You see that's what they do. So, yes, time management, but it is a whole other level of time management.

Kamau: From the standpoint of a graduate student whose primary goal is to receive his/her Ph.D., would you advise them to hold off researching Black topics due to the possible backlash that he/she may receive from their committee?

Dr. White: What I would advise them to do is, if they are going to research a Black topic for their dissertation, use inside networks. If there is no Black psychologist at your college, use networks outside of the College (i.e. ABPsi). Get the biggest and "baddest" brother or sister in that field on your side. You can have outside members on your committee. If that does not work, they can advise you and write letters stating that you are on the right track. You play the power game. So if a student is doing something on Black identity, the student should be in touch with William Cross. Have William Cross check out his research. Meet him at conventions and perhaps have Cross fly down for the student's oral examination or defense. Once the committee knows that you have someone behind you they will back off. But if you are just out there by yourself and you are nothing but twenty-three or twenty-four years of age, then you may have to back down. You always want to make it to the next level. The battleground is not in graduate school. The battleground is in the real world.

If you have a solid topic with a great deal of data (i.e. identity), and you have some people behind you, then do it. If you are just all alone out there, and you are trying to research a new area, then you should back off. I'm not saying that Black graduate students have to sacrifice their identity, but they have to understand the power game.

Kamau: In some of the points that you have been making throughout the conversation you have mentioned the issue of identity. Using the Cross' Nigrescence Model,[3] which has postulated that identity development progresses in a series of stages, do you think that there is a degree of identity development in graduate school?

Dr. White: Yes. I think there is a degree of identity development in graduate school. I think what happens in graduate school is that you come in with vague notions of who you are and what it is that you want to be. You also may think that if you are smart enough, that you can be one of them. And you may work and work and work only to discover that there are certain doors that are closed to you. That then may give you a little shock. From that initial shock you may begin to think about what it really means to be Black in America. It some cases overt racism, discrimination, and prejudice may be subtle. Nobody is going to burn a cross on your lawn. Nobody is going to openly call you names. They do little stuff. For example when the professor and students see you researching a Black topic they may say, "Well when are you going to study the real psychology?" They are telling you something. So I think that graduate school will make you question who you are, and when you come out of graduate school you should have a good notion. Identity development continues after you get out of graduate school. Some brothers, especially some "bowtie" brothers, thought that when they got their Ph.D. the man would not bother them anymore. But when they attempt to make a change they find out that this is not true. So I think we go through these re-appraisal stages throughout our adult life.

Kamau: So now when you say "reappraisal" of one's identity do you mean a recycling of stages?

Dr. White: Yes. They move faster and you may not have to go through all the stages sequentially each time.

Kamau: Is that what Parham suggested when he expanded the Nigrescence Model to include the concept of recycling through stages?[4]

Dr. White: Yes. But it is not so much as the stages. Cross feels now that part of this cycling is that people are moving towards wisdom. You're going through the same thing, but in a deeper way.

Kamau: There seem to be multiple interpretations of wisdom. For our readers can you define the term *wisdom* in the context that you are using it?

Dr. White: Wisdom means a kind of deep understanding of the ebb and the flow of life coupled with the ability to move through unexpected events (i.e., tragedies) and keep it in perspective. To get through something like that you have to come to a deeper understanding of love, spirituality, and the meaning of life. You can only get it by going through that stuff. That is what wisdom is. Books can teach you knowledge, but wisdom comes from life. It comes from understanding Black psychology . . . the real Black psychology . . . grass roots Black psychology.

Kamau: In the book co-authored by James Cones and yourself, *Black Man Emerging,* you stated that "the real role model for young Black males are not TV stars or super athletes but people in their everyday lives whom they can see, reach out to, and touch" [White & Cones, 1999]. Looking from the standpoint of Afrikan American graduate students and newly minted Ph.D.s, who may rarely come into contact with a familiar face at a PWI in terms of mentorship, who do we turn to? What are our other alternatives?

Dr. White: Well what you have to do is outreach. If they are not there then you have to try to go find them where they are. Sometimes you go to meetings and conferences. Sometimes you may have to write letters and e-mails. But if the opportunity does not present itself in the environment you have to be very creative in seeking out opportunities. That goes for brothers at all stages—from eight, nine, ten years of age and on—trying to reach out and find things in the environment that may not be visible. For example I became the third Black clinical psychologist in America, so I had no role model ever. I never had a Black teacher from grade school through the Ph.D., so I had to be constantly on the alert. "Here is a brother who may do something important. He may not be a psychologist, but this brother is putting it together. Here is somebody over here." After finding bits and pieces I was able to fashion not *a* role model but some people I could reach out and touch. That is all a part of being Black in America. The ability to be innovative, imaginative, creative, and to put pieces of things together that may not be visible. It is called improvisation. It is the first principle of Black psychology.

Kamau: There seems to be consensus that the progress of Afrikan Americans that was witnessed during the 60s has experienced some setbacks. Some scholars, like John McWhorter, place the blame on the victims by implying that Afrikan Americans suffer from the "cult of anti-intellectualism" [McWhorter, 2001]. Others like you cite the system of racism. Within the past couple years many have cited that Afrikan Americans are just simply losing the race. In the context of education, are we really losing the race? If so, what can we do to ensure survival in this obstacle course we call "academia?"

Dr. White: I'm going to break that question down into the progress and education part. If you look at the history of Afrikan Americans in America since 1619, that is 382 years roughly. Progress never did occur in a straight line. That was one of the biggest mistakes that I've made. In White psychology, everything moves in a straight line. Progress has periods where we are moving forward. Then there are periods of resistance followed by periods of renewed struggle. Each time we come to a period of renewed struggle, then we have to go back to the seven principles and come back up with a new creative model. So in the 60s Martin Luther King Jr., Thurgood Marshall, and Malcolm X came up with a model that was marked by improvisation, creativity, and spirituality, the whole nine yards. Now this generation has to come up with a new model. They can't redo what we did in the 60s because that time period is over with. So know we are in between models. So every time we make some progress, then the White folks resist, then it takes us another half generation to come up with a new model. So we are stuck in between two models right now.

Now the McWorhters and the Clarence Thomas's of this world—we will always have them. In education we have to figure out a way to help Afrikan Americans (especially brothers because sisters are doing better than brothers), to be down with the 'hood and at the same time master the skill necessary to participate in the twenty-first century economy. How can they be down with the 'hood, which to me means identity, and at the same time master the skills that will allow them to participate in the twenty-first century economy? They have not been able to pull those two together. To them that looks like a "either/or" situation. Either you are down with the 'hood or you master the skills, "acting white" and "dissin" the brothers. We don't have a way of helping the ten-, twelve-, and fourteen-year-old Black boys in the critical stages of development. So now put those two together. How can you be a "down" brother but at the same time master algebra? The school system is not designed to help them resolve this dichotomy. The school wants to stamp out their identity and educate them. As a result, they lose them in the process. And the school must also figure out how to make learning fascinating. How to make learning make sense. I run into the inner city boys who cannot read, but at the same time they know every rap song and what it means. How in the hell can they learn all of that, make up raps and yet cannot read. It does not make sense to me. And in the rap they show all the signs of intelligence. They show concept formation, comprehension, and the ability to move rhythmically with the music (mind-body connection). They show all that and have internal motivation to learn to do it. But yet you set them in a classroom and they just go blank.

Kamau: We live in a society that is dominated by the need to experience immediate gratification. Consequently many males seem to be hesitant to pursue terminal degrees. Why should Afrikan Americans pursue these terminal degrees?

Dr. White: For Black males it is not so much the need for immediate gratification. They do not believe that if they go for the long haul that the man will give them the pot of gold at the end of the race. You cannot trust American society to live up to its promise. We have a long history of America not living up to its promise.

I busted my ass for my first 28 years trying to get my tickets punched. I did my two years in the military. I was in higher education for nine years. I was the best graduate student at Michigan State. Once I graduated, then the man would not rent me a house. I could not rent an office. I had to argue and damn near shot some people. I said to myself, "What the hell did I spend all my time delaying gratification for?" When I come out and work twice as hard to go half as far does not make sense." My mother told me that you had to be twice as good because that is how society is. The younger brothers say to themselves, "Why should I go all that long way to have the man argue and hassle me when I attempt to get a job, tenure, and everything else? Why should I do all that? Brothers don't believe in the contract. If the brother could be assured that the contract would be fulfilled, then he would put a couple more hours of studying in when he is sixteen or nineteen. But since he does not believe in the contract, why should he sit up there and study some dull book?

That takes us back to principle one, improvisation. If you want an equal range of choices in America and you are Black, especially male, then you have to put yourself in a position to create those choices. You have to be innovative, imaginative, and seek opportunity. There is a way of narrowing the gap, but it won't be handed to you. So you have to have it in your head when you leave graduate school that even though you delayed gratification until you were twenty-eight or twenty-nine, the battle is far from won. You are still on the battlefield. You see, I got my head all messed up, man. It took me about three or four years to recover.

Kamau: One of the stages of the Nigrescence model is the encounter stage. Would you say that your experiences after graduate school marked the beginning of the encounter stage?[5]

Dr. White: The encounter stage was after I got out of graduate school. I don't know where I had been living. Don't ask me where I had been living. I thought I knew what was going on until I moved to Long Beach. Once I arrived in Long Beach, man, I could not rent a house or an office. People at the University (California State University, Long Beach), where I was one of the first Blacks there, did not want to issue me my faculty library card. I said, "What is wrong out here?" Man, I went through three-to-four years of shock. At the time I lived right down the street form Long Beach Poly High School. The man asked me to come down there, and I found kids who were in the eleventh grade reading at the third and fourth grade level, and I asked myself, "What is going on around here?" So I went into shock.

Kamau: So it took you three or four years to recover from that?

Dr. White: Right! I had spent my whole life aiming for one goal; I thought that I was on my way to the promised land, and I ended up in hell. I asked myself, "How in the hell did I get here!"

Kamau: Can the intensity and severity of the shock vary from person to person?

Dr. White: Yea! Even though I had been Black for twenty-eight years, for some reason I must have had tunneled vision. I was playing sports, hanging out, doing things other than thinking about being Black. Until it hit me right straight up side my head. Other people tried to tell me; they said, "Joe, now you're still going to be another minority in America." Malcolm X told me that. "I don't care how many Ph.D.'s you get." I said, "Oh I don't want to hear that stuff."

Kamau: So you just brushed Malcolm off?

Dr. White: Yes. This was of course before Malcolm was famous. I did not realize that I had been arguing with somebody who would later be famous.

It was not until I got out of college when I began to understand what he was saying.

Kamau: What are the benefits of pursuing a terminal degree, and how does it impact the Black community?

Dr. White: The benefits of pursuing a terminal degree is that is gives you options. It gives you a whole range of options. You may not have the same options that White people have, but you have a whole lot of options. I have been able to do everything. Teach. Consult. Work in politics. Write. A whole number of things. I have been able to influence two generations of young scholars. The teaching and mentoring opportunities would not have been there if I did not have that degree.

Kamau: We often see images and hear stories of athletes and other superstars giving back to the community, yet we are seldom exposed to the roles that Afrikan American scholars fill in the community. Looking from a "kinship" or "collectivist" perspective, what is the role and/or niche of the Black scholars in the community?

Dr. White: The niche of the Black scholar is that we have to write and produce ideas and materials that people can understand. Sometimes when we get in our academic niche and there are nine or ten of us at a meeting, we are talking a whole lot of abstract stuff. I brought my brother to a Black meeting of academics one time. After sitting back and listening to the conversation he turned to me and said, "Man them folks are crazy, Joe!" Like others in the community, my brother did not understand what the Black scholars were talking about. So he does not believe it. So I think the Black scholars have a responsibility to break it down to the point where the people in the community can understand what we are about. Some members think, like my grandmother once did, that we are educated fools who have the book knowledge but lack the understanding of life.

With athletes it is obvious what they are doing. They are running up and down the field or shooting up a basketball. The athletes are highly visible, but the brothers that are the scholars have to make their work a little more visible. We have to make sure that people understand what we're doing, even if that means that we have to write it twice—once for the people at the college and again for the community. When I wrote that article "Toward a Black Psychology" in *Ebony* magazine [White, 1970], my goal was to do it in such a manner that Black folks in the community could understand what I was talking about. Sometimes in academics I read some of these books, and I don't want to call any names, but I don't understand what these brothers are talking about—and I have a Ph.D. coupled with forty years of experience. "What are you talking about bro?" Finally when I come to the point where I understand it I say to myself, "Brother, why couldn't you just say that?"

Kamau: My generation has a saying, "Keep it real." Be real with us and inform us of the academic, social, and climate issues effecting the plight of Afrikan American students and faculty in higher education.

Dr. White: The plight of Afrikan American students is that we have chosen to live in a house that we don't control. When you live in a house that you don't control, you have to be very innovative, resourceful, and astute in order to get your message out there. The students and younger faculty feel a sense of alienation. They feel that the institution is not really meeting their needs. That is the truth. The senior faculty (my generation) have the responsibility of teaching you how to work the institution so that it becomes somewhat responsive to your needs. But it will never become totally responsive. So we have to teach you how to get some of your needs met inside of the institution and then outside of the institution by forming organizations like Brothers of the Academy and the Association of Black Psychologists.

Kamau: Discuss with me, if you will, the positive and gratifying experiences that have prolonged your tenure in academia.

Dr. White: The most two gratifying experiences that I have had are, first of all, the opportunity to work with some fantastic young people who are now senior scholars, professors, and vice president at various universities. This has been fantastic. These kids come from all walks of life.

The second part that has been very gratifying is this Black psychology movement. I had never even thought of Black psychology in graduate school. I was just going to graduate school doing what all the others was doing. But when I went through the encounter stage, I concluded that what I had been taught did not fit. Then after I struggled for a while, I said "Hey, I must know something about Black people. I grew up in a Black neighborhood. My family was Black, so let me address that." At the time I did not understand where that was going. From that came all this cross-cultural psychology and everything else. People were jumping up and down, ripping and running. I said, "Hey man what's going on?"

Kamau: Some of your former students often comment on your routine closing of a lecture or class session in which you state, "Keep the faith," a statement that seems to enhance the motivation of your students. If you were giving a motivational speech to all the sisters and brothers of the Academy, what three main points would you make?

Dr. White: One of the points that I would make is to be consistent in the pursuit of excellence. If you are going to do something, then be the best you can be. I don't care if you want to be a Black psychologist, a White psychologist, whatever. You be the best that you can be. If you are the best that you can be, people will recognize it, and that will protect you from a lot of things. When the man sees that you have your stuff together, then he is going to go home and think about.

I would also encourage them to construct their lives based on the concepts of love and spirituality. You have to have a base of love and spirituality to make it through the long haul. A lot of these brothers and sisters about thirty-five or forty years of age are angry and bitter, and pretty soon they can't love anybody or themselves for that matter. Sure, I understand what has happened to them. Some of their anger is justified. But at the same time it is destroying them.

Last, but by no means least, I would encourage the brothers and sisters in academia to keep the faith. That is, the darkest hour is right before dawn. Martin Luther King, Jr. said, "No matter how dark the hour, there's going to be a brighter tomorrow." I've always remembered that. "Keep the Faith" came from Congressman Adam Clayton Powell. Powell used to say, "Keep the faith baby; it's going to get better bro."

Notes

1. The author has consciously chosen to spell the word Afrikan with the letter 'K' rather than the traditional 'C'. The logic behind the spelling is due to the absence of the letter 'C' in the many indigenous Afrikan languages. Therefore throughout this text the word Afrika will be spelled the way it is in most Afrikan languages, rather than the colonial British way.

2. The deficit deficiency model is supported by the genetic inferiority and the cultural deprivation hypothesis that have been advanced by American scientists.

3. William Cross developed the Nigrescence Model to conceptualize the development of an Afrikan American identity. Using this model, Cross theorizes that identity development progresses in a series of four phases that include: The Pre-encounter, Encounter, Immersion-Emersion, and Internalization stages. For further information regarding this model, see W. E. Cross, Jr. (1978). The Thomas Cross models of psychological Nigrescence: A review. *Journal of Black Psychology,* 5(1), 13–31.

4. For more information regarding the lifespan of the Nigrescence model and the concept of recycling through stages of identity, see W. Cross, T. Parham, & J. Helms, (1992). The stages of Black identity. development: Nigrescence models." In Reginald L. Jones (ed.), *Black psychology.* Berkeley, CA: Cobb and Henry Publishers.

5. The encounter stage is the second stage in Cross's model. A person enters this stage when they experience an event that challenges their existing belief that racism does not exist.

References

Akbar, N. (1985). *The community of self.* Tallahassee: Mind Productions & Associates.

Akbar, N. (Spring 2000). Personal Communications.

Kwaku, P.-L. (1996). *First word: Black scholars, thinkers, warriors: knowledge, wisdom, mental liberation.* New York: Harlem World Press.

McWhorter, J. (2001). *Losing the race: Self-sabotage in Black America.* New York: Perennial.

Welsing, F.C. (1991). *The Isis papers: The keys to the colors.* Chicago: Third World Press.

White, J. (1970). Toward a Black psychology. *Ebony,* September, pp. 44–45, 48–50, 52.

White, J. (1984). *The psychology of Blacks: An Afro-American perspective.* Englewood Cliffs, NJ: Prentice Hall.

White, J., & Cones, J. (1999). *Black man emerging: Facing the past and seizing a future in America.* New York: WH Freeman and Company.

William H. Watkins

William "Bill" Watkins was born in Harlem, New York and raised in South Central Los Angeles. A product of the Los Angeles public school system, Watkins attended Los Angeles City College and transferred to the California State University at Los Angeles. He obtained a B.A. degree in political science–pre law in 1970. Relocating first to Brooklyn, New York then to Chicago, Watkins attended graduate school and began teaching. He received a M.A. masters of education degree in 1979 from the University of Illinois at Chicago. His masters specialty was Curriculum: Programs for Schools and Institutions. He completed the Ph.D. in public policy analysis/education from the University of Illinois at Chicago in 1986.

After ten years of teaching high school social studies and history, Watkins accepted a joint faculty appointment in the College of Education and the Department of African American Studies at the University of Utah where he remained for nine years. In 1995 Watkins returned to the University of Illinois at Chicago as a tenured associate professor in the College of Education.

Watkin's areas of specialization include sociology of education, African American education, history of curriculum, multicultural education, and curriculum movements. In addition to teaching, Watkins lectures on matters of politics, race, education and social justice to universities, schools, workplaces and community audiences throughout the nation.

Watkins is senior editor and a contributing author in the recently published book *Race and Education: The Roles of History and Society in Educating African American Students* (2001) and the author of *The White Architects of Black Education: Power and Ideology in America 1865-1954* (2001). In addition to several book chapters, other recent publications have appeared in the *Journal of Interdisciplinary Education, The International Encyclopedia of Education, The International Encyclopedia of Curriculum,* the *Harvard Educational Review, Educational Theory,* and the *Encyclopedia of African American Education.*

Watkins has presented academic papers in East Africa, Japan, Thailand, Amsterdam, Cuba, Canada, and throughout the United States. He has traveled extensively throughout Europe, the (former) Soviet Union, the Peoples Republic of China, the Caribbean, Central America, Vietnam, and West Africa.

Watkins currently serves on leadership bodies of the American Educational Research Association, the Research Focus on Black Education Special Interest Group, and the World Council for Curriculum and Instruction and the Education for Liberation Conference.

8

UNDERSTANDING THE SOCIALIZATION PROCESS

William H. Watkins

Today the number of African American males receiving the doctoral degree and obtaining appointments in major universities exceeds any other time in our history. Unaccustomed to today's still relatively small numbers of Black faculty, predominantly White universities as well as their new professors have been challenged. Therein lies the issue for consideration. The Academy socializes new Black faculty and, simultaneously, those faculty challenge the university.

Conventional scholarship on socialization most often explores how the organization inducts the individual into its ranks. Owing to the sociohistorical and cultural dynamics of Black people and today's Black scholar, our socialization process is a complex one. I view this process as a dialectical interaction where Black people bring an antithetical culture to the Academy. Often our very presence is a problem. Thus they not only socialize us, but we also socialize them in the process.

In this brief discussion I would like to acknowledge and cite some of the fine scholarly work addressing (Black) faculty socialization in recent years, however, I would also like to be personally reflective. As a post-World War II baby boomer from a blue collar family who attended undergraduate school in the late 1960s and completed graduate work in a major White university, I am representative of a significant demographic. Equally important, I was ideologically shaped by the militant racial politics of my generation. In another essay (Watkins et al., 2001) I refer to us as the "post-Malcolm scholars."

In addition to my own urban upbringing and education, for the last sixteen years I have served as professor at two large White universities, one with less than 1 percent African American students and the other with around 5 percent African American students. Both these universities have few Black faculty members. In short I am part of the story I write about.

Will the Real University Please Stand Up?

To contextualize the complexities of the socialization process for Black males in the White Academy, we must first establish a clear sober picture of what the Academy stands for. The university occupies an exalted position in our society. We need to understand its evolved mythology, which provides a haze that surrounds, and often distorts, the realities of its purpose.

In the larger society it is viewed as a hallowed training ground for the intellectual elite, a launching pad for a professional career, and the agency capable of providing upward mobility for its graduates. Attending college is the dream of every parent for their child.

Those in training for the professorate also have images of the Academy. It is often viewed as a marketplace of ideas and free thinking where a community of scholars pursue science and truth, impart those truths to students, and help create tolerance and understanding.

The realities of the university are quite different. Smith (1990) argues that higher education in America is the product of an individualistic and theological ideology rooted in the Protestant Reformation led by Martin Luther and John Calvin. Far from free thinking, education in Calvin's view aimed to seek out a proper understanding of God's intentions for human beings. Despite liberalization and secularization, the university continues to embrace a "medieval tradition of learning" (Smith, 1990 p. 23). The early liberal arts, trivium, quadrivium, and other curricula were forged around the "classics" and the study of antiquity. A scholastic philosophy emphasizing a grand system of thought or canon evolved. The university's claim to offer enlightenment and progress through reason cloaks what is really academic imperialism!

The canon provides the organizing idea of university study. The political, sociological, and economic influences of colonialism, industrialization, racism, and ethnocentrism have contributed to the contemporary paradigm of Western thought. In this paradigm Europe is viewed as the civilizing and ordering force in the modern world.

Over time the American university has taken on a modern identity. Professors, who have replaced the ancient priests, must possess the Ph.D., which serves as a union card to the academy. The Ph.D., a teutonic invention, represents the outward credential of legitimacy. The long and tedious process of obtaining the Ph.D. provides the first step in the socialization process. Although gaining some familiarity as a graduate student, the African American professor who joins a university faculty today will likely find an organization more complex than (s)he imagined.

So, You Want to Be a Professor?

Many benefits and opportunities, however, await the new Black professor. Office space, open access to computers, copiers, scanners, shredders, audio-visual equipment, and a wide array of resources dazzle the new arrival. Time to think, research, and write are inviting. Above all else, a new status as university professor places the individual in rarified air where few of his people have gone before.

Within a short time reality strikes. Faculty scuttlebutt and politics suddenly dull some of the luster. The new Black professor is suspect. Is (s)he really a scholar or did the department need a minority? How many committees can we put him on? Let's put him in that course where we need coverage. The false face is soon stripped away as those White and white-haired professors who appear so intelligent and worldly lapse into guttersniping, backstabbing, and murdermouthing in polysyllabic prose. The new professor quickly discovers that university faculties are what Paul Goodman called "jealous dukedoms."

Personal reflection: My biggest shock as a new professor was observing the never-ending bickering among the White professors. I discovered that some feuds had been going on for years. I uncovered alliances and social cliques among professors. The squabbling for power and influence was accompanied by great personal antagonism. I quickly found out that some of these people genuinely despised one another. How would they treat me?

Beyond debilitating faculty politics, a more in-depth understanding of university culture and power is soon obtained. The university is revealed as a keeper of the flame structured to guard the gates against the "barbarians." An academic fundamentalism flourishes where, as Alfred North Whitehead pointed out a "scheme of orthodoxies" prevails. At a deeper level it can be argued that the twentieth century American university is under the full influence of Eurocentrism, capitalism, and the military-industrial complex.

Understanding the socialization process now becomes a major objective. The Black professor must find out what the university culture is about and how to negotiate a sometimes hostile system. Those who study university socialization, for example Hendricks and Caplow (1998), Manning (1997), and Tierney and Rhoads (1994) note that socialization is the process wherein the organization imparts its structure, culture, values, and goals to new members. The new member is introduced to the hierarchy of the organization. Through social interaction the new member learns the rules and is expected to embrace the culture. Successful socialization suggests that the new member is integrated into the organization.

The socialization process occurs in two stages (Tierney and Rhoads, 1994). The first stage is graduate school where the future professor is preparing and the second stage is on the job itself. Studies suggest that the socialization process for African Americans is fraught with problems from graduate school onward. Hendricks and Caplow (1998) found that only three of nineteen Black professors interviewed were encouraged by their professors to go beyond undergraduate study. Only six of the nineteen were encouraged to pursue academic positions beyond graduate school.

That same 1998 study, as well as another conducted by Lawrence and Patton (1997) found that new Black faculty encountered negative and preconceived attitudes from the White faculty and staff who questioned their worthiness for the position. Blacks quickly felt marginalized.

Personal reflection: I was a new assistant Professor at a very White university during the Oliver North-Iran-Contra hearings in Washington. Just as in the recent terrorist airplane crashes, America was riveted to television. As a political science major and political person with many doctoral level courses in poly sci., I was extremely well informed and interested in this matter. During the height of the drama I found myself at a mountain retreat with a half dozen male White faculty colleagues. They eagerly anticipated discussing the issues gripping the country, but felt inadequate to discern the complexities. I informed my colleagues that I was well up-to-speed on the matter and I repeatedly attempted to initiate discussion. No one would respond. For nearly five hours I sat with my colleagues drinking beer while they waited for one professor to make his way to the mountain cabin to lead the discussion. Upon his arrival we all found out that he was bright and informed, but his knowledge of the matter never approached mine.

Race, Respect, and Research

While some African American scholars engage in research not oriented to race, the history, drama, and emotion of the "Black struggle" makes the study of race compelling for many. Thus from the outset Black professors stand out from their White colleagues. They claim to be engaged in the pursuit of scientific phenomenon, while the Blacks can't seem to get beyond their passions. They can't understand why we are so preoccupied with the study of our people. Although the "Negro question" is at the heart of all American social science, our research gets devalued and is often viewed as propaganda or polemics (Braddock, 1978). When Whites study Blacks it is viewed as scholarship, but when Blacks study Blacks it is emotion.

Interestingly enough this scholastic devaluation always accompanies our placement on every university committee imaginable. The university seems to want to hear the Black voice on everything from parking to affirmative action to campus beautification. We are simultaneously viewed as narrow in scholarship and essential to democratic governance.

Personal reflection: As a young Assistant Professor my research interests focused on the history and political sociology of curriculum movements in the nineteenth and twentieth centuries. I did not plan to focus on, or ignore, African American issues in the process. Immediately I found that my department viewed me as an expert on everything "Black." I was assigned courses in multicultural education where I had no background. The curriculum courses I wanted to teach were the property of senior professors. I found within a short time that I had better shift my research focus to matters "Black" where I was being assigned courses and was expected to excel.

Publishing and the Road to Tenure

Nothing is more intimidating to the Black male professor than the tenure process. It determines whether or not you attain lifetime employment or are sent packing. Tenure is at the heart of the socialization process. It enforces conformity, discipline, and most importantly, it influences ideology as the new professor must enter the strange and vexing world of publishing.

Publishing is perhaps the most formidable of all academic challenges. What do I write about? What journal do I submit to? Why does the review process take so long? How do I make recommended revisions to an article I worked on for a year and said what I wanted to say?

We know that Black folks value oratorical skills, but we quickly learn that the White academy cares little for our ease with the spoken word. We now have to write for a living. Beyond forced writing, we must learn to write in the manner of White scholarship. We find that the scholarly journals are gated communities where friends take care of friends and the same names re-occur on article after article.

For many young Black professors, this is the ultimate challenge and often the breaking point. Our writing is often criticized as conversational. We don't use "journal speak." "Why can't they write about anything except issues of race, oppression, and social justice?" Academic imperialism and scholastic elitism are more prominent here than any other place. Many of us are buried in this process, never to recover.

The Black Response: Accommodate, Adjust, or Assert

In the face of overwhelming stress and the lack of institutional support, many African American professors opt out. Opting out often means obtaining employment in other agencies or seeking consulting positions. Others opt out by remaining within the university system, but instead building their careers in administration, service to the university, or service to the community. Many of us have seen the anemic curriculum vitas of veteran colleagues who ingratiate themselves to the university and/or the larger community.

Sutherland (1990) summarizes coping strategies of Blacks in White Academies. She notes that some Blacks become "deracinated," joining Whites in social and ideological circles. Such Blacks avoid other Black faculty and, especially, Black issues. Others develop individual strategies such as divorce from the campus, seeking instead support and acceptance from outside the university.

Today more and more Black faculty are asserting themselves in new ways. A critical mass of Black scholars has now successfully matriculated through the most prestigious White universities in the country. We now have our own networks, co-authors, caucuses, grants, mentors, and support. Armed with confidence and standing on a solid tradition of Black intellectual thought, many are breaking through old barriers. Black scholars are forcing their way into the erudite journals, onto editorial boards, into leadership positions, and, most importantly, into the intellectual dialogue.

This brand of assertiveness has dramatically altered the socialization process. It suggests that they are not simply inducting us, we are also altering their institutions. We are at the forefront of infusing scholarly paradigms with racial and political consciousness. We are insisting that equity and social change issues count as legitimate avenues of inquiry. We are challenging Eurocentrism, essentialism, and academic imperialism at every turn. We are expanding research paradigms of qualititative inquiry, ethnography, and research for social amelioration.

Afterthoughts

Issues surrounding universities, Black professors, and socialization are embedded in much greater economic, social, political, cultural, and racial dynamics. The world is changing rapidly. The globalization, restructuring, and reallocation of the world economy is leading to narrow concentrations of wealth, unspeakable poverty, renewed racism and hatred, huge displacements of people, shifting alliances, threats to civil liberties, and convulsions in the United States and the world over.

Hegemonic circles feel the need to manage knowledge, information, and people as never before. What will be the role of the university in the changing world order? Now ideologically and financially married to corporate order, can the university open up, become more socially relevant, hear new voices, and take in new populations or will it close ranks, retreat, and recommit to antiquity?

It could be that African Americans are the hope of the university. Our ongoing historical exclusion, oppression, and treatment make us the conscience of America. Our treatment is usually a barometer of change. Perhaps it is ordained that we serve as the moral compass for the university and, perhaps, even the nation.

References

Braddock, J. H. (1978). Internal colonialism and black American education. *Western Journal of Black Studies, 2,* 236–243.

Hendricks, A. D. & Caplow, J. A. (1998, November). African American faculty perceptions of the academic culture and their professional socialization. Paper presented at meeting of the Association for the Study of Higher Education, Miami, FL. Eric Document 427 617.

Lawrence, J. H. & Patton, D. C. (1997). Work satisfaction and faculty departure among African-American faculty. Paper presented at meeting of the Association for the Study of Higher Education Annual Meeting, Alburquerque, NM.

Manning, P. K. (1997). Talking and becoming: A view of organizational socialization. In Blankenship, R. L. (ed.). *Colleagues in organization: The social construction of professional work.* New York: John Wiley and Sons. pp. 181–205.

Smith, P. (1990). *Killing the spirit: Higher education in America.* New York: Viking.

Sutherland, M. E. (1990). Black faculty in white academia: The fit is an uneasy one. *Western Journal of Black Studies, 14,* 17–23.

Tierney, W. G. & Rhoads, R. A. (1994). *Enhancing promotion, tenure and beyond: Faculty socialization as a cultural process.* Association for the Study of Higher Education, Washington DC Eric Document 368 321.

Watkins, W. H., Lewis, J. H. & Chou, V. (2001) (eds.). Preface. In *Race and education: The roles of history and society in educating African American students.* Boston: Allyn & Bacon.

Irving Pressley McPhail

Dr. Irving Pressley McPhail is the chief executive officer of Maryland's largest community college system, consisting of three campuses at Catonsville, Dundalk, and Essex, and extension centers at Owings Mills, Hunt Valley, Towson, and White Marsh. Upon assuming the chancellorship of the Community College of Baltimore County (CCBC) in February 1998, McPhail set an ambitious agenda for the college to become a premier, learning-centered, single-college, multi-campus institution. Trustees and members of the college community embraced McPhail's vision and the college's five-year strategic plan, LearningFirst. Building upon CCBC's unique strengths and powerful partnerships, McPhail has moved steadily and aggressively toward this vision of the learning college. His advocacy has brought CCBC recognition and distinction as a leader in this national movement to create learning-centered community colleges, where learning occurs anytime, anyplace, and anyway.

In addition to being a leading advocate for the learning college, McPhail is a noted expert on literacy, urban education, and test performance for African American students. He is the author of *Test-Wiseness Curriculum* (Kamilah Educational Enterprises), and he has published more than 25 scholarly articles, book chapters, and monographs. An educator for the past quarter century, McPhail was president of St. Louis Community College at Florissant Valley and LeMoyne-Owen College in Memphis, Tenn. He was provost of Pace University and dean of Arts and Sciences at Wayne County Community College. He held faculty, administrative, and research posts at Delaware State University, Morgan State University, Johns Hopkins University and the University of Maryland at College Park. He also served as chief operating officer of Baltimore City Public Schools from 1984–95.

The native New Yorker has a bachelor's degree in sociology from Cornell University, a master's degree in reading from Harvard, and an Ed.D. in reading/language arts from the University of Pennsylvania. He was an American Council on Education Fellow in Academic Administration, and is a graduate of Harvard's Institute for Educational Management and the Presidents Academy of the American Association of Community Colleges (AACC).

9

CULTURE, STYLE, AND COGNITION

EXPANDING THE BOUNDARIES OF THE LEARNING PARADIGM FOR AFRICAN AMERICAN LEARNERS IN THE COMMUNITY COLLEGE[1,2]

Irving Pressley McPhail

Abstract

Culturally diverse students, especially African Americans, are generally not successful in classrooms that ignore cultural differences. This paper presents research, theory, and practice that indicate different cultures have different cognitive styles, ways of processing information, knowledge, and experience and that culturally diverse students become successful learners when these differences are taken into account in the classroom. This theory of culturally mediated education enriches the conceptual basis of the learning paradigm (Barr & Tagg, 1995) making it a powerful alternative to the widely used unmediated instruction, or teacher/content-centered, paradigm. The paper describes the Nairobi Method's successful culturally mediated approach to education and discusses the implications for the community college.

The application of existing theories of learning and instruction has not improved the academic performance of presently under-served populations, most especially African American learners. A fundamental tenet of the learning (outcomes-centered) paradigm (Barr & Tagg, 1995) is that colleges must do more for under-represented groups, such as African Americans, than open doors to higher education; colleges must take responsibility for producing student success. The current theory base for Barr and Tagg's learning paradigm, which frames learning holistically, offers a powerful alternative to the atomistic model of the instruction (instructor- and content-centered) paradigm. However, a new theory more directly linking culture, information processing, instruction, and how the brain learns is needed to transform classroom practice for culturally diverse learners. Such a theory of cultural mediation in instruction extends the conceptual base underlying the learning paradigm and offers the promise of student success for African American learners.

This paper will explore issues that have not been covered in a minority context, and will identify current research and examine the implications for classroom practice for community colleges. Specifically, the paper will answer the following questions:

- What are the characteristics of African American cognitive style?
- What are the linkages between how the brain learns, culture, information processing, and instruction?
- What are the components of a theory of cultural mediation in instruction?
- How does a theory of cultural mediation in instruction extend the conceptual base of the learning paradigm?
- How does practice based on a theory of cultural mediation in instruction offer concrete solutions to improving classroom practice for African American learners in the community college?

Characteristics of African American Cognitive Style

The learning process involves interpreting sensory events, categorizing the information into familiar categories, searching memory for similar experiences and ideas to which the information relates, and manipulating ideas, images, and concepts. A learner's approach to perception, memorization, thinking, and using any type of knowledge is inextricably bound to the patterns of activity, communication, and social relations of the culture of which he/she is a member (Cole & Scribner, 1974).

In an impressive body of original research on the cultural foundations of African American thought, Shade (1978, 1981, 1982, 1983, 1986, 1989; Shade & Edwards, 1987) has argued that all learners are not alike, cannot be treated in the

Table 1.   Characteristics of African American Cognitive Style

- Prefers to acquire knowledge through visual and kinesthetic/tactile mode and is especially responsive to sensations and perceptions as they seem to affect self.
- Construes the world in its totality, often ignoring specific parts of factors which might be relevant.
- Tends to use and rely on approximation rather than exactness.
- Has an excellent ability to attend to and interpret body language or facial expressions.
- Can see relationships and can synthesize or integrate ideas into a larger whole without necessarily understanding parts.
- Must have a context or scheme into which concepts can be incorporated to be understood and learned.
- Seems to prefer a multiplicity of stimuli to which to attend, which results in short, quick, attention focus and the gathering of only the bare essentials.
- Engages in creative, intuitive thinking using the trial-and-error approach; thus prefers spontaneity, novelty, and improvisation in interaction with ideas, concepts, people, events.
- Has own specific world view through which information is filtered, thereby often arriving at answers or behaviors which may vary from the socially accepted norm.
- Has excellent awareness of nonverbal, environmental factors, i.e., moods, climate, feelings, and ideas held by others.

Note: Adapted from *Alternatives to I.Q. Testing: An Approach to the Identification of Gifted Minority Children* by A. G. Hilliard, 1976, and "Afro-American Cognitive Style: A Variable in School Success?" by B.J. Shade, 1982, *Review of Educational Research, 52*, pp. 219–244.

same manner, or exposed to the same instructional methodologies. The focus on cognitive style—along with a focus on brain-based education (Barinaga, 1995; Caine & Caine, 1997; Fischbach, 1992; Gregory, 1987; Healy, 1994; Hull, Rose, Fraser, & Castellano, 1991; Jacobs, Schall, & Scheibel, 1993; Jensen, 1998; Kandel & Hawkins, 1992; Martinez & Martinez, 1987; Milgram, MacLeod, & Petit, 1987; Petit & Markus, 1987; Rose, 1988, 1995; Smilkstein, 1993, 1998; Sylwester, 12/1993–1/1994, 1995; Zinn, 1980)—does, however, suggest that all learners can learn the same content and information when educators are willing to fit it to their students' particular—and culturally determined—cognitive and affective behaviors and to how the human brain naturally learns.

   An examination of the culture and Weltanschauung of African Americans reveals a culturally specific method of organizing and processing information (see Table 1). African American learners utilize strategies that are

Table 2.   Characteristics of Eurocentric Cognitive Style

- Can process visual information analytically, i.e., has good visual discrimination skills, has good figure-ground discrimination, has good attention focus, has good visual memory and has good visual imagery skills.
- Can listen to verbal explanations and follow oral directions.
- Can give elaborate, elongated verbal explanations of ideas, events, or objects.
- Can engage in cause-and-effect thinking.
- Can create order/structure out of assignments/or information when presented in a disarray.
- Can handle and manipulate ideas/objects, events, without a significant context for reference.
- Can/seems to prefer a limited number of stimuli on which to focus.
- Has the traditional background experience through which to filter materials and explanations; therefore, the processor arrives at the expected and socially accepted answers.
- Has good problem solving skills, i.e., can observe and use all relevant facts; is not confused by irrelevant facts; is reflective and systematic in the examination of possible solutions.

Note: Adapted from "Conceptual Styles, Culture, Conflict, and Nonverbal Tests of Intelligence" by R. Cohen, 1969, *American Anthropologist, 71,* pp. 828–856.

rather universalistic, intuitive, and, most importantly, person-oriented. This cognitive style contrasts markedly from that of learners who are most successful in the Eurocentric schooling process, and who employ an information processing strategy that is sequential, analytical, or object-oriented (see Table 2).

Viewed from another perspective, the comparison of African and European philosophical assumptions (see Table 3) suggests that African American learners tend to view things in their environment in entirety rather than in isolated parts, seem to prefer intuitive rather than deductive or inductive reasoning, tend to approximate concepts of space, number, and time rather than aiming at exactness or complete accuracy, prefer to attend to people stimuli rather than nonsocial or object stimuli, and tend to rely on nonverbal as well as verbal communication (Anderson, 1988, 1992, 1995; Heath, 1982, 1983; Hilliard, 1976). The evidence that learners might not learn in the same manner and might, in fact, develop rather diverse cognitive strategies for processing information provides clear impetus for proposing ways to develop culturally compatible classrooms and other learning situations that incorporate all

Table 3.   Comparison of African and European Philosophical Assumptions

	African	European
Orientation	Naturecentric	Eurocentric
Norm(s)	Human Nature	Middle-class, Male Caucasian
Conception of "Self"	Transpersonal Self	Individual Self
Human Goal	Self-perpetuation	Gratification
Conception of "Time"	Cyclical, Phenomenal	Linear, Futuristic
Ontology	1. Spiritual Essence	1. Physical/Material Essence
	2. Collectivism/ "We-ness"	2. Individualism/ "I-ness"
	3. Interdependence	3. Independence
	4. Survival of the Community	4. Survival of the Fittest
	5. Oneness of Being/ One with Nature	5. Dichotomy of Being/Control over Nature
Epistemology (Knowledge of "What Is")	1. Affect/Symbolic	1. Object/Measure
	2. Immersion in Experiences	2. Observation of Experiences
	3. Fluid and Flexible	3. Rigid and Fixed
	4. Diunital Logic	4. Either/or Logic
	5. Complementarity of Differences	5. Duality of Opposites
Axiology (Value of "What Is")	1. Cooperation/ Harmony	1. Competition/Conflict
	2. Preservation of Life	2. Control of Life
	3. Affiliation (Human-to-Human)	3. Ownership (Man-to-Object)
	4. Collective Responsibility	4. Individual Rights
	5. Self-Knowledge	5. Acquiring Information

cultures and learning styles as well as the brain's natural learning process. Until and unless we find ways to make classroom and institutional practices in the community college multicultural, multicognitive, and brain-based, the vision of the learning-centered community college shall remain ephemeral for African American and other learners of color.

How the Brain Learns and Linkages with Culture, Information Processing, and Instruction

This section describes the brain's innate learning process and the effect of this process on how and what a person learns and thinks. It also focuses on the relationship between the brain's learning process, a person's culture, how a person processes information, and implications for instruction.

The brain is a physical organ in the body; and, like every other body organ, it has evolved to perform—indeed, is impelled to perform—specific functions; it innately knows what to do and how to do it. The brain has a wide range of functions, from maintaining the body's temperature to regulating all the body systems. However, of most importance to educators is that three of the brain's major functions are to learn, think, and remember. Neuroscience research shows that the brain's impulsion and ability to perform these functions are indeed innate and natural. For example, five- to twelve-week-old infants are "capable of perceiving, knowing, and remembering [and] begin to grasp the complexities of their world" (Bransford, Brown, & Cocking, 1999). Healy (1994), in reviewing the research, reports the same phenomenon: human beings are natural and apt pattern-seekers, thinkers, and learners from birth.

Brain research gives us a clear picture of what happens in our brain when we are learning. As—and *because*—we experience, explore, interact with, practice, become familiar with, try to make sense of the objects of interest or phenomena in our environment, whether family, community, or classroom, specific physiological events naturally occur in our brain. Some of our approximately one hundred billion brain nerve cells (neurons) grow fibers (axons and dendrites). These fibers reach out and make electro-chemical connections (synapses) with other neurons and their fibers. This growing and connecting of fibers construct increasingly more complex neural networks. The growing, connecting, and constructing of these physiological structures *is* learning, and the new neural networks that are constructed *are* our understanding and knowledge of any and every experience, phenomenon, concept, skill, or body of information. Thinking about what is being learned, or has been learned, results from the activities of the electro-chemical pathways between neurons. The brain does this physiological work on its own. We do not yet fully understand how the brain knows where and how to grow dendrites, create synapses, construct neural networks, and activate these structures to perform learning, thinking, and memory functions.

However, the first rule or requirement for learning is that new dendrites, synapses, and neural networks (i.e., new knowledge) must physiologically grow from what is already there (what is already known or present in the brain). These physical knowledge structures do not just appear, growing out of nothing—no more than a tree branch can grow unless it grows out of a structure (a branch or trunk) that already exists. Piaget (1973), the biologist and child psychologist who "founded the field of cognitive development as we know it" (Bjorklund, 2000,), identified the original structures preceding all subsequent learning as the innate instincts or reflexes with which babies are born:

> Between the newborn child's almost entirely reflex behavior . . . and the appearance of language or of the [abstract thinking] function, there exists a series of levels. . . . In the first of these stages, certain complex reflexes, like those of sucking, give rise to a kind of exercise and of internal consolidation due to their functioning, which announce the formation of [the knowledge structure of this action]. (pp. 65–66)

According to Piaget, it is only from earlier knowledge structures that higher-level knowledge structures can grow and develop, leading to higher and higher levels of skill and understanding. Do all students have general structures in common or does each student have an individual, idiosyncratic foundation of knowledge and function structures or do students from the same culture have a similar, culture-based foundation or is it some combination of these? An extensive study of the newest findings in educational and neuroscience research suggests an answer (Bransford, Brown, & Cocking, 1999). "The key finding [in this two-year study] is the importance of experience in building the structure of the mind by modifying the structures of the brain: development is not solely the unfolding of preprogrammed patterns" (p. xvi). More specifically, the study finds that:

> Participation in social practice is a fundamental form of learning. Learning involves becoming attuned to the constraints and resources, the limits and possibilities that are involved in the practices of the community. Learning is promoted by . . . social environments, through the kinds of activities in which adults engage with children. These activities have the effect of providing to toddlers the structure and interpretation of the culture's norms and rules, and these processes occur long before children enter school. (p. xii)

Further, Bransford et al. report that "[n]euroscience . . . is showing how learning changes the physical structure of the brain and, with it, the functional organization of the brain" (p. 4). Thus, not only do environmental experiences and caregivers shape children's capacities, but "[d]evelopmental processes involve interactions between children's early competencies and the environmental supports—[physiologically] strengthening relevant capacities and pruning the early abilities that are less relevant to the children's community, [l]earning is promoted and regulated by both the biology and the ecology of the child" (p. xv). In other words, by the time children get to school, knowledge structures that infants might have developed that are not supported or reflected by their culture have disappeared. In short, children's brain structures have been *physiologically altered* to make them conform to the functions and knowledge structures of their culture. This, of course, has profound implications for how students process information and for instruction.

In terms of instruction, Bransford et al. identify the "foundational role of learners' prior knowledge in acquiring new information . . . [and] the importance of social and cultural contexts in learning" (p. xix). Moreover, "[w]ork in social psychology, cognitive psychology, and anthropology is making clear that all learning takes place in settings that have particular sets of cultural and social norms and expectations and that these settings influence learning . . . in powerful ways" (p. 4).

Consequently, educators need to be aware that each student brings to school his or her own foundation of specific, culture-based functions and structures, and it is only from this foundation of knowledge and skills that the student's new learning can develop: "Effective instruction begins with what learners bring to the setting; this includes cultural practices and beliefs. . . . [L]earners use their current knowledge to construct new knowledge and what they know and believe at the moment affects how they interpret new information" (p. xvi).

If the functions and structures that students of whatever age bring to school are not compatible with, are not expected by, are not provided for nor respected and valued in the curriculum and pedagogy of the classroom, then the students will be at a critical academic, emotional, and social disadvantage in that unfamiliar world. These students will not be just less successful than those students whose functions and structures are adapted to—have been tailor-made for—that classroom, they will not be just less educated nor uneducated; they will actually have been *miseducated*. The antidote is the student-centered learning paradigm.

Ladson-Billings (1995) has observed the following:

> "[L]earner centered" refers to environments that pay careful attention
> to the knowledge, skills, attitudes, and beliefs that learners bring to

the educational setting. This term includes teaching practices that have been called "culturally responsive," "culturally appropriate," "culturally compatible," and "culturally relevant" . . . . Teachers who are learner-centered recognize the importance of building on the conceptual and cultural knowledge that students bring with them to the classroom (pp. 465–491).

Toward a Theory of Cultural Mediation in Instruction

Hollins has proposed a theory of cultural mediation in instruction to explain the relationship between culture and instruction. The theory of cultural mediation in instruction, although focused on K–12 populations, offers a powerful alternative for community college educators committed to designing classroom and institutional practices that are both multicultural and *multicognitive,* and responds to the challenges presented in the preceding discussion.

A full explication of the classic and contemporary research supporting the theory of cultural mediation in instruction is beyond the scope of this paper. Readers are directed to the seminal work of Hollins in this area (Hollins, 1982, 1990, 1996; Hollins & Spencer, 1990). Hollins (1996) offers the following rationale for the theory:

> The basic premise underlying the theory of cultural mediation in instruction has two components based on the centrality of the students' home-culture in framing memory structures and mental operations. First, teaching and learning are more meaningful and productive when curriculum content and instructional processes include culturally mediated cognition, culturally appropriate social situations for learning, and culturally valued knowledge. Second, the authenticity of schooling is validated for students by the interactions and relationships between adult members of their community and school personnel. (pp. 137–138)

Culturally Mediated Cognition

Culturally mediated cognition in instruction refers to approaches using the ways of knowing, understanding, representing, and expressing typically employed in a particular culture (Hollins, 1996, p. 139). As is evident in the comparison of African and European cognitive style and philosophical assumptions (see Tables 1–3), there are variations among cultures in the ways of knowing and understanding (see also Hall, 1989). Culturally mediated cognition requires knowing and using these differences in classroom instruction.

Culturally Appropriate Social Situations

Culturally appropriate social situations for learning refers to relationships among students and between teachers and students during classroom instruction that are consistent with cultural values and practices (Hollins, 1996, p. 139). For example, Hoover, McPhail, and Ginyard (1992) describe a culturally appropriate literacy approach for adults, the Nairobi Method, that emphasizes group approaches to reading and writing instruction. Such an approach builds on the ontological (collectivism/"we-ness"), epistemological (affect/symbolic), and axiological (cooperation/harmony) assumptions of the "African way of knowing" and demonstrates the centrality of social arrangements to effective learning (see also McPhail, 1979).

Culturally Valued Knowledge in Curriculum Content

Culturally valued knowledge in curriculum content refers to the inclusion of knowledge valued within the students' home-culture (Hollins, 1996, p. 139). McPhail and Morris' (1986) application of cultural content such as popular rhythm-and-blues song lyrics and the poetry of African American writers to raise the reading achievement levels of inner-city junior high school students is an example of this approach. Hoover's (1982) use of themes in African American culture in teaching basic (and other) critical communications skills to African American college students has resulted in substantial growth in basic skills levels in just one year of developmental education. Finally, Spears-Bunton (1996) documents the power of multicultural and multicognitive classroom strategies through the introduction of African American literature in an eleventh-grade honors English class. African American and European American students were able to cross perceptual, gender, and cultural lines as they responded to literature and confronted difficult issues of race, sex, and class.

This approach works because it is compatible with how the brain learns. The brain is best able to start learning new materials, concepts, and skills when learners can make a connection between the new object of learning and something they already know or have experienced and are invited to do their own thinking about this connection. Giving students the opportunity to start where they are, to interact with materials and ideas with which they can make a personal connection and about which they can do their own thinking, is the essential first step in the brain's natural learning process. Starting with this kind of activity makes it possible for students of whatever culture, gender, cognitive, and perceptual style to begin to successfully learn new material and ideas, i.e., grow and connect new neural fibers and construct new neural networks.

Extending the Conceptual Base
of the Learning Paradigm

Barr and Tagg (1995) have defined the theoretical foundations of the learning paradigm which, in turn, support the aims, values, and purposes of "the learning college" (O'Banion, 1997a, 1997b). Barr and Tagg (1995) argue that:

> A paradigm shift is taking hold in American higher education. In its briefest form, the paradigm that has governed our colleges is this: A college is an institution that exists *to provide instruction*. Subtly but profoundly we are shifting to a new paradigm: A college is an institution that exists *to produce learning*. This shift changes everything. It is both needed and wanted. (p. 13)

Table 4 presents a comparison of the educational paradigms at the level of Learning Theory.

Table 4.   Comparing Educational Paradigms

The Instruction Paradigm	The Learning Paradigm
Learning Theory	
• Knowledge exists as a separate entity.	Knowledge exists in each person's mind and is shaped by individual experience.
• Knowledge comes in "chunks" and "bits" that can be acquired through the senses.	Knowledge is constructed, created, and "gotten."
• Learning is cumulative and linear.	Learning is a nesting and interacting of frameworks (neural networks)
• Fits the "storehouse of knowledge" metaphor	Fits "learning how to ride a bicycle" metaphor.
• Learning is teacher-centered and controlled.	Learning is student-centered and controlled.
• "Live" teacher, "live" students required.	"Active" learner required, but not "live" teacher.
• The classroom and learning are competitive and individualistic.	Learning environments and learning are cooperative, collaborative, and supportive.
• Talent and ability are rare.	Talent and ability are abundant.

Note: From "From Teaching to Learning: A New Paradigm for Undergraduate Education," by R. B. Barr, and J. Tagg, 1995, *Change, 27* (6), p. 17.

The learning paradigm frames learning *holistically*. It also incorporates the brain's natural learning process. The congruence of this holistic, brain-based approach to learning with the cognitive preferences and cultural practices of African American learners is apparent in Table 5. The two perspectives outlined in Table 5 provide the input for the theory of cultural mediation in instruction. Such a theory, when combined with an understanding of how the brain learns, posits a powerful pedagogy for framing classroom practice for African American learners in the learning-centered community college.

From Theory to Practice

We return to Hoover, McPhail, and Ginyard (1992) for a fuller explication of the Nairobi Method, a concrete example of the theory of cultural mediation in instruction as applied to adult literacy instruction. Development of the Nairobi Method began in 1969 in a community-oriented, independent African American college (Nairobi) located in East Palo Alto, California. The pioneering work of Mary Rhodes Hoover resulted in an approach to learning that incorporates *culturally mediated cognition, culturally appropriate social situations,* and *culturally valued knowledge in curriculum content* in adult literacy instruction with miseducated, culturally and linguistically different African American adults. "Miseducation" implies that instruction proven to be effective for African American learners has not been provided to them in school (see also Woodson, 1933). This is a problem caused by the educational system, not by the learners. To date, we have verified that the Nairobi Method has been used in a variety of academic settings, including adult literacy centers, General Educational Development (GED) programs, two- and four-year colleges, developmental programs, reading labs, prisons, community agencies, and JTPA programs.

Heath, in her groundbreaking ethnographic studies (1982, 1983), provides evidence that validates Hoover's view. Heath identified the cause of the less-successful academic performance of working-class African American students in a newly integrated Southern elementary school. She discovered that the socialization of children in the area's working-class African American community (e.g., they learned through stories and personal-experience-based interaction) was different from the socialization of children in the area's middle-class—both African American and European American—communities (e.g., they learned through question-and-answer interaction) and that the integrated school expected all students to come to school socialized in the middle-class way. Students who had not been so socialized were, thus, at a significant disadvantage.

Table 5. Learning Paradigm Theory and Cognitive Style/Philosophical Assumptions: A Matrix

Learning Paradigm Theory	Cognitive Style/ Philosophical Assumptions
• Knowledge exists in each person's mind and is shaped by individual experience.	• Has own specific world view through which information is filtered, thereby often arriving at answers or behaviors which may vary from the socially accepted norm. • Immersion in experiences • Self-knowledge
• Knowledge is constructed, created, and "gotten."	• Engages in creative, intuitive thinking using the trial-and-error approach; thus prefers spontaneity, novelty, and improvisation in interaction with ideas, concepts, people, events.
• Integrates ideas into a larger whole without necessarily understanding parts.	• Fluid and flexible • Diunital logic • Complementarity of differences • Construes the world in its totality, often ignoring specific parts of factors which might be relevant. • Can see relationships and can synthesize.
• Fits learning how to ride a bicycle metaphor.	• Seems to prefer a multiplicity of stimuli to which to attend, which results in short, quick, attention focus and the gathering of only the bare essentials. • Must have a context or scheme into which concepts can be incorporated to be understood and learned. • Cyclical, phenomenal
• Learning environments and learning are cooperative, collaborative, and supportive.	• Collectivism/ "we-ness" • Interdependence • Survival of the community • Affect/symbolic • Cooperation/harmony • Affiliation (human-to-human) • Collective responsibility • Transpersonal self • Has excellent awareness of nonverbal, environmental factors, i.e., moods, • Climate, feelings, and ideas held by others. • Survival of the community
• Talent and ability are abundant	• Collectivism/ "we-ness"

The Laboratory of Comparative Human Cognition (1982) came to the same conclusion: "[C]hildren . . . act on and interact with their environment. What they come to know is the form of this interaction. . . . Cultures may differ in the extent to which their particular practices provide opportunities for experiences [of the kind expected and assumed by the educational system]" (p. 665).

Philosophy

The Nairobi Method is rooted in a philosophy that is designed to encourage miseducated, culturally and linguistically different adults to believe that a literacy education can make a positive difference in the way they live their lives. The philosophy recognizes that a lack of promotion of the miseducated's culture and history suggests that they do not have a background from which to grow and develop.

Another aspect of the philosophy recognizes that miseducated adults can be motivated through intellectual excitement, knowledge of the educational system, and their history. Moreover, research on the brain's natural learning process shows that students are motivated to learn when they have the opportunity to learn the way their brain naturally learns (Smilkstein, 1998); intellectual excitement is manifested in classrooms using natural-learning curriculum and pedagogy. Even in classes not exclusively using natural-learning curriculum, intellectual excitement is manifested through lessons, slogans, posters, speakers, and pep talks. Such excitement was seen in the Nairobi Method by Coombs (1973). He states: "I was taken by their interest, their enthusiasm for their work, and their refusal to be intimidated even if they knew their answers were incorrect. . . . " (p. 42). Learners were taught to cope with the system by developing upper-level literacy and survival skills. Also, they were taught to use their skills to help others who were less fortunate. Finally, learning about the history of African Americans was a must in the Nairobi Method. In academic courses and in assemblies, learners were constantly exposed to the history of Africans' and African Americans' achievements (Van Sertima, 1983). They were introduced to the fact that the first alphabet with vowels was invented by Ethiopians (Williams, 1974); that universities existed in Timbuktu while other groups were living in "cultural deprivation;" and that the belief that African American and other underrepresented groups in the U.S. come from illiterate cultures is not true.

A third aspect of this method's philosophy includes "going the extra mile" to convince learners that someone has a genuine concern for them. That concern includes (a) calling learners every day to remind them of their classes or whenever they miss a class; (b) picking up learners in order to counsel with them to and from their classes; (c) helping with all details of the learners' lives; for example, doctor's appointments, delivery of children, personal problems; (d) immersing the learners with pep talks (Hoover & Fabian, 1979); and (e) educating students about how their brain naturally learns and teaching accordingly.

Finally, the method's philosophy promotes a value system oriented toward the masses of African Americans—the expelled, suspended, and alienated ("View from Nairobi," 1969). Every student was encouraged to commit himself/herself to a lifelong goal of helping others. To get started, learners became engaged in such community service projects as tutoring in the public schools, helping organize community forums, and running errands for the elderly.

Staff

To ensure an all-staff endorsement of high expectations, the staff was given a series of workshops to instill in them a strong belief in students' ability to learn. (Based on brain and natural-learning research, this belief is absolutely realistic. The brain is the learning organ: it knows how to learn, has an innate imperative to learn, and loves to learn, feels good when learning—endorphins, the pleasure chemicals, are produced in the brain during learning.) Learners were thus imbued by every staff person in classes and assemblies with these high expectations. Learners were informed that though they had been deprived of basic skills in the past, they will learn these skills now. They were encouraged to adopt Malcolm X's vigilance in pursuing upper-level literacy (X & Haley, 1966). Moreover, if the staff shows students how the brain learns and that they are natural learners (Smilkstein, 1989), the staff is giving students facts that can further increase their confidence and motivation.

Techniques

Audience and language: The techniques used in the Nairobi Method stressed audience participation, a key element in the learning-centered constructive approach (Healy, 1994; Jensen, 1998; Perkins, 1999; Smilkstein, 1991). While most adult literacy programs value individualization, most of the activities in the Nairobi Method were group-oriented and geared to an audience-participatory style. For example, learners read pattern-practice word lists with partners, played prefix/suffix games, corrected dictation with partners, and paraphrase read. Paraphrase reading was one of the major comprehension exercises. For practice, learners were placed in small groups where they read a sentence of a paragraph orally and then paraphrased the sentence in their own words. This exercise not only improved comprehension skills, but vocabulary skills as well.

Because most of the learners in classes for miseducated adults were bidialectical (i.e., exposed to two dialects, usually standard English and another variety such as Ebonics (a language variety spoken by African Americans and other Americans), a semiforeign language approach (Hoover, Politzer, & Lewis, 1980) to reading was used. With this approach, a systematic exposure to the most regular and frequent spelling patterns in English was provided. This language approach has been effective in teaching African American and other bidialectical learners to read (Guthrie, Martuza, & Seifert, 1979; Hoover, 1978; McPhail, 1982, 1983; Weber, 1971).

Before learners were assigned compositions to write, they discussed how features of their spoken language might influence their written language. To do that, learners studied Ebonics; it includes features of West African language patterns (Dillard, 1973; Scales & Brown, 1981). Their study enabled them to understand why certain language patterns such as "he come" might appear in their written work. Further, they learned that the reason why there is no third person singular "s" on many of their verbs is that there are very few syllables ending in consonants in most West African languages. Once learners understood their language pattern was rule governed like any other language pattern, they wrote freely.

Word attack: In the Nairobi Method, learners were provided a systematic, programmed, linguistic approach to acquire word-attack skills. A linguistic sequence (140 English spelling patterns), with selections written in the pattern provided, was used to avoid the failure inherent in presenting a long list of phonic skills with no opportunity for practice in actual reading situations. A linguistic sequence also gives adults many patterns beyond the usual consonants, blends, short vowels, etc. Morphemic, accent, and syllabication patterns were presented for use in analyzing multisyllabic words. Finally, spelling practice of pattern words was provided through dictation by the teacher.

Structured vocabulary: Learners were provided with a structured approach to word attack, spelling, and vocabulary through the presentation of 200 Greek and Latin prefixes, suffixes, and roots. They were given five to ten affixes or roots each day and quizzed on them the following day. An evaluation of their knowledge of these word parts was handled through tests. Afterwards the word parts were discussed in whole words with a given context.

A game, "Automatic Flash" (Hoover & Fabian, 1979), designed to assist learners' memories was played daily. The affixes/roots thus provided several skill benefits. Among them were (a) *word attack*—the affixes/roots were presented according to their spelling patterns, that is, short vowels first, then long vowels, then "r's"; learners thus improved their knowledge of English orthography and spelling; (b) *vocabulary*—the affixes/roots also represented meaning units so the learners' vocabulary level increased; and (c) *security*—learners previously taught by an ineffective reading method did not realize that English has a structure and set of rules. They enjoyed discovering the structure and patterns of words.

Reading comprehension: Most of the reading comprehension materials used in the method incorporated generative words and themes (Freire, 1970). An example of a generative word is *cadillac*. From cadillac, learners generated discussion of the term and generated such syllables as *cad, ked, kid, cod, cud, dall, dell, dill, doll, dull, lack, leck, lick, dock* for study. Other reading materials included themes that were culturally and politically relevant. Culturally relevant books, for example, included *The Color Purple* (Walker, 1982) and *The Earth Did Not Devour Him* (Rivera, 1987). Other formats and genres of interest to adults used were magazines, newspapers, and job-related materials. These materials related to learners' personal struggles with illiteracy, the educational system, and sexism and racism.

Controlled composition for motivation: Learners were given a program of controlled composition. The daily composition assignments were designed to give miseducated learners a sense of security. As a first assignment, learners orally composed a paragraph on the topic "I Have a Number of Strengths." Techniques from the Language Experience Approach (Van Allen, 1976) were incorporated as a guide for learners. They learned that, collectively, they had a number of strengths. They recited their strengths and put them into a form letter. The following example, taken from such an oral composition activity, demonstrates this process:

> I have a number of strengths. I am a hard worker. I learn quickly and I am very dependable. As listed above, I am a hard worker. For example, I improved my vocabulary skills in a program I attended six hours a day. At the same time, I was raising my family as a single parent and working part-time as a babysitter. Another strength I have is that I learn quickly. Though I never tutored before, I picked up the skills to tutor my own children by attending Project Success. My third strength is that I am very dependable. In my last job, I never missed a day unless I was extremely ill—and that was only once.

This form letter was modified to fit each student's circumstances. Learners then used the letter (a) as a model of English grammar and organization;

(b) as the basis for several questions usually asked on applications and interviews for jobs; and (c) for self-esteem purposes.

Learners memorized the letter so that they would always have a few perfect paragraphs for job interviews and as introductions or conclusions to papers they must write. The letter was also used as a vehicle for grammatical practice. One activity was for learners to rewrite the entire paragraph in the past tense, change the "I" to "we," thus changing from singular to plural, and other similar exercises.

Other topics for controlled composition were "Why I Am Unique," "Why My Culture Is Unique," and "Why This Program Is Unusual."

Composition based on generative themes: Not only reading but also composition methodologies were used in the Nairobi Method. The composition methodology (Hoover et al., 1986; Lewis, 1981) stressed the use of prose, poetry, and speeches from African American authors. They also stressed such topics as apartheid, racism, miseducation, protest, and Ebonics. The method combined emphasis on a writing process with work on grammar in the context of African American literature.

Standard English grammar: A brain-based, natural-learning textbook for teaching standard English grammar, *Tools for Writing: Using the Natural Human Learning Process* (Smilkstein, 1998), though not part of the Nairobi Method, has successfully helped miseducated African American adults succeed at learning to write with the standard grammar expected—even required—in mainstream academic and professional environments. For example, the following pre- and post-tests were written by a forty-five-year-old African American woman enrolled in a 12-week community college basic grammar course that used this textbook. All errors in the samples have been retained.

Three prompts constituted the pretest: (1) What are your strengths as a student? (2) What are your problems as a student? (3) Write something about yourself.

1. More time to read.
2. My problems as a student are the same as above.
3. I would like to learn how to concentrate to keep the mine from wandering while I am trying to read. About myself I am a very hard worker, but I love doing thing with my family. My family is very nice, daughter marry son going to college another son principal list.

The post-test prompt was a moral dilemma: A professional woman loses her job when her company goes out of business. She wants to return to college to retrain for another profession. Her husband tells her they cannot afford her not working and that she should immediately get any kind of job. You are a marriage counselor. What do you think about this situation?

> I think that the couple should get counseling. If she isn't happy in her present job, she will have little self-esteem. The marriage may not work under any circumstance. If she goes back to college, it may be hard now, but later in life it could be helpful to her.

The students in this challenging community college developmental English course seemed to increase not only their grammar but also the sophistication of their thinking as well as their spelling and vocabulary—even though spelling, vocabulary, and critical thinking were not directly addressed in the course. The reason for the students' astounding success is that their high level of intelligence had just not been accessible through their untutored writing and remained inaccessible until they had the opportunity to learn to write the way the brain naturally learns.

Test-wiseness: Teaching learners to develop questions and find answers to the questions were the core components of a test-wiseness strategy taught to learners in the Nairobi Method. Specifically, learners read a passage, asked questions about the passage, and found answers to their questions. Secondly, for each question written about the passage, learners wrote statements that they believed answered their questions. Only one statement was considered as the most complete answer. Third, learners wrote questions based on such comprehension skills as main ideas, details, and vocabulary in the passage. Finally, they reviewed their questions in the context of the passage (McPhail, 1981b).

Conclusions

We support the learning paradigm and the vision of the learning college. However, if African American learners are to benefit from this important paradigm shift in the community college, the following recommendations for classroom practice deserve careful consideration:

- Each learning facilitator must explore his/her values, opinions, attitudes, and beliefs in terms of his/her cultural origin.

- Each learning facilitator must believe that all people can learn.
- Each learning facilitator must create an empowerment culture for learners in the classroom and beyond by doing the following:
  - ~ Increasing his/her knowledge of the culture of their African American learners.
  - ~ Listening to the voices of their learners.
  - ~ Weaving the realities of their learners' lives into the curriculum.
  - ~ Rethinking instructional delivery systems to include positive representations of the African American cultural heritage in the curriculum.
  - ~ Informing students about the brain's natural learning process and about their being natural learners, and teaching in light of the brain's natural, constructive learning process.
- Each learning facilitator must revise, extend, and reformulate the theory of cultural mediation in instruction over time and with additional research.

Finally, we hope that the presentation of the theory of cultural mediation will generate the type of discussion and debate that will improve practice and help us to realize the vision of the learning-centered community college for *all* learners.

Notes

1. An earlier version of this paper received the Maryland Association for Adult, Community, and Continuing Education (MAACCE) Research Award for 2000.
2. Earlier versions of this paper were presented at the 1998 and 1999 Learning Paradigm Conferences, San Diego, CA, and the 1998 AACC Convention, Miami Beach, FL.

References

Anderson, J. (1988). Cognitive styles and multicultural populations. *Journal of Teacher Education, 39*, 2–9.

Anderson, J. (1992). Acknowledging the learning styles of diverse populations: Implications for instructional design. *Teaching for diversity*. San Francisco: Jossey-Bass.

Anderson, J. (1995). Toward a framework for matching teaching and learning styles for diverse populations. In R. Sims & S. Sims (eds.), *The importance of learning styles.* Westport, CT: Greenwood Publishing Group.

Barinaga, M. (1995). Dendrites shed their dull image. *Science, 268,* 200–201.

Barr, R.B., & Tagg, J. (1995). From teaching to learning: A new paradigm for undergraduate education. *Change, 27* (6), 13–25.

Bjorklund, D.F. (2000). *Children's thinking: Developmental function and individual differences* (3rd ed.). Belmont, CA: Wadsworth/Thomson Learning.

Bransford, J.D., Brown, A.L., & Cocking, R.R. (eds.), (1999). *How people learn: Brain, mind, experience, and school.* Washington, DC: National Academy Press.

Caine, G., & Caine, R.N. (1997). *Unleashing the power of perceptual change: The potential of brain-based teaching.* (The Brain Store, 4202 Sorrento Valley Blvd., Suite B., San Diego, CA 92121).

Cohen, R. (1969). Conceptual styles, culture, conflict, and nonverbal tests of intelligence. *American Anthropologist, 71,* 828–856.

Cole, M., & Scribner, S. (1974). *Culture and thought: A psychological introduction.* New York: John Wiley & Sons.

Coombs, O. (1973). The necessity of excellence: Nairobi College, *Change, 5* (3), 39–43.

Dillard, J.L. (1972). *Black English.* New York: Vintage.

Fischbach, G.D. (1992). Mind and brain. *Scientific American, 267* (3), 48–57.

Freire, P. (1978). *Pedagogy of the oppressed.* New York: Seabury Press.

Gregory, R.L. (ed.). (1987). *The Oxford companion to the mind.* Oxford: Oxford University Press.

Guthrie, J.T., Martuza, N., & Seifert, M. (1979). Impact of instructional time in reading. In L. Resnick, & P. Weaver (Eds.), *Theory and practice of early reading,* (pp. 153–178). Hillsdale, NJ: Lawrence Erhlbaum.

Hall, E.T. (1989). Unstated features of the cultural context of learning. *The Educational Forum, 54* (1), 21–34.

Healy, J.M. (1994). *Your child's growing mind: A practical guide to brain development and learning from birth to adolescence.* New York: Doubleday.

Heath, S.B. (1982). Questioning at home and at school: A comparative study. In G. Spindler (ed.), *Doing the ethnography of schooling: Educational anthropology in action.* Prospect Heights, IL: Waveland Press.

Heath, S.B. (1983*).* Ways with words: Language, life, and work in communities and classrooms. New York: Cambridge University Press.

Hilliard, A.G. (1976). *Alternatives to I.Q. testing: An approach to the identification of gifted minority children.* Sacramento: California State Department of Education.

Hollins, E.R. (1982). The Marva Collins story revisited. *Journal of Teacher Education, 32* (1), 37–40.

Hollins, E.R. (1990). Debunking the myth of a monolithic white American culture; or, moving toward cultural inclusion. *American Behavioral Scientist, 34* (2), 201–209.

Hollins, E.R. (1996). *Culture in school learning: Revealing the deep meaning.* Mahwah, NJ: Lawrence Erlbaum.

Hollins, E.R., & Spencer, K. (1990). Restructuring schools for cultural inclusion: Changing the schooling process for African-American youngsters. *Journal of Education, 172* (2), 89–100.

Hoover, M.R. (1978). Characteristics of Black schools at grade level: A description. *Reading Teacher, 31,* 757–762.

Hoover, M.R. (1982). A culturally appropriate approach to teaching basic (and other) critical communication skills to Black college learners. *Negro Educational Review, 33,* 14–27.

Hoover, M.R., & Fabian, M. (1979). *Patterns for reading manual.* Belmont, CA: Star Publishing Company.

Hoover, M.R., Lewis, S., Daniel, D., Blackburn, R., Fowles, O., & Moloi, A. (1986). *The one/two/three method: A writing process for bidialectal learners.* Edina, MN: Bellweather Press.

Hoover, M.R., McPhail, I.P., & Ginyard, L. (1992). Literacy for miseducated Black adults: The Nairobi method, a culturally appropriate approach. In A.M. Scales & J.E. Burley (Eds.), *Perspectives: From adult literacy to continuing education* (pp. 212–218). Dubuque, IA: William C. Brown.

Hoover, M.R., Politzer, R.L., & Lewis, S. (1980). A semi-foreign language approach to teaching reading to bidialectal children. In R. Shafer (ed.), *Applied linguistics and reading* (pp. 63–71). Newark, DE: International Reading Assocation.

Hull, G., Rose, M., Fraser, K.C., & Castellano, M. (1991). Remediation as social construct: Perspectives from an analysis of classroom discourse. *College Composition and Communication, 42,* 299–329.

Jacobs, B., Schall, M., Scheibel, A.B. (1993). A quantitative dendritic analysis of Wernieke's area in humans. II. Gender, hemispheric, and environmental factors. *Journal of Comparative Neurology, 327,* 97–111.

Jensen, E. (1998). *Teaching with the brain in mind.* Alexandria, VA: ASCD.

Kandel, E.R., & Hawkins, R.D. (1992). The biological basis of learning and individuality. *Scientific American, 267* (3), 78–86.

Laboratory of Comparative Human Cognition, University of California, San Diego (1982). Culture and intelligence. In R.J. Sternberg (ed.), *Handbook of Human Intelligence* (pp. 642–719). Cambridge: Cambridge University Press.

Ladson-Billings, G. (1995). Toward a theory of culturally relevant pedagogy. *American Educational Research Journal, 32,* 465–491.

Lewis, S. (1981). Practical aspects of teaching composition to bidialectal learners: The Nairobi Method. In M. Whiteman (Ed.), *Variations in Writing:*

Functional and Linguistic-Cultural Differences. Hillsdale, NJ: Lawrence Ehrlbaum.

Martinez, J.G.R., & Martinez, N.C. (1987). Are basic writers cognitively deficient? *Journal of College Reading and Learning, 20,* 16–23.

McPhail, I.P. (1979). A study of response to literature across three social interaction patterns: A directional effort. *Reading Improvement, 16,* 55–61.

McPhail, I.P. (1981). Why teach test-wiseness? *Journal of Reading, 25,* 32–38.

McPhail, I.P. (1982). Toward an agenda for urban literacy: The study of schools where low-income minority children read at grade level. *Reading World, 22,* 132–149.

McPhail, I.P. (1983). A critical evaluation of George Weber's classic study of schools where low-income minority children read at grade level. In L.M. Gentile, M. Kamil, & J. Blanchard (Eds.), *Reading research revisited* (pp. 549–558). Columbus, OH: Charles E. Merrill.

McPhail, I.P., & Morris, P.L. (1986). A new look at reading/communication arts in the inner-city junior high school. *Reading Improvement, 23,* 49–60.

Milgram, N.W., MacLeod, C.M., & Petit. T.L. (eds.). (1987). *Neuroplasticity, learning, and memory.* New York: Alan R. Liss.

O'Banion, T. (1997a). *Creating more learning-centered community colleges.* Mission Viejo, CA: League for Innovation in the Community College and People Soft.

O'Banion, T. (1997b). *A learning college for the 21st century.* Phoenix: Oryx Press.

Perkins, D. (1999). The many faces of constructivism. *Educational Leadership, 57* (3), 6–11.

Petit, T.L., & Markus, E.J. (1987). The cellular basis of learning and memory: The anatomical sequel to neuronal use. In H.W. Milgram, C.M. Macleod, & T.L. Petit (eds.), *Neuroplasticity, learning, and memory* (pp. 87–124). New York: Alan R. Liss, Inc.

Piaget, G. (1973). *The child and reality: Problems of genetic psychology.* (A. Rosin, trans.). New York: Grossman Publishers.

Rivera, T. (1987). *Y no se lo trago la terra [And the earth did not devour him].* Houston, TX: Arte Publico Press.

Rose, M. (1988). Narrowing the mind and page: Remedial writers and cognitive reductionism. *College Composition and Communication, 39,* 267–302.

Rose, M. (1995). *Possible lives: The promise of public education in America.* Boston: Houghton Mifflin.

Scales, A.M., & Brown, B.G. (1981). Ebonics: An English language pattern. *Negro Educational Review, 32,* 252–257.

Shade, B.J. (1978). Social-psychological characteristics of achieving Black children. *Negro Educational Review, 29,* 80–86.

Shade, B.J. (1981). Racial variation in perceptual differentiation. *Perceptual and Motor Skills, 52,* 243–248.

Shade, B.J. (1982). Afro-American cognitive style: A variable in school success? *Review of Educational Research, 52,* 219–244.

Shade, B.J. (1983). Cognitive strategies as determinants of school achievement. *Psychology in the Schools, 20,* 488–493.

Shade, B.J. (1986). Cultural diversity and the school environment. *Journal of Humanistic Education and Development, 25* (2), 80–86.

Shade, B.J. (1989). *Culture, style, and the educative process.* Springfield, IL: Charles C. Thomas.

Shade, B.J., & Edwards, P.A. (1987). Ecological correlates of the educative style of Afro-American children. *Journal of Negro Education, 56,* 88–99.

Smilkstein, R. (1989). The natural process of learning and critical thinking. *Gamut, 1,* 26–29, 38. (ERIC Document Reproduction No. ED 382 236)

Smilkstein, R. (1991). A natural teaching method based on learning theory. *Gamut, 2,* 12–15, 36. (ERIC Document Reproduction No. ED 382 237)

Smilkstein, R. (1993). The natural human learning process. *The Journal of Developmental Education, 17* (2), 2–10.

Smilkstein, R. (1998). *Tools for writing: Using the natural human learning process.* Fort Worth, TX: Harcourt Brace.

Spears-Bunton, L.A. (1996). Welcome to my house: African-American and European American learners' responses to Virginia Hamilton's House of Dies Drear. In E.R. Hollins (ed), *Transforming curriculum for a culturally diverse society* (pp. 227–239). Mahwah, NJ: Lawrence Erlbaum.

Sylwester, R. (12/1993–1/1994). What the biology of the brain tells us about learning. *Educational Leadership, 51* (4), 46–51.

Sylwester, R. (1995). *Celebration of neurons: an educator's guide to the human brain.* Alexandria, VA: ASCD.

Van Allen, R. (1976). *Language experiences in communication.* Boston: Houghton Mifflin.

Van Sertima, I. (1983). *Blacks in science.* New Brunswick, NJ: Transaction Books.

View from Nairobi. (1969, December 6), *Newsweek,* pp. 74, 79.

Walker, A. (1982). *The color purple.* New York: Pocket Press.

Weber, G. (1971). *Inner-city children can be taught to read: Four successful schools.* (Occasional Papers No. 18). Washington, DC: Council for Basic Education.

Williams, C. (1974). *The destruction of Black civilization.* Chicago: Third World Press.

Woodson, C.G. (1933). *Mis-education of the Negro.* Washington, DC: The Associated Publishers, Inc.

Wynn, K. (1992). Addition and subtraction by human infants. *Nature, 358,* 749–750.

X, M., & Haley, A. (1966). *The autobiography of Malcolm X.* New York: Grove Press.

Zinn, H. (1980). *A people's history of the United States.* New York: Harper-Collins.

Nathan McCall

Nathan McCall currently serves as a distinguished visiting professor at Emory University in Atlanta, GA. He was born in Norfolk, Virginia. One of five children, he graduated from Manor High School in Portsmouth and attended Norfolk State University, where he received a bachelor of arts degree in journalism in 1981. Nathan has worked as a reporter for *The Virginian Pilot-Ledger Star* in Norfolk, Va., *The Atlanta Journal-Constitution,* and *The Washington Post,* where he worked until taking a leave of absence to work on his best selling autobiography, *Makes Me Wanna Holler, A Young Black Man in America. Makes Me Wanna Holler* was a *New York Times* bestseller and won the Blackboard Book of the Year Award for 1995.

McCall's latest publication, released in 1997, is a series of personal essays titled *What's Going On.* With the same personal authority and exhilarating directness he brought to his account of his passage from a prison cell to the newsroom of *The Washington Post,* Nathan McCall delivers a series of front-line reports on the state of the races in America today.

He is currently working on a new book.

Tony Anderson

M. Anthony Anderson is currently a graduate student at Florida State University. He received his bachelor of arts degree from Xavier University in Cincinnati, Ohio, in music performance. He is the executive director of Vizionary Productions and Sound Vizion Music camp. His research is dedicated to assessing the potential effects of music-centered instruction (primarily hip hop integration) on urban youth, specifically African American males.

10

THE ROLE OF BLACK COLLEGES IN EDUCATING AFRICAN AMERICAN MEN

An Interview with Nathan McCall

Nathan McCall and Tony Anderson

Anderson: Can you give some background information about yourself and how and why you decided to pursue a career in education?

McCall: I am originally from Portsmouth, Virginia, around the Tidewater area. I grew up in a working-class family; there were five boys and no girls. I am the next-to-the-youngest child, and we were raised by my mother and stepfather. I completed high school and then went to an historically black university, Norfolk State University in Norfolk, Virginia. I am the only person in my family who has graduated from college.

Anderson: What was the motivating force that inspired your educational pursuits?

McCall: The motivating force that inspired my educational pursuits would have to be my incarceration. I actually went to college after I spent some time in the penitentiary. It was at that time that I realized that knowledge really is power and if I was to go out in that world and compete, particularly against White folks I needed to be sufficiently armed. I realized that I was not armed, not with knowledge anyway. I was not armed before then, and that was largely what resulted in my circumstances. There was a college in my area (Norfolk State University), and before I got out of the "joint" I had already given some thought to attending Norfolk State. I also had heard or read somewhere that Dr. Na'im Akbar was teaching there. When I was locked up I read his books, particularly, *The Community of Self,* and *Psychology and Human Transformation.* So I thought to myself that if this brother is teaching at Norfolk State, I might have an opportunity to take a class or some classes under him. I had gotten a lot from his books, and that was part of my thinking. I decided I wanted to write, so I wrote the head of the journalism program at Norfolk State. I explained to him my situation, and he was gracious enough to enter me into a writing contest. Ultimately I was awarded a scholarship to attend Norfolk State University. I don't believe I would have been afforded that opportunity at a predominantly White institution.

Anderson: Dr. Akbar often speaks about the Academy as the place where reality is defined. Given your experience at Norfolk State, do you feel that Historically Black Colleges and Universities (HBCUs) accurately prepare African Americans for a predominantly Eurocentric workforce?

McCall: I do believe that HBCUs accurately prepare African Americans for the world and the workforce, and in some cases more accurately than PWIs (Predominantly White Institutions). I think that is primarily because predominantly white institutions move on the assumption that if you equip students with training and skills that they will be prepared to go out in the world and compete. Comparatively, HBCUs function on the premise that African Americans will have to be additionally armed to go out and compete and meet the challenges of race and discrimination that they will surely encounter in the workplace. I think that has been part of HBCU's mission historically. I think that has modified to some degree because of the downfall of segregation. During segregation HBCU's primary function was to provide an education for African Americans who couldn't otherwise get an education. After the end of segregation I think that mission was modified so that they would provide an opportunity for those to attend college who could not afford to financially or otherwise. However, one of the primary foci has been to arm African Americans so that when they go out into the workforce and they encounter racial challenges and/or discrimination they will be prepared. In my professional life I have seen the difference in those African Americans who have come into the workplace and encounter problems with race and are able to handle those challenges because they were prepared beforehand. I have also seen African Americans who have come into the workforce unprepared. They often tend to be the ones who are traumatized when they encounter problems. They are often taught to believe that race is now irrelevant, and that is the simply not the case. A person can have fifteen degrees and be qualified and overqualified, ten times over, and there are still going to be certain challenges they will have to encounter and those degrees will be of little help to them.

Anderson: Sometimes African American students who attend PWIs view students who attend HBCUs as living on an "island," almost like a fantasyland. Often times the argument is made that the student who attends an HBCU talks about what the real Eurocentric world is like, whereas the student at the PWI experiences it head-on. Therefore the African American student who attends a PWI has a more accurate understanding of the complexities and realness of racism. For example African American students who attended Ole Miss, Louisville, and Auburn Universities encountered what I would consider the most accurate depiction of America's conscience in reference to African Americans. (Alluding to the incident where White students wore black faces at each respective university for Halloween, along with other derogatory depictions of African Americans.) Comparatively, students who attend HBCUs will not encounter that type of blatant racism during their tenure at their respective universities.

McCall: That's a good point. That speaks to the complexity of this. You are right—African American students who attend HBCUs are often taught about the challenges that they will encounter, whereas African American students at PWIs begin experiencing it from day one, once they arrive at those institutions. By and large I think you get some African American students at PWIs that go through that experience and come out of it better armed. However, I believe that those are students who had solid foundations before they entered those college institutions. Those students who go into PWIs without solid foundations such as a strong sense of their identity and a sense of what they will encounter often become traumatized and don't recover from it. By the time they graduate, they are in pretty bad shape. Now the pluses are that some of the students learn to build networks among themselves and begin to gravitate to African American faculty and people that will help provide support for them. Many students find ways to survive. But I think the key is that the college age is still an emotionally delicate age, and given a choice between the two I would opt for an environment that provides the most support. There are pros and cons to each one. On the flip side I have seen students graduate from HBCUs and go out into the world and experience a culture shock. They have often times been insulated throughout their college experience. There are all kinds of variables there. I think the key piece is finding which environment enables the student to get the guidance and support they need during that critical stage of their lives and development. I think at the PWIs one may clearly get superior training in many respects, but there is also higher risk that when you come out you will be damaged goods. That is not a guarantee. I think that risk, in fact, is lessening somewhat as we move along in time, and as people at PWIs begin to understand the need to create and provide support mechanisms for African American students. At Emory University where I teach, they have a fair number of African American faculty on hand for students, but they also have an Office for Multicultural Affairs. The purpose of that office is to provide supplemental support for students that might not receive support in that environment. There are plusses and minuses to each. Students at HBCUs and those at PWIs are sort of back-and-forth on that issue, but it almost comes down to a case-by-case basis. I think there are more support mechanisms in place at PWIs currently than there have been in the past, and at HBCUs the mechanisms are already there.

Anderson: The climate of PWI's intrinsically requires for there to be a relationship forged between African American faculty and students. Is the role of mentoring as pressing at an HBCUs?

McCall: There absolutely is a need for mentoring for all college students. I think that White students receive mentoring to a certain degree, but I think they also receive reinforcement throughout society in various ways. At predominantly Black institutions there is a need for mentoring because even though students are post-high school age it is still a critical stage in their development. They need the support systems. They need the support that they receive from faculty. When I went to Norfolk State, I met several professors who took an active interest in me, not only academically but in my overall wellbeing. I recently attended the presidential installment of Dr. Algenia Freeman at Livingstone College in Salsbury, North Carolina. She was a former teacher of mine. I took a course under Dr. Freeman, and she took an interest in me. She invited me to her home for dinner. She understood that I was troubled and had issues, and she worked with me on that. There were other professors who did the same. So we not only developed those relationships and they became my mentors, but we still maintain those relationships today.

That was very important to me to be able to have those types of relationships. I think African American students at PWIs have fewer opportunities for those kinds of experiences with professors.

Anderson: Can you talk about some of the roles you play at Emory University in Atlanta, GA?

McCall: At Emory I know and understand that I serve a dual purpose and role. I think the administration knows and understands that as well. My role is primarily that of an instructor, but it is also that of a mentor. There are African American students who automatically gravitate to me, and I understand that because of my own experience. African American students often feel isolated at PWIs. I spend time with them; I have them over to my home. We watch films together and talk about those kinds of things. I see them on campus and talk about their futures and that sort of thing. It is important that I have a direct role. I serve a direct role as mentor and an instructor, as well as a role model. I know that it is important to see an African American male operating in a predominantly White institution and doing it well. It is important for them to see that. It is also important for White students to see that as well. They need to understand that, contrary to what they might have been taught, the world is not solely theirs. There are people of other races that are capable of teaching them anything that White professors can teach them.

Anderson: The average tenure of a president of a predominantly White institution is eight years versus the average tenure of a president of a historically Black college or university, which is fifteen–seventeen years. Can you speak about that disparity, as well as the overall management of HBCUs?

McCall: I think if the average tenure of presidents at HBCUs is fifteen–seventeen years that is too long. I think that when you stay around too long your ideas become stale, and there is a strong risk of complacency setting in. When you look at some HBCUs and how they operate, that becomes apparent. As important as their role is, many do not use the creativity and aggressiveness needed to bring in Black leadership to stimulate the student bodies at the universities. When you look at many of the so-called public intellectuals—the Michael Eric Dysons, the Cornel Wests, the Henry Louis Gates Jr. and many others—you find that they are teaching at predominately White institutions, and I do not know that its because they don't want to teach at HBCUs. Perhaps its because the HBCUs have not been as aggressive in recruiting them as the White institutions have. Emory University, where I work, is a predominantly White institution. Many students often ask me why is it that I come with such a strong pro-Black message, but teach at a PWI. I have to explain to them that I made numerous efforts to teach at HBCUs but for some reason it didn't happen. I believe it didn't happen because no one made it happen. I was the one who initiated the discussion. A professor at Clark Atlanta

University in the Atlanta University Center was unable to get her dean to schedule a meeting to make that happen. I have since talked to other people around the country who have experienced something very similar. For some reason there has been an inability or unwillingness of HBCUs to reach out to folk. I understand that economics might be a factor. HBCUs can't afford to compete with the salarys that PWIs offer. However, I think that if they tried hard enough and were creative enough they might come up with a system where institutions might share the services of a Na'im Akbar or a Cornel West. Students need to see people who have national prominence and are highly respected. They need to see those people on their campuses and to hear those people in their classrooms. That, again, was one of the main reasons I attended Norfolk State University. When I heard that Dr. Na'im Akbar was teaching there, that became one of the considerations in my going there. When I got to Norfolk State University I encountered numerous students from around the country who had come there because Dr. Akbar was teaching in the psychology department. So when you bring in someone with national stature, it serves as a great recruitment tool. Also when those people go out on their various speaking engagements, those people represent the university. That is excellent advertising throughout the county. At Emory University, you have Kathleen Clever, former member of the Black Panther party, Wolei Sulyinka, the Nigerian playwright, and myself on staff. I'm sure people wonder why we are across town and not at the Atlanta University Center, and it's a legitimate question.

Anderson: What do you think about White students receiving minority scholarships to HBCUs?

McCall: I feel ambivalent about White students receiving minority scholarships at HBCUs. I think that there is a tendency for us in this country to play games around the issue of equality and opportunity, and that may represent an example of that. While I don't doubt that there are White students who are financially strapped and cannot afford to go to college, I'm not sure that they are without an opportunity at PWIs throughout the country. I think when you look at the history of African Americans in this country you have to acknowledge that we been placed at a disadvantage for a long time. I think that if we are going to rectify the disadvantages that have been handed down to us through generations, then we have got to provide special accommodations. I think one of those accommodations is preserving HBCUs for those Blacks that need the opportunities to attend those universities. Another example of the gamesmanship that is played around the issue of equality is here in the state of Georgia; the University of Georgia was recently taken to court. Some White students were upset because they were passed over for admission and some Black students with lower GPAs or test scores were admitted. Those students took the case to court and won. So the courts then decreed that the University could no longer use race as a primary consideration in its admission policy, however, they left an interesting loophole. They said that the president of the university could provide special admissions for people, such as athletes. So the ruling really was an insult to people's intelligence because we know that the loophole was provided so that Black athletes can be admitted to universities such as the University of Georgia and help make hundreds of millions of dollars for their football programs. So here you have the institution wanting to benefit on the backs of Black folks, but yet not give Black folks benefits that might be due to the general population. So we can be admitted under special consideration as athletes, but not be admitted under special consideration as scholars. So that sends the same message that we have received historically. We are valued for our physical labor, and in this case our athletic labor, more so than we are valued for what we have to offer intellectually. It's ridiculous, and it's a farce, and it would be wonderful if African Americans—particularly athletes—had strong enough consciousness to withdraw their services from all the predominantly White colleges and universities in this country until Black folks are admitted in broader numbers for academic achievement. The courts might go back and rethink that issue.

Molefi Kete Asante

Dr. Molefi Kete Asante is professor and former chair, Department of African American Studies at Temple University. Considered to be one of the most distinguished contemporary scholars, Asante is the author of 40 books, including *Favorite African American Names* (with Renee Muntaqim); the revised and expanded *The Afrocentric Idea; African American History: A Journey of Liberation; African Intellectual Heritage* (with Abu Abarry); and *Love Dance,* a book of poetry and illustrations.

He has published more scholarly books than any contemporary African author and has reently been recognized as one of the ten most widely cited African Americans. Asante received his Ph.D. from UCLA at the age of 26 and was appointed a full professor at the age of 30 at the State University of New York at Buffalo. He created the first Ph.D. program in African American Studies in a major institution and has directed more than 60 Ph.D. dissertations in communication and Africology, making him one of the principal producers of Ph.D.'s in the nation. He has written more than 200 scholarly articles for journals and is the founder of the theory of Afrocentricity. Indeed, his books *Afrocentricity, The Afrocentric Idea,* and *Kemet, Afrocentricity and Knowledge* are the key works in the field. Sought after as a speaker and consultant, nationally and internationally, Asante was born in Valdosta, Georgia, one of sixteen children. He is a poet, dramatist, painter, and gardener.

He appears regularly on shows like Nightline, BET, MacNeil-Lehrer News Hour, Today Show, the Tony Brown Show, 60 Minutes, NightTalk, and Nightwatch. He has received honorary degrees for his community and educational work. Asante is the founding editor of the *Journal of Black Studies* and was the president of the Student Nonviolent Coordinating Committee at UCLA in the 1960s.

Recently he was made a traditional king, Nana Okru Asante Peasah, Kyidomhene of Tafo, in Akyem, Ghana.

I I

AFROCENTRICITY AND THE AFRICAN AMERICAN MALE IN COLLEGE

Molefi Kete Asante

I graduated from college during the Freedom Summer of 1964. This was the beginning of my awakening, although I had marched in demonstrations led by Diane Nash, a college student leader of Fisk University, while I was a high school student in Nashville, Tennessee. But it was the Freedom Summer that brought about an exhilarating feeling that somehow we were on our way to a society of justice and equality. Martin Luther King's speech at the Washington March in August, 1963, still rang in my ears. I had driven to Washington with my college roommate, John Lye of Singapore, to participate in the great outpouring of optimism. We knew, at least we thought we knew as college students, that the end of racism, discrimination, and the doctrine of white supremacy was in sight.

Soon Malcolm was dead, and Martin was killed a few years later. Our optimism had turned sour. This was the moment of realization that something more had to be done. The battle lines had been drawn in the society by the reactionary forces that controlled most of the institutions, including the colleges, of the country. African American students entered college, ill-prepared to deal with the racism that confronted us at every turn. Yet we were able to successfully deal with most institutions from the standpoint of rational argument and debate. What was not expected was that reaction would lead to confusion on the parts of African Americans. We would be under attack from our own quarters by those who neither understood nor cared to understand the depth of White racial oppression in the university.

Afrocentricity emerged during the late 1970s as a way to construct identity and be for-ourselves, culturally, without advice from Europe. This was in many ways the beginning of wisdom. It took a giant leap with the publication of *Afrocentricity* in 1980 by a small company in Buffalo, New York. Subsequently, *Kemet, Afrocentricity and Knowledge* (1990) and *The Afrocentric Idea* (1998, 2nd edition) were written to provide theoretical and methodological support for the idea that African people had to become agents and actors in order to transform ourselves and society. I also wrote scores of articles for magazines and journals detailing the ways behavior and identity could be impacted by the simple process of orienting ourselves as Africans to our own agency. In many ways Afrocentricity was seen as a response to racism, but this was a limited, provincial response to the movement begun by the advent of Afrocentricity (Schlesinger, 1991). The concern with racism was a valuable liberal democratic response to the conditions of African Americans (West, 1992; Marable, 1995). But this was not the intention of Afrocentricity. In the first place, Afrocentricity would have been necessary for a mature people, even if there were no White people to produce White racism. Secondly, Afrocentrists have claimed that the proper response to this moment in world history is a campaign against White racial domination, that is, the doctrine of White world triumphalism. This is a response that will be necessary for a long time because the elements that produce racism appear to be long lasting (Bell, 1992).

When I was asked to write this essay about African American male college students and Afrocentricity, I could not help but think of the totality of our experiences, male and female. While there are some unique expressions of the male's presence on campus, the mis-education that has taken place affects all of us. This is why, as a child of the 1960s, I say that curriculum is the most important area to be dealt with by students. We had to transform the curriculum in many areas. Our young males must train themselves to be able to do no less.

The demand to teach an Afrocentric curriculum is more important now than ever in America's history, or else we will continue to slip deeper into two dangerous racial camps. No nation can long exist that does not teach accurate history to its people. We have failed to give African children a full understanding and appreciation of the experience of African Americans. How else can a Korean or a Turkish American feel what it truly means to be an American citizen if they do not share in the knowledge of how this nation came to be, what it is, and how it is today?

Every African American male student must understand the enslavement experience of Africans in detail. This will give logic to the Los Angeles conflagration and the many other rages that we have seen and will see. From this angle we will be able to construct a true future based upon a common knowledge of history.

Afrocentricity is the perspective that centers us within our own historical context, but also allows us to be agents within our own sphere. We are not spectators to Europe; we are actors. Our history is replete with the best examples of heroism in the world. Why should we give deference to anyone? We should neither ask for it nor give it. Our college students, particularly our male students, must redouble the efforts to preserve the culture and to make it work for them as a source of inspiration.

We do not harbor fury out of some irrational need, some insane desire for anarchy and havoc. Our rage is legitimate and rational (Hacker, 1992). Indeed if we did not have anger it would be the most illogical, irrational, insane response a people had ever made to an oppressive history. Our anger is not shaped out of a will to harm others, but out of a will to protect ourselves against deceit and lies. This is precisely the reason our students and White students should be taught the truth of the brutal enslavement of Africans in this country.

Writers with rather opaque views of American history—white-washed to highlight a monocultural reality—do not find comfort in the idea that all Americans should study the impact of the European slave trade and enslavement of Africans. This is an educational therapy; we need to move our own selves out of the insanity that leads to all forms of nihilism. In fact we must study ourselves to find a breakthrough in the walls of oppression, and there is no more profitable study for African American male college students than our own cultural bases. This is always the first level of attack upon the incessant propaganda of European supremacy. If a student attends college in America and does not ask the right questions or pursue the correct course, he or she will return home without depth or possibility.

The brothers on the campus should hear, indeed must hear, the story of how the barbaric treatment began, of how the African's dignity was stolen, how cultures were destroyed, and how death swam next to the ships in the dreaded Middle Passage. A few Africans recorded their experiences: Jacob and Ruth Weldon, an African couple, give the most detailed account ever found. They wrote that the African, having been captured and brought onto the ships, was chained on the deck, made to bend over, and branded with a red hot iron in the form of letters or signs dipped in an oily preparation and pressed against the naked flesh until it burned a deep and ineffaceable scar, to show who was the owner.

The Weldons say that those who screamed were lashed in the face, breast, thighs, and backs with a cat-o-nine-tails wielded by White sailors. Every blow brought the returning lash pieces of grieving flesh. They say that they saw "mothers with babies at their breasts basely branded and lashed, hewed and scarred, till it would seem as if the very heavens must smite the infernal tormentors with the doom they so richly merited."[20]

According to their very poignant account of the abuse of Africans, the male slaves were chained two-by-two, at the arm and leg. Women were stowed away without chains, but naked, and all were packed away in the holds of ships for the five-to-eight-week trip across the sea. The Africans could not even sit upright, the space between the decks being only two feet in height. On fair weather days Africans were allowed to come on deck and dance for exercise. This they did with leg irons and chains to prevent them from escaping. Even some of the slave ship captains said the "groans and suffocating cries for air and water coming from below the deck sickened the soul of humanity."

Compelled to moan the long hours of night away, with no water to quench their tormenting thirst, and just enough oxygen to prolong their suffering, I have faith enough to believe that Africans vowed in those dark, damp, dank hell holes of horror that we would be free one day to teach the world the meaning of humanity. It is true that the weak perished and that the strong stayed alive. Their sleeping and resting places were often covered with blood and mucous; the horrid stench of the dead, breeding yet others for death, was everywhere. Those who survived often looked upon the dead beside them and intoned, "Gone to she own country" or "gone to he own friends."

The slavers spared not even children and infants from this terror. The Weldons tell of a child of nine months being flogged because it would not eat. This failing, the captain ordered the child's feet placed in boiling water, which dissolved the skin and nails, then the child was whipped again. Refusing to eat, the child had a piece of mango wood tied to his neck as punishment. When nothing would make this baby eat, the captain took him and dropped him from his arms upon the deck. The child died instantly. The mother was called and asked to throw the dead body over board. She refused and was beaten. Then she was forced to take it to the ship's side, where "with her head averted so she might not see it, she dropped the body into the sea."

If the African American males of this nation were educated as they ought to be about the history of Africans in this country, they would find a renewed sense of purpose and vision. Of course I must believe that if the entire society knew this, rather than the pablum of deceit that is normally given about the European slave trade, they would rise up and not only see differently but work to create a better place. If African American males knew that one captain of a ship with 440 Africans on board had 132 thrown overboard in order to save water, they would have a different attitude about human life. Nowhere in this nation filled with the bogeys of the right and bogeys of the left is the story of the African presence really taught to our students.

When those ships reached land, whether in the Americas or the Caribbean, whatever the condition, the Africans thought nothing could be as bad as the Middle Passage, with it long bloody night of violence and terror. Here on land the situation was often worse. Mothers were often forced to leave their children alone in the slave shacks while they worked in the fields. Unable to nurse these children or to care for them, they often returned from work at night to find their children dead. This was not suffering produced because of our religion, our previous class (and many were royalty), but because of our race. Neither class nor religion could sustain the level of persecution and violence inflicted against Africans. Our ancestors came ashore to the uncertainty of life, but the certainty of pain.

If young men who are most susceptible to violence and the committing of violent actions could really read history and understand the relationship of Africans to cotton, they would have a different view of life. The time was when men, women, and children worked until the blood ran from the tips of their fingers where they had been pricked by the hard pod of the cotton. I believe that if Wilderness dweller and Promise dwellers could appreciate how my ancestors dragged their cotton baskets, all trembling, to the scale, for fear their weight should be short and they would be whipped, they would have a common understanding of the trials that made our history. I know that if Promise dweller learned about the foundations upon which their privileges were based—that is, my ancestors bent double with constant stooping and scourged on their bare backs when they attempted to rise to straighten themselves for a moment—they would want to treat each human being with respect and dignity.

This nation is only one nation if we make it so; there is no magic to the declaration of unity itself. Those who have tried to declare one nation by insisting that we all become Anglo-Germanics have failed. There is no returning to the past. There is fury everywhere, but it is a righteous anger that seeks to right the wrongs of an unjust society. What Afrocentric young men must ask themselves is the following, "Do we go forward with a mission for harmony and unity or do we persevere in creating structures of racism and walls inherited from the romantic Camelots of the past?" The answer can only be that we go forward seeking the path to harmony and peace. In this journey, however torturous, together we might find the maturity to become the nation the Dreamer dreamed and, hence, to erase racism.

References

Asante, M.K. (1980). *Afrocentricity.* Buffalo: Amulefi.

Asante, M.K. (1990). *Kemet, Afrocentricity, and knowledge.* Trenton: Africa World Press.

Asante, M.K. (1998). *The Afrocentric idea.* Philadelphia: Temple University Press.

Bell, D. (1992). *Faces at the bottom of the well: The permanence of racism in America.* New York: Basic Books.

Hacker, A. (1992). *Two nations: black and white, separate, hostile, unequal.* New York: Scribner's.

Marable, M. (1995). *Beyond black and white: Transforming African American politics.* New York and London: Verso.

Schlesinger, A. (1991). *The Disuniting of America: Reflections on a multicultural society.* New York: Whittle Communications.

West, C. (1992). *Race matters.* Boston: Beacon Press.

Clarence "Skip" Ellis

Dr. Clarence A. Ellis is professor of Computer Science and director of the Collaboration Technology Research Group at the University of Colorado. At Colorado, he is a member of the Institute for Cognitive Science. He is involved in research and teaching of groupware, coordination theory, and operating systems. Dr. Ellis has worked as a researcher and developer at MCC, Xerox PARC, Bull Corp, the Institute for the Future, Bell Telephone Labs, IBM, Los Alamos Scientific Labs, and Argonne National Lab. His academic experience includes teaching at Stanford University, MIT, University of Texas, Stevens Institute of Technology, Johannes Kepler Institute in Austria, and at Chiaotung University in China.

Ellis is on the editorial board of numerous journals, and has been an active instigator and leader of a number of computer associations and functions; he has been a member of the National Science Foundation Computer Science Advisory Board; chair of the NSF Information Technology and Organizations working committee; and chair of the ACM Special Interest Group on Office Information Systems (SIGOIS). Ellis was chair of the recent ACM Siggroup Group-2001 Conference. His interests include affective computing, CSCW, jazz programming, groupware, workflow systems, collaboration theory, distributed systems, modeling and simulation, Java and object-oriented programming, and social informatics. Ellis has published over 100 technical papers, written several books, lectured in more than two dozen countries, and was selected, in 1998, as an ACM Computer Society Fellow.

12

AFFECTIVE COMPUTING

THE REVERSE DIGITAL DIVIDE

Clarence "Skip" Ellis

Abstract

This document introduces the kid, Skip Ellis, and his odyssey through computer science. This is an autobiographic document presenting personal history and observations of a Black computer scientist. It is about successes, failures, and affective computing. This document discusses concepts of the digital divide, reverse digital divide, and directions of need in computer science.

Introduction

It was obvious to any unbiased observer that the kid born in May, 1943, should be a mathematician within the Academy. However, there were no unbiased observers; the kid was Black, and born in the Chicago ghetto. In the year 1969, the kid got his Ph.D. in computer science (the first African American to get this). In the year 1998, the kid was inducted as an ACM computing fellow (the first African American to get this) for his pioneering contributions to social computing. This article is a brief chronicle of the growth and maturation of the kid; and of computer science.

The Beginnings

The kid was named Clarence "Skip" Ellis. He obtained his first computer job in 1959 as a computer operator near downtown Chicago. The actual chances of getting this—or any computer job at that time—were quite slim, but his mother kept encouraging the kid to keep "pushing against the wind." When Skip applied for the job, he stated that he had a strong interest in computers, but no direct experience. He was surprised to learn that he had gotten the job and was excited to begin hands-on work with a real computer. On the first day of work, he asked his boss why he was selected for the job. His boss replied, "You were the only applicant. Nobody else was stupid enough to come to this dangerous part of town to work the graveyard shift. Your job is to walk around the building all night, and be visible in the picture windows so that nobody will break in and harm the computer. Also, whatever you do, never touch the computer."

In those days computers were a new phenomenon. They were very big, expensive number-crunchers that could only be owned and operated by large, rich companies and large, rich governments. This computer was vacuum tube technology (2,400 vacuum tubes!) with punched cards as input and output, so it filled an extremely huge room. As was sometimes the custom in those days, the company wanted to show off the computer by displaying it to the world from behind a large picture window. My job was to help protect this computer during and after the midnight hour. Needless to say, it was very disappointing that my job titled *computer operator* had a restriction of *never touch the computer.*

Nevertheless, I had lots of time during the nights to get to know this computer in an intuitive, and somewhat awestruck way. I read and reread all of the two dozen computer manuals and learned the ins and outs of the machine using all of my senses except touch. By the time that I left this company, I could sense the state and the well-being of the computer by simply walking around it and observing its hundreds of blinking lights and listening to its sounds. It was an awesome and enjoyable combination of my logic and my intuition. It kindled the beginnings, for me, of what I call "affective knowing" in computer science.

For example two months after I began the job, the company had an emergency. They needed to process payroll before 8:00 AM, but had no unused punched cards. I showed them how to recycle their used punched cards (sometimes called IBM cards or, more properly, Hollerith cards) by lifting the hood of the computer, and disabling the parity check circuitry. This simple act saved the day for them and made me a minor hero. After this they began asking me whenever the computer had problems, and soon I was operating and programming the machine for them.

This first computer job and many others to follow were eye-opening, self-learning experiences. A dream for the future began to shape in my mind's eye. I could see the day that computers would not only be used to aid large companies and governments, but would be used by all kinds of people all over the world to benefit individuals, families, groups, tribes, and humanity in general. I was envisioning (somewhat idealistically) the personal computer!

Student Life and Activism

During the 1960s the kid was in college, earning his bachelors degree (in physics), masters degree (in mathematics), and doctorate degree (in computer science). He was also kicked out of school at times because of his civil rights activities, and because of need to earn money for his family.

My almost-all-Black high school in my almost-all-Black neighborhood of Chicago was woefully inadequate preparation for my college studies. Much of my scholastic time in various colleges and universities was catching up with the knowledge and techniques of others. This was arduous and difficult work requiring strong persistence. My first years at college were indeed tough and lonely times; I can still hear my mother saying, "Kid, keep pushing against the wind." I succeeded in the predominantly White environments partly because I was basically a loner and an introvert, partly because of my supporters, partly because I was good at computers, and especially because the civil rights movement exploded just as I was about to explode. Explicit acts of racism that I encountered in my academic life tended to motivate me to accomplish more rather than to discourage me.

Although there were no degrees in computer science at the beginning of the 1960s in most schools, I could sometimes substitute computer lab projects for physics lab requirements. At Beloit College I was a student and also became director of the computer lab when the college received a gift of an IBM 1620 computer. At the University of Illinois I received the exciting opportunity to engage in leading edge research on hardware and software of the Illiac computers during my undergraduate and graduate years. In those days the University of Illinois had an ongoing set of research projects building and programming novel computing systems: Illiac 1, 2, 3, and 4. Illiac 1 was a vacuum tube computer completed in 1952. Illiac 2 and 3 were transistor computers built in the early 1960s. Illiac 4 was a supercomputer (the world's largest at the time) begun at Illinois in 1965. I received my Ph.D. from the University of Illinois in 1969 in the areas of theoretical computer science and supercomputing. I greatly enjoyed my computer experiences during my student years, although school was mostly a lonely endeavor.

The 1960s was an exciting era because the civil rights movement took on major proportion and changed the face of racism in America. For me, it totally fulfilled the adage, "May you live in interesting times." I fully participated and emerged from this decade as a much fuller and wiser person. I was engaged, scarred, and active. The debates, the protests, the times in Selma, Alabama, and Washington, D.C. were all an important education and awakening. I learned to engage my intuition and emotion as well as my logic. Time in a jail cell always affects a person; I emerged as a skeptical philosopher. Ultimately my Ph.D. thesis was really about life, computing, and philosophy (Ellis, 1969) from a skeptic's perspective. At the entrance to the 1960s decade I was narrowly interested in mathematical computing; at the exit from this decade I was broadly interested in society's problems and affective computing.

The studies, research, and writings of the Ph.D. dissertation were a surprisingly positive and empowering experience. The topic was one conceived and fully explored by myself; and one that synthesized formal mathematics with affective computing. In 1969 Clarence (Skip) Ellis completed his dissertation entitled "Stochastic Languages and Automata" at the University of Illinois. It was a monumental feat, and it felt good to be *the* expert in this blossoming new area. This thesis was not simply a study topic for me; it was my passion and my life's philosophy wrapped in hard cover. When I was awarded the Ph.D. degree in 1969 I was ready to escape from America; I decided to live and teach for a few years in China (Ellis, 1998).

Industry and Officetalk

With a Ph.D. in computer science in the 1970s, a plethora of opportunities was available, ranging from Chinese language translation research in China, through 3-D hydrodynamics research at Los Alamos in New Mexico, to creating new distributed computer systems at MIT in Cambridge. I participated in all of these and much more during the 1970s and 1980s. I alternately worked in industry and in academia. My work allowed me to live for periods in France, Brazil, Austria, and Ghana. Each time, when the kid returned to America, it was starkly apparent that America has its unique set of pressing social problems, including racial inequality. It was also starkly apparent that each society in the world has its set of pressing social problems.

Computing degrees open doors for those who attain them. Although Skip never followed the unspoken rules for obtaining university tenure, he was a faculty member at MIT, at University of Texas, at Stanford University, and at other institutions. One of the doors opened to me by the Ph.D. degree was the door to enter PARC, the exclusive Palo Alto Research Center in the heart of Silicon Valley, California. This was the high tech research center sponsored by Xerox Corporation, located in the industrial park adjacent to the Stanford University campus where Ethernet, Smalltalk, Iconic user interfaces, and the personal computer were created and developed (Smith, 1988). During the nine years at PARC and Stanford University (1976–1984), I participated in this technical revolution. I helped to realize the shared dream of "Computers for the People" and create technology that could be afforded and used by the majority of people in America. My other half of this dream is to make it available and useful to all of humanity, including the Third World survivors in Africa, China, America, and everywhere. This part of the dream has not yet come true, and the kid is still pushing against the wind here. Indeed, life is filled with successes and with failures from which we learn.

Among many endeavors at PARC, I worked on Smalltalk and headed a group to invent and develop Officetalk. Officetalk was a distributed office information system; it was an early research prototype—the first to use graphical icons and Ethernet to allow groups of people to collaboratively interact from a distance (Ellis, 1980). A goal of Officetalk was to allow users (noncomputer specialists) to use a visual programming language to tell their computer what they wanted it to do. This project was one of the first to push into the area of collaborative, social computing; many clones of this (called workflow systems) are in common use by offices and organizations today.

Our research group was not simply technical engineers building a system, but an interdisciplinary team of computer scientists, social psychologists, engineers, ergonomists, business consultants, and cultural anthropologists that was trying to conceptualize, model, build, deploy, and evaluate technology. Thus after building our research prototype, part of our team mission was to observe and evaluate the computer system in everyday use by "ordinary office people." Thus we delivered our new computers and network to a commercial sales office to see how "real users" would react to this new technology. I recall pre-delivery meetings with the work staff to get them interested and to train them in usage of Officetalk. One office manager was an older African American lady to whom I enthusiastically explained Officetalk. After patiently listening, she informed me, "Young man, I have been competently handling this office for twenty-eight years without a computer, and I do not need your new fangled device to do my work." I said to her, "But it will make things easier, more reliable, and you will get a personal computer, a bitmap display, and a mouse." She exclaimed, "Eeek, I hate mice!!" I then realized how far out our project was; not only was the personal computer unheard of in the 1970s, but the only mice that office workers knew at that time were the living, squeaking animals. At that time, as well as today, it turned out to be extremely important to have the non-computer specialists (social scientists) working on our team. They were integral to the success of our project. Over the years I became more and more involved in the *people* aspects of computing. Indeed these are the most complex and fascinating aspect of computing.

The Digital Divide

There is a noticeable separation between those who are internet-connected and those who are not. Those on the disconnected side of this connection are losing out. This separation is termed the digital divide (iAAEC, 2000; Gordin et al., 1995). In the USA, the disconnected tend to be poorer, less educated, and disproportionately African American, Hispanic, and women. A number of efforts are underway to decrease this separation (Fishman, et al., 1995).

In those old days when I began computing, there was no digital divide; there was an inescapable chasm between the few scientists who could use the computer because they studied and knew a lot of math and engineering, versus the rest of the world. In those days networked computers were a rarity, not a common commodity as is the case today. During my time at PARC, I took one year leave of absence to introduce computers to the Black neighborhood across the tracks (across highway 101) from Palo Alto, California. It was an enlightening and frustrating year. Although high tech companies had professed their willingness to donate computers to the elementary and high schools across the tracks, there were obstacles ranging from tax writeoffs, through security of computer labs, through ownership battles within the school district, to very unenthusiastic students. On this latter point, many of the students at the predominantly Black junior high school developed a defense mechanism; instead of working hard, they simply decided to say, "I would rather be playing music and basketball, and get famous."

After this experience and similar ones elsewhere, I firmly believe that it is not sufficient to teach our younger generation how to be users of computers (and consumers of technology in general). After all, these technological systems are mostly conceived and developed by White America for White America. We must give our children of color positive experience as creators, designers, and engineers of systems that are relevant and empowering to them. Only then will we be able to overcome the digital divide.

Affective and Effective Computing

We understand that different people have different sensitivities, different learning styles, and different ways of knowing (Belensky 1986). Molefi Asante (and others) speaks of three different ways of knowing (Asante, 1998). These ways of knowing (cognitive, conative, and affective) turn out to be quite relevant to computing and computer science. Furthermore the third way of knowing is not well recognized for its high value, and is in danger of extinction!

Cognitive is an adjective referring to logical thinking. *Cognitive knowing* refers to use of logic and analytic thinking to know an idea. The scientific method, and much of mathematics, is based upon this way of knowing. For example, if asked, "How many 1 foot by 1 foot square tiles does it take to cover a 3 foot by 3 foot floor?" one might apply math and logic to attain the answer ($3 \times 3 = 9$). This way of knowing the answer is the normal expected methodology in the Western world. An alternative might be to take a stack of tiles to a 3×3 floor, and get the answer by actually doing the covering. This is the conative way of knowing.

Within computer science, one can think of the building of computers (electrical and mechanical engineering) and the instruction of computers (programming) as highly cognitive activities. A fundamental concern at the heart of computer science is algorithms (Brookshear, 2000). Algorithms are an abstract and fundamentally cognitive way of knowing. Thus computer science is fundamentally based in cognition.

Conative is an adjective referring to purposeful action. *Conative knowing* refers to experiential knowing. It is concerned with knowing/learning by doing. For example one learns to ride a bicycle by hands-on trial-and-error, not simply by cognitively studying the equations of motion. Many good learning strategies and, indeed, many engineering successes are predicated upon the ideas of conative knowing.

Conative knowing is, unfortunately, a second class citizen in many scientific communities of the Western world. Math and science are frequently taught as cognitive disciplines, ignoring the fact that many great generalities were motivated by, and derived from, conative experience. Scientific presentations are sometimes considered less excellent if they intermingle conative fluff with the cognitive substance. When I was taking graduate math courses, the emphasis was usually upon mathematical theorems and proof; the proofs were presented in elegant and precise fashion. Professors typically ignored the conative aspects; consequently, students were not given insight into the process (sometimes long and arduous) of the original invention of the theorems and proofs. This excellent conative preparation for a research career was unfortunately missing from formal lectures. Important ingredients within my research education were the informal interactions that formed context for the formal lectures.

I believe that it is clear that conative knowing is an important element in many creative endeavors of math and science. In computer science we find conative knowledge in every good programmer. The sub-discipline of software engineering is a good example—it is concerned with the engineering of large software systems. A million-line program cannot be written by a single person. We find that team-writing of large programs is partly an art with human unpredictability in it. As most professional software engineers know, you really get to be a professional at this via conative learning by doing. My experience as a computer operator in Chicago taught me at an early age that cognitive and conative learning must be combined. My Ph.D. thesis experience combined affective learning. In my research and in this document, I assert that affective knowing must also be combined.

Affective is an adjective meaning "related to, or arising from, intuition, or feelings, or emotions." Thus *affective knowing* is knowing via intuition. There are numerous examples in everyday life that involve affective knowing. One salient example involves an experience that I had when visiting my host family in Ghana. The extended family lives under one roof there. In the middle of the night, one older relative (great grandma) began yelling uncontrollably; everyone awoke and went to determine the problem. The relative said, "My son in Zimbabwe just died!" My first thought was, "How do you *know* this?" However, the family did not need to ask this question; they immediately began consoling her at the loss. They all knew that she knew. It was not until many weeks later that official notice arrived. It verified the event, the date, and time as previously known by great grandma.

This example illustrates that people are capable of affective knowing— that is knowing by feeling and intuition. Furthermore, in this Ghanaian household, everyone accepted (and encouraged) this affective knowing as valid (first class) knowledge. I was quite moved by this affective incident and others that I observed in Africa.

Unfortunately affective knowing has negative associations within the Western world. It is sometimes associated with mysticism, black magic, cults, and crackpots. In the world of computing (and indeed in science and technology generally), I claim that affective knowing plays a very important role (Ellis, 2000). Unfortunately, in the Academy of the western world this way of knowing is becoming lost and discredited. As computers become ubiquitous, computer science technologies and methodologies are being applied in a huge variety of situations. Today computing and communications technology try to provide solutions to problems ranging from language translation to urban planning. For example in urban planning a computerized traffic study might pinpoint a dozen city roadways that should be significantly widened to allow automobile traffic to flow optimally. This engineering solution should be augmented by intuition, however, that says wider roads may imply and encourage more autos and more pollution, so that the negative effects will not disappear. People living locally also have feeling and intuition that widening roads can be quite destructive to neighborhoods. All this suggests that a careful look at alternative solutions that encourage people to use alternative transportation may be more appropriate. Los Angeles can be cited as living proof that narrow scientific solutions (such as building more and more freeways) tend to be inadequate, and sometimes disastrous. Science and technology is greatly in need of more affective knowing.

The Reverse Digital Divide

There is another pressing problem that is facing America in computing and generally in technology areas. I call this problem the *reverse digital divide*. This is concerned with the social implications of technology, and the dehumanization of the human race. In 1992 I joined the University of Colorado as a tenured Professor of Computer Science and Cognitive Science to start the Collaboration Technology Research Group. My purpose was to specifically address the problem of the reverse digital divide. In this section I briefly describe this problem. See other documents (Ellis, 2000) for further elaboration.

Computers have a reputation and tendency to push people away from humane directions toward mechanistic solutions. Western society is moving in the direction of logical cognitive processes and discouraging our affective senses from growing. Computers also have a reputation for being isolationistic. Many children spend many hours with computer games and isolationistic video entertainment. These are hours that would, in the past, have been spent playing with friends and interacting with family.

I term this loss of affective skills as the "reverse digital divide" because many disenfranchised third world and minority populations have the well developed affective skills that are needed. Perhaps they can lead the First World nations to affective understanding.

Acknowledgements

Thanks to many people who helped along the way as I was "pushing against the wind." To numerous teachers who encouraged and stimulated me. To colleagues within the Institute for African American Electronic Culture (iAAEC)

(iAAEC, 2000) who have been a joy to work with. Although I have never met him, I would like to gratefully acknowledge the work of Molefi Asante. His thinking pervades this document and my life.

I take this opportunity to offer gratitude to the women in my life: To my mother in Chicago who steered an errant "the kid" in positive directions. To my older sister who first got me involved in the civil rights movement and in life. To my loving daughter who is a great inspiration. Finally, my utmost love and thanks to Yang Ying, my assistant, my encourager, my critic, my lover, and my wife. Although she passed away on May 26, 2001, she is with me in spirit and influences this document drastically.

Summary

This document has introduced the kid, Skip Ellis, and his odyssey through computer science. This is an autobiographic document presenting personal history and observations of the first African American Ph.D. in computer science. It is about successes, failures, and affective computing. This document has presented concepts of the digital divide, reverse digital divide, and directions of need in computer science. It is my hope that work on removing the digital divides will be continued and stimulated by the words in this document. I want other brothers to make their waves by also getting a Ph.D. or doing whatever needs to be done. Keep pushing against the wind.

References

Asante, M. (1998). *The Afrocentric idea.* Temple University Press.

Belensky, M.F. (1986). *Women's ways of knowing.* New York: Basic Books.

Brookshear, J.G. (2000). *Computer science: An overview.* New York: Addison-Wesley.

Ellis, C. (1969). Probabilistic languages and automata, Ph.D. Thesis, University of Illinois, Department of Computer Science, June.

Ellis, C. (1980). Office information systems and computer science, in ACM Computing Surveys, 12,1, March.

Ellis, C. (1998). The state of computing in china, ACM SIGOIS Bulletin 16,1.

Ellis, C. (2000). Ameliorating the reverse digital divide, CU-CS Technical Report. June. Boulder, Colorado.

Fishman, B., Gomez, L., Pea, R., & Gordin, D. (1995). Using the WWW to build learning communities in K–12 settings, Part II: The next generation of web servers to support learning communities. In The Global Network Navigator [Electronic Document].

Gordin, D., Gomez, L., Pea, R., & Fishman, B. (1995). Using the WWW to build learning communities in K–12 Settings, Part I: The current state of the art in web-based technology for K–12 Education. In The Global Network Navigator [Electronic Document].

iAAEC. (2000). The Institute for African American ECulture, *www.iaaec.org. Beyond the digital divide.*

Smith, D.K. & Alexander, R.C. (1988). *Fumbling the future.* New York: W. Morrow.

Frank W. Hale, Jr.

Dr. Frank W. Hale, Jr. is vice provost and professor emeritus at Ohio State University where he served from 1971 to 1988. Hale is a graduate of the University of Nebraska where he was awarded a B.A. and M.A. in communication, political science, and English in 1950, and a Ph.D. in communication and political science from Ohio State University in 1955. He was awarded the "Certificate in English Literature" from the University of London in 1960.

Serving in the field of higher education for forty-one years (1951–1992), Hale has held full professorships at Central State University (Ohio), Oakwood College (Alabama) and Ohio State University. In 1957, Dr. Hale was a Visiting Professor of Communication at Potomac University (Maryland). He served as chair and professor of the department of English (1959–1966) at Central State University (Ohio). Before coming to Ohio State, he was president of Oakwood College (1966–1971) in Huntsville, Alabama. From 1971 to 1978, he was associate dean and chairman of the Fellowship Committee of the Graduate School of Ohio State University. Dr. Hale was appointed vice provost for minority affairs in 1978, a position which he held until his retirement from Ohio State in 1988. He also served as special assistant to the president at Kenyon College from 1989 to 1992. In the summer of 1995, he was visiting professor of communication at the University of Nebraska-Lincoln. He was appointed distinguished university representative and consultant at Ohio State University in May 1999.

As a scholar, researcher, author, teacher, administrator, consultant, and civil rights crusader, Hale was the engineer of many new initiatives at Ohio State University. He founded the Graduate and Professional Schools Visitation Days program in 1971 and its undergraduate counterpart, the Minority Scholars Program in 1982. Through his efforts, nearly $15 million in graduate fellowship awards were granted to approximately 1,200 minority students. Eighty percent of these fellowship recipients earned master's and/or doctoral degrees. With the awarding of full tuition scholarships through the Minority Scholars program to high school seniors, the university was able to attract a "Community of Minority Scholars" numbering more than 500 during Hale's tenure. As a capstone to his illustrious career, the Ohio State University Board of Trustees voted him vice provost and professor emeritus, naming in his honor the Frank W. Hale, Jr. Black Cultural Center.

13

VISUALIZING THE FRAMEWORK FOR ACCESS AND SUCCESS

DEMOCRACY DEMANDS THAT WE CARE*

Frank W. Hale, Jr.

The ways and means of "expanding opportunities for access and success in higher education are varied and complex." Perhaps we need to be reminded once again that our journey into the important areas of access and success require, at this juncture in our historical experiences, far more courage and will than practical knowledge. The civil rights victories of the 1960s have enabled us to focus our attention over the last four decades toward achieving greater access for people of color and other marginalized populations. Enlightened academics by now should recognize the need to transcend rhetoric into positive action.

Recognizing the dramatic shifts in the nation's demographic profile should help us to focus on the urgency of moving forward in a more sustained and effective way to make our society reflect the dreams, aspirations, and possibilities of all of its citizens.

---

*Thoughts from a presentation that was delivered June 25, 2001, at the Annual Summer Meeting of NASULGC (Commission on Human Resources and Social Change). Theme: "Expanding Opportunities for Access and Success in Higher Education."

Any framework for access and success must be couched in the interrelatedness of parental involvement, community involvement, and the impact of practices and processes of elementary and secondary education. Success or failure at one level inevitably surfaces at another. It was Alexander Astin, decades ago, who reminded us that we need to begin preparing our youth to be successful early on in the educational pipeline. To the extent that these schools are successful in elevating achievement, the success of their graduates in the pursuit and persistence in higher education will be improved.

It follows, then, that we must begin new approaches that will enable us to be far more successful in both admitting and retaining nontraditional students. It is important that we comb through the academic and personal files and profiles of students whose success would not be compromised were we to admit them.

Not long ago I was pleased to gain an overview of Freeman Hrabowski's excellent work on *Beating the Odds: Raising Academically Successful Males,* and he championed the successes of the Meyerhoff Scholars Program, created in 1988 at the University of Maryland, Baltimore County, for talented African American college males interested in research careers in science and engineering. The Meyerhoff program addresses the shortage of African American males in college and the national shortage of African American males earning Ph.D.s in science and engineering. The first group of nineteen young men were enrolled in the program in the fall of 1989. The program has expanded to include women, and has now reached a steady state enrollment of approximately two hundred students from across the nation. The program has already graduated over a hundred students, almost all of whom are succeeding in graduate and professional programs in the sciences and medicine.

As institutions are becoming increasingly selective, it is important to have programs in place that will enable those who are admitted to benefit from significant welcoming and positive experiences that will enable them to perform at the level of their successful counterparts. Borrowing from the calculus workshop approach developed at the University of California at Berkeley, the Meyerhoff Scholars Program focuses on (1) creating an environment that offers rewards for academic achievement; (2) providing opportunities for young males to come together to talk about their performance in school; (3) giving the parents of young males opportunities to gather to discuss issues of mutual interest, common problems, challenges, and proven solutions; (4) encouraging regular interaction between young Black males and role models; and (5) forming study groups, composed of both these young males and others who are not necessarily of their racial group. These elements are also augmented by a six-week summer bridge program component that includes math, science, group study, and training in analytic problem solving as well as social and cultural events. (See Hrabrowski p. 199, 171)

Vincent Tinto's research (Tinto, 1993), punctuated in his very fine work, *Leaving College: Rethinking the Causes and Cures of Student Attrition,* underscores the promise, prospect, and value of collaborative and cooperative learning for both student learning and retention. Numerous institutions have begun training their faculty and restructuring their courses to require students to work together in structured cooperative settings. "The faculty and students often join together as collaborators in dealing with the content of the courses in a manner which provides both for therapeutic unity and synthetic wholeness," according to Tinto. He cites the experiences of the University of Oregon, Brown University, Long Island University-Brooklyn campus, the University of Washington, the University of Maryland, Duquesne University, and the University of Minnesota as examples of institutions that have applied cooperative-learning teaching strategies to classroom settings.

We must do all that we can to eliminate the inequitable distribution of people of color and women at the various levels and in the various disciplines and types of postsecondary education. Hopefully the time will come when we will no longer have to divine programs to address the special needs of those whose educational preparation was inadequate in the first place. Such palliatives only promote blanket stereotyping and are psychologically damaging to the very students whom we seek to serve.

It goes without saying, nevertheless, that there is so much more involved in the access and success of people of color, women, and other marginalized groups than their potential and their educational preparation. While making demands upon students and faculty, the institution needs to be responsible itself in creating a welcoming, creative, supportive environment of high expectations. It is one thing "to admit and hire people; its quite another to accept them." Barbara Sizemore of the University of Pittsburgh collected research and data on "effective schools" nearly two decades ago and documented the fact that strong leadership was instrumental in setting the tone of the school, helping to decide on instructional strategies, organizing and distributing the school's resources, and in bringing the disparate elements of the school together and developing a consensus among the school staff around high achievement as a goal for all the children in the school (Weber, 1971). It has been well established that effective schools challenge the students to be the best that they can be, holding high expectations for them. Thus teacher's expectations for student performance contribute both to the students' achievements and to each student's success in persisting to the point of graduation. In higher education we must come to realize that the progress of students is affected by the type of welcoming environment they receive from the institution and its personnel.

Attracting faculty of color into the Academy has become an increasingly difficult challenge. Institutions need proactive programs to be effective in their diversity efforts. Even when the administration "gets it" in terms of a healthy diversity agenda, pockets of resistance can make it appear that the institution "speaks with forked tongue." Institutions that have been most successful are those that have not succumbed to those negative attitudes that noncommitted institutions use as alibis to justify their poor records of hiring people of color, women, and other underrepresented groups. Achieving faculty diversity requires extraordinarily creative and aggressive efforts. There should be comprehensive approaches to addressing the supply problem. Most diversity efforts in higher education have come as a response to a crisis-based rationale after student protests. It is indeed ironic that we like to think of ourselves as a rational community of scholars, but often react only after there has been what some might consider, irrational behavior (student protests, sit-ins, boycotts, etc.).

The new explosion of people of color in the nation's population provides us with an historic opportunity and rationale for achieving faculty diversification. Because we know that there is a limited pool of trained professionals among people of color, we must go beyond good intentions to make a difference. We need to solicit the views and experiences of those institutions that have designed institutional policies and practices that focus on setting new goals for achieving diversity.

There is absolutely no substitute for strong leadership that will make the point that systemic change is an institutional imperative. Such leadership will not fall into the trap of symbolic "feel good, cathartic" support. Accountability is key throughout the chain of command. Recognizing the importance of educating students and faculty to live and work in an increasingly diverse society, our institutions need to frame their visions and their agendas to weave diversity into the fabric of the university as an essential component of excellence. Goals for faculty diversity are best realized when leaders are not afraid to make it clear that diversity is high on their agenda and that they will not be intimidated by the naysayers. They should be encouraged by the recent report of "The Americans For Fair Chance," and the release of a new book by the civil rights project at Harvard University. The book, *Diversity Challenged: Evidence on the Impact of Affirmative Action,* argues that when colleges and universities employ policies to create more racially and ethnically diverse student bodies, all students benefit from broader educational experiences and better preparation for careers in a multiracial democracy. The public opinion polling in behalf of AFC found that 64 percent of Americans support overall affirmative action for women and people of color. According to George Orfield, co-director of Harvard's civil rights project and editor of *Diversity Challenged,* ". . . affirmative action policies have major benefits not only in overcoming the history of the exclusion of minorities, but also in creating a richer educational experience for all students and faculty and in injecting new ideas and understandings into discussions, debate and research on campus."

Nevertheless, for many college and university presidents the issue of diversity continues to be a scary one. In citing his experience prior to becoming president of Teachers' College at Columbia University, Dr. Arthur E. Levine directed management-training programs for senior higher education administrators. Each summer he taught ninety-five presidents, vice presidents, and deans. When he confronted the group with the issue relative to diversity and inquired about what they wanted to see happen, he found that, regardless of the race, gender, or age, the answer was usually the same, "I want it to go away!" (Levine, 2000)

I am sure that we all know by now that the issue won't go away. The new wave of immigrants, as well as those women and people of color who are a historical and important part of the mosaic of this country, are determined that this "government of the people, by the people and for the people" will include them and not deny them their inalienable rights as American citizens.

Fortunately we have committed and stalwart presidents like my own highly respected leader, Dr. William Kirwan, who are insistent that a wider range of cultures, their opinions and insights, and their representatives have a place at the university's table. From the very beginning of his presidency at the Ohio State University, he has championed the theme that his focus will be on "Achieving Excellence Through Diversity."

It was one year ago this month that our diversity action plan was released after having the benefit of the suggestions and recommendations of a wide range of constituencies on campus. The plan urges and encourages the university family "to aggressively and publicly defend the principles of affirmative action in admissions, financial aid, curriculum development, library acquisitions, cultural and extracurricular activities, budget decisions, and in the hiring and promoting of faculty, staff and administrators." And there are other institutions that are making particular strides in meeting the challenges of diversity. Georgia Institute of Technology is now the number one producer of Black engineers. Among traditionally White institutions (TWIs), Southern Illinois University, University of Maryland, College Park, Florida International University, and Georgia State University had dramatic increases in the number of Black degree recipients. Purdue University's Graduate School's Office of Minority Affairs has been very successful in its outreach program in attracting students of color to pursue graduate degrees in science and technology. It is refreshing to observe that some institutions are seriously attempting to close the gap between the rhetoric of diversity on one hand, and the engagement of the administration, the faculty, the staff, the students, the alumni, and the trustees on the other.

We've got to do better and we must. It was a decade ago that I developed an inventory for assessing an institution's commitment to diversity programming. At its center was administrative leadership, out of which radiated a number of areas that are factors that contribute to effectiveness in providing a dynamic pluralistic environment. These included the development and implementation of strategies to facilitate diversity in the areas of admissions, recruitment, financial assistance, support services, curriculum, campus environment, graduate and professional programs, and hiring.

Any fundamental program that is to be made for expanding opportunities for access and success in higher education should embrace these goals on a continuing basis, otherwise we will, as has happened so often before, fall into the trap of crisis-oriented band-aid efforts that assume that negative practices that are well-entrenched are regarded as simply as temporary institutional aberrations. Such contradictions can only lead to chaotic consequences.

James Boyer, in his thoughtful approach entitled *Multicultural Education: From Product to Process,* emphasizes the five As or stages of development in diversity education. He states that before an institution can realize its goal of true diversity, it must develop a sense of *awareness* in historical perspective; *analyzing* its philosophy, its policies, its programs, its practices; *accepting* the purpose of diversity unconditionally; *adopting,* examining, and revising its practices and its approaches to inclusion; and *actualizing* by visualizing and creating new paradigms for embracing diversity as a way of life.

Over the span of the last three decades I have been able to develop a skeletal scheme for achieving access and success in higher education. In order to make headway in the area of diversity, each institution should:

- Formulate a forthright vision and commitment to access and diversity by the president and members of central administration.

- Make diversity and access among the *highest priorities* on campus.

- Know that *courage* and *will* are often more important than practical knowledge to accomplish institutional goals.

- Pursue goals on basics rather than on the basis of trends or fads.

- Recognize the *interrelatedness* of home involvement, elementary and secondary school preparation, and racial and ethnic cultural patterns.

- Design unique programs that focus on *cooperation* and *collaborative* teaching and learning.

- Motivate targeted students to consider disciplines where there is a *limited pool* of people of color.

- Identify programs that *work* and *why*. It is not always necessary "to reinvent the wheel."

- Hold faculty accountable in terms of being *socially sensitive* to student needs, abilities, and possibilities.

- Recognize how important it is for people of the same racial and ethnic backgrounds to want to spend time together, and have a *designated space* for that purpose.

- Understand the *symbiotic* relationship between the presence of faculty and administrators and students of color.

- Make *rational* decisions that benefit students and faculty of color because it is right to do so, not because of some crisis situation that has erupted.

- Let what is right and best *funnel down* from the institution before waiting for things to *bubble up*.

- Make *accountability* the glue that will keep the institutional programs of access viable and productive.

- Recruit at Historically Black Colleges and Universities and at educational institutions with high concentrations of Hispanic/Latino students and faculty.

- Educate the community to understand that "affirmative action is the use of *race-conscious remedies* to address *race-conscious inequities.*"

- Pursue the process of access and diversity through the following stages: *awareness, analysis, acceptance, approval, actualization,* and *advocacy.*

- Work with local school officers to design programs that will *reward and recognize academic scholars* with the kind of publicity and promotion that is given to student athletes.

- Establish a Professional and Assistance Leadership (PAL) Program that will pair middle school and high school students with community professionals and college professors over a number of years in disciplines where students of color are seriously under-represented.

- Examine and evaluate the following areas to determine to what extent your institution needs to improve in the area of equal educational opportunities:

  - administrative leadership

  - admission and recruitment

  - financial assistance

  - student support services

  - curriculum

  - campus environment

  - graduate and professional programs

  - hiring

There is so much that corporate America can teach us. A 1998 society of human resource managers survey showed that companies increasingly have diversity programs in place and that the larger the company, the more likely it is to have an established program. Seventy-five percent of the Fortune 500 companies have a diversity program in place and another 8 percent are planning to implement a program. Unfortunately there are companies that have not profited from the legal issues surrounding Coca-Cola, Texaco, Denny's, and Nationwide Insurance Company, among others.

And so our greatest challenge in higher education is to bring all of our campus constituencies on board. When the nation has understood the rich possibilities inherent in the concept of *e pluribus unum,* it has come to the fore in championing women's rights, civil rights, gay-lesbian rights, veterans' rights, the rights of the disabled, and children's rights, all of which are encompassed in the broader spectrum of human rights.

The nation has a history of people coming together as allies to face up to those injustices that plague both the oppressor and the oppressed. During the nineteenth century, there were Black and White allies in the struggle for the emancipation of Blacks. Such notables as William Lloyd Garrison, Charles Sumner, Wendell Phillips, Elijah Lovejoy, Theodore Weld, and Salmon Portland Chase joined hands with Black advocates for justice to help in redirecting the nation's thinking of what true democracy should be.

The same was true in the 1960s. The Montgomery Boycott, the Little Rock Nine, the March on Selma, and the March on Washington were examples of similar cooperative and collaborative efforts.

Nowhere was the impact of Blacks and Whites coming together more dramatic and effective than the March on Washington. Though the idea of having a march was batted back and forth among the civil rights leaders, it was probably the voice and advocacy of A. Phillip Randolph that tilted the decision in favor of the march. The collective support of the civil rights organizations, religious leaders, and the unions, as well as the endorsement of the Kennedys, added respectability and momentum to the idea.

I was there and sponsored several carloads of students from Central State University in a caravan of cars that scurried all night long from Wilberforce, Ohio, to the nation's capital in order to be a part of what we knew would become a revolutionary part of American history. And we were not disappointed as more than a quarter of a million people gathered, stretching themselves along the lagoon that leads to the Lincoln Memorial. It was a significant manifestation of goodwill as Blacks and Whites, labor and management, rich and poor, corporate America, and religious and secular institutions melded their respected interests to create a coalition of conscience, concern, and support in behalf of equality of opportunity for all of America's citizens. It was this massive effort that led to the turn of events that cumulated in the passage of the 1964 Civil Rights Act. Its passage had special relevance to the significance of what can happen when Americans, putting race and racism aside, create vehicles for the achievement of equality for all citizens. The greater challenge remains, as it appears that we are witnessing a downswing of national conscience and effort in promoting and achieving cultural and racial diversity on our campuses. We must never forget that, "Education Demands That We Care."

References

Banks, J.A. (1997). *Educating citizens in a multicultural society.* New York and London: Teachers College, Columbia University.

Banks, J.A. (2001). *Diversity within unity.* Seattle: Center for Multicultural Education, College of Education, University of Washington, Seattle.

Boyer, J. (1983). *Multicultural education: From product to process.* Washington, DC: National Institute of Education.

Cox, W., & Matthews, F.L. (1991). Diversity in higher education: Can we meet the challenge? (Live Video Conference) Fairfax, VA. Black Issues in Higher Education.

Cox, W., & Matthews, F.L. (1992). Enhancing race relations on Campus. (Live Video Conference) Fairfax, VA. Black Issues in Higher Education.

Cox, W., & Matthews, F.L. (1998). Blacks and latinos in higher education. (Live Video Conference) Fairfax, VA. Black Issues in Higher Education.

Hrabowski, F. (1998). *Beating the odds: Raising academically successful males.* New York: Oxford University Press.

Levine, A.E. (2000). The art of diversity. *Black issues in higher education,* 17 (14), 17–23.

Matthews, F.L. (August 31, 2000). *The art of diversity.* Fairfax, VA: Black Issues in Higher Education, Volume 17, No. 14.

Tinto, V. (1993). *Leaving college: Rethinking the causes and cures of student attrition.* Chicago: University of Chicago Press.

Weber, G. *Inner city children can be taught to read: Four successful schools.* No. 18. Washington, DC: Council for Basic Education.

Wade W. Nobles
(Nana Kwaku Berko I
aka Ifagbemi Sangodare)

Dr. Wade W. Nobles, a professor of Black studies and the founder and executive director of the Institute for the Advanced Study of Black Family, Life and Culture at San Francisco State University, is a renowned experimental social psychologist and a prominent theoretical scientist in the fields of African psychology and cross-cultural and ethno-human functioning. Nobles received a Ph.D. in psychology from Stanford University, and is the recipient of numerous awards for his work, including the first Scholarly Research Award and the Scholarship Award from the National Association of Black Psychologists and the Congressional Award for Outstanding Contribution to the Community, the State and the Nation from the 99th Session of Congress.

14

FROM NA EZALELI TO THE JEGNOCH

THE FORCE OF THE AFRICAN FAMILY FOR BLACK MEN IN HIGHER EDUCATION

Wade W. Nobles
(Nana Kwaku Berko I aka Ifagbemi Sangodare)

Definition of an Elder
An Elder is a person, who is still growing, still a learner, still with potential and whose life continues to have within it promise for, and connection to the future. An Elder is still in pursuit of happiness, joy and pleasure, and her or his birthright to these remains intact. Moreover, an Elder is a person who deserves respect and honor and whose work it is to synthesize wisdom from long life experience and formulate this into a legacy for future generations.

—The Live Oaks Project

The key crisis and challenge in African life is one of culture. It is a crisis resulting from a worldwide phenomena of African domination and dehumanization. In recognition that the critical feature of African domination has been our de-culturation, the fundamental challenge of all people of African ancestry is to rescue and reconstruct the best of African culture and to use it as a paradigm for a renewed, modern African human authenticity. This in effect is the fundamental charge and moral responsibility of the Black academician. Only in this way can we, as Karenga (1990) notes, speak our own special truth to the world. Only in meeting the requisites of culture and the imperatives of being human can we make our own unique contribution to the forward flow of human history. Such a task requires that we stand, as Fu-Kiau (1991) says, on our own ground. What does it mean, to stand on our own ground? Too often we are located in the shifting sands of other people's stuff, and then we wonder, no matter what our position or status, why "things" just don't make sense. We must stand on our own ground and speak from our own sense of human authenticity. Given this perception, what ground do we stand on when we speak of elder brothers in higher education? For me, it must be upon African ground.

The African Sense of Elder

In the Amara Society of East Africa, persons over the age of sixty are known as "Shimagle" (male Elder) and "Baltet" (female Elder). The primary work of the Elder is to advise, guide, and oversee the work of various other councils ("Shimgilina"). The Elders are the guardians of the culture, traditions, and history of the people. They continually engage in the teaching of those who are younger. The experience and wisdom of the Elder is readily sought and freely shared with others. They serve as a link between the past and the present while guaranteeing that our way of life is extended into the future.

In the Yoruba tradition, the Council of Elders is called the "Osugbo" or "Ogboni Society." The Osugbo (Ogboni) Society is a society of male and female Elders responsible for the selection, installation, and burial of kings. They also render judgment and stipulate punishment in cases of serious crimes in the society. As in most African cultures, the Council of Elders is one of the most important institutions created. Sitting on the Council of Elders requires wisdom and the ability to express what needs to be said in a way that is not socially disruptive or alienating. Integrity, wisdom, articulateness, subtlety, tactfulness, and being listened to by others are all qualities of an Elder. The Council of Elders ideally consists of the eldest and wisest male and female Elders of the community.

The symbol of the West African Ogboni Society (Council of Elders) is the "Onile." It is represented by two iron figurine spikes (one male, one female) that are joined at the head with a chain. The Yoruba believe that the head is the site of the spiritual essence of the person. The Onile symbolizes the sacred bond shared between the male and female members of the Council of Elders and the importance of "the couple." The emphasis on sexual attributes of the Onile are designed to convey the mystical power of procreation and the omnipotence of the Elders. The importance of the complementarity between men and women is similarly reinforced by the Ogboni Society's unique gesture of placing the left (feminine) fist on top of the right (masculine) fist, with the thumbs concealed, in front of the stomach. This gesture represents a sign of giving blessings, as well as the recognition of the dominance of spiritual, sacred matters—and the primacy of the spiritual over the material.

Na Ezaleli and the Spirit of Blackness

Na Ezaleli is a Lingala word from the Bantu-Congo peoples of Central Africa (Obenga, 2001). Almost forty percent of our ancestors came from this region. The phrase "Na Zali Na Ezaleli" means "I am with existence or essence." Na ezaleli literally means "with existence" or to be mixed inextricably with your own essence. Hence the title of this discussion, "From Na Ezaleli to the Jegnoch," represents the intention to understand the importance of going from one's own essence (Na Ezaleli) to the position of elder (Jegna). The use of this Bantu-Congo term, in effect, represents a deeper ontological feeling for African people. It reflects the spirit of Black people. In many ways we are the "Na people." At the level of the streets, we are the people of the "hook up." Our *modus operandi* is seemingly driven by the desire to hook someone up in order to connect with someone or to get something done. As the "Na people," the spirit of Blackness is to be "with" people. Whether the issue is fixing someone up with a date, solving a marital problem, or getting a deal on some purchase, the spirit that drives the behavior is in making the "connection"—to be in (with) the mix. At the more esoteric level, we are a people whose way of life requires living in a way that is always "mixed up" (Na) with our own stuff, with our own essence or energy (Ezaleli). When our ancestors were forced to speak English, they mixed (used) African linguistic rules "with" English language forms and created a distinct language system (i.e., Ebonics). Even in submitting to Christian religious conversion (domination), we Africanized both the interpretation of the doctrine and the practice of the faith. From slave hollers, to the blues, gospel, and jazz, and all the way up to R & B and hip-hop, we mixed our own essence "with" the new or alien forms. We, in effect, will make it (i.e., language, religion, fashions, music, etc.) Black no matter what. What makes this difficult to see or understand is the on-going process of African de-spiritualization or de-Africanization, which has contaminated our process of self-knowledge and identity.

In this regard one can simply point out, for example, that in the critically acclaimed and equally critically flawed BBC documentary, *Africans in America,* the viewers were informed that the first African child born in America was named William Tucker. He was born in 1624. While attempting to describe the events and evolution of chattel slavery in America, the documentary tries to give the viewer a first hand account of this American experience by taking excerpts from the autobiography of Olaudah Equiano (1996). The film shares Olaudah's personal account of his enslavement and freedom by introducing him as "a kidnapped African who becomes British and marries a British wife." In the actual writing of his autobiography, Olaudah completes his saga by signing his book as "Olaudah, an enslaved African." This brief commentary on the BBC documentary helps us to see several important points. The first point, which is substantiated by the necessity to pass the fourteenth Amendment to the U.S. Constitution, is that each and every African American today, like William Tucker, is technically only an American by the location of our birth and secondly by an act of law that makes us citizens. Who or what is being located and whose citizenship had to be ratified into law is the African. The second important observation in the documentary is that, while the myth-makers want us to believe that the Africans, along with our culture and spirit, somehow were mysteriously transformed into something other than African, the authentic voice of Olaudah recognizes that he remains an African, albeit "an enslaved African." The essential issue to note in this regard is that neither time, circumstance, conditions of cruelty and oppression, nor adopted legal status, change us from being African. None of these factors have destroyed the Spirit of Blackness, and the "Na Ezaleli approach" to living in the world. In effect we are all William Tuckers. We are all Olaudah Equianos. We are Africans whose birthplace locates us in America. We are elder brothers (Africans) whose occupation locates us in the Academy. Unfortunately, we are, in many respects, especially mentally, still enslaved Africans. It has in fact been the Spirit of Blackness, the Na Ezaleli, in us that has been the constant, although disrespected, unrecognized, and most often misunderstood aspect of our strength and humanity.

Similarly, in the book, *Souls of Blackfolks* (1982), Dr. W.E.B. Dubois made the classic and prophetic observation that the problem for the twentieth century was the problem of the color line. Dr. Dubois went on to identify the dual consciousness of the Negro (sic), which consisted of two warring dark idols, one American and one Negro (errata African) whose dogged strength alone keeps us from being torn asunder. Dr. Dubois' observation is funda-mental in two distinct ways. First, it directs our attention to the duality of our lived experience—an experience that is simultaneously African and not African (i.e., American) at the same time. Second, it most importantly directs our attention to the African essence, whose dogged strength keeps us from being torn asunder.

As we enter the new millennium, it is paramount that we return to, revisit and recast Dr. Dubois' prophetic observations. In returning to Dr. DuBois' observation we should now recognize that the problem in America was not simply a color line. The problem in America from the colonial times to the present was and has been what to do with the African. In America there has been and remains a deep psychological fear of Black people (African people). A fear of pathological proportions resulted in an almost complete obsession with the question, "What shall be done with the African?" The historical and on-going answer to this seemingly perplexing question was to "de-Africanize" the African. The objective was simply to make African American people ashamed of being Black and African and, ultimately, to convince us that our very humanity was connected to our declaration that we were not African at all. It was, however, Black people's response to the experience of de-Africanization or dehumanization, that DuBois noted, acknowledged and, in a sense, celebrated as the "dogged strength." This "dogged strength," which refused to be torn asunder, was, I would argue, our racial instinct, our Spirit of Blackness, to refuse to be "de-Africanized."

In revisiting Dr. DuBois' observation, it seems that the Elder brothers in the Academy have a special duty to consciously claim the responsibility for seeing the world and ourselves as African people. We must speak our own special truths and claim our own special meaning as human beings. Our meaning can no longer be in reaction to second class citizenship, to the racist illusions of White people, or to our own inner fear of being who we really are (i.e., African).

The task of the next millennium for African American people is to be authentically African and, in so doing, create time, place, and space on the stage of humanity's future. Ours is to be African by understanding the African spirit, which keeps us from being torn asunder. In fact, our fundamental task, as we enter the next millennium, is to address the dual challenge of our existential problematic. By that I mean we must simultaneously resist our de-Africanization (deculturalization), while we retain our sense of Africanity (African spirit) in a non-African or, more correctly, an anti-African environment.

This charge simply means that we have a profound and deep responsibility to understand what makes us human and what kind of geopolitical, sociocultural reality is necessary to support and advance our human possibility, probability, and potential. For elder brothers in the Academy, ours is not the small limited question of teaching (civil rights), tenure (citizenship), promotion (equal opportunity), or student advising (political advancement). All these things we do as part of the academic experience, however, they alone are not our full responsibility. To be one with our own essence, to be African, to be the "Na people," requires that we also address the more fundamental question of the human authenticity of our colleagues, our students, and ourselves.

This is a critical concern because worldwide White supremacy, especially as experienced in the Academy, is not simply a system of segregation, discrimination, and disenfranchisement. Worldwide White supremacy was and is the philosophical and ideological foundation for implementing the systematic and systemic negation and nullification of the humanity of African people throughout the world. This negation and nullification is the singular and sole goal of the "Maafa." The Maafa, as noted by Marimba Ani (1994) is a Kiswahili word for "disaster." Many equate African enslavement with the Jewish holocaust. Such a comparison is erroneous. The Maafa is a continual, constant, complete, and total system of human negation and nullification. Fundamentally, the Maafa is the "denial of the validity of African people's humanity," accompanied by a collective and ever-present total disregard and disrespect for the African and people of African ancestry's "right to exist." It gives license to the continual perpetuation of a total systematic and organized process of spiritual and physical destruction of African people both individually and collectively (cf. Nobles, 1994). Hence we cannot be lulled into believing that the experiences of oppression, discrimination, and dehumanization of African American people are past history (ending with the passage of civil rights legislation). Our past in America is a prologue for the future unless we seize the authority and authorship of the definition and meaning of our collective well-being. Our essential humanity is at stake.

However, to be African in an anti-African society requires that we seize control of all the instruments that determine the lived experience and quality of life of our people. As a campaign, "to be African" clarifies and refocuses our human imperative. Can we be African in a pathogenic, hostile, and anti-African society? My answer is unequivocally yes. Not only is the answer yes, but the expanded implication of the question translates to the ultimate recognition that the real issue for us is "to be African or not to be." To not be African, philosophically, culturally, spiritually, aesthetically and psychologically, in a society of African negation and nullification, can only result in our collectively not being (Nobles, 1997). In such a space, all that we can be is the deviant or the nothing. The psychological liberation of the African mind and the worldwide development of African people (including African American people) requires that we, as a people, take responsibility for defining, maintaining, and controlling every institution that influences and/or impacts on the agency of African people.

The Tradition of the African Family

Character is the mark of someone or something that signifies its distinctive quality. One's character is the complex of mental and ethical traits marking a group or nation. It is the detectable expression or evidence of the processes that control and is essential to the transmission of one's hereditary information and nature. Is there an African character, an African spirit, and an African essence? Can we detect the evidence and expression of a recognizable African beingness and see the transmission of this African "stuff" from one generation to the next? For me, the obvious answer to all these queries is yes. Without falling into the nonsensical debate as to the Blackness of the ancient Kemites (Egyptians), we can point, for instance, to the thinking of these ancient Africans who taught us that Man or Beingness is composed of a mortal element—the KHA—the body, physical and an immortal element—the Akh— the spirit; the Ba—the soul and the Ka—the double or shadow. The visible (mortal, physical) and the invisible (immortal, spiritual) are one and the same even though the invisible (spiritual) is far greater than the visible (physical). Kemetic symbolism and spirituality helps us to understand the process of Being and Becoming that translates or reveals itself as Selfhood. Kemetic selfhood is revealed in the symbolism of MAAT and the spirituality of the Pharaoh. MAAT was believed to be the proper quality of all being and becoming. It is found ruling the cosmic, metaphysical and physical planes of reality. In its cosmic (spiritual) expression, MAAT represents harmony, order, stability (unchanging), and security (eternal). In its metaphysical expression, MAAT represents uprightness, righteousness, truth, and justice. In its physical expression, MAAT represents levelness, evenness, straightness, correctness, regularity, and balance.

As cosmic law, MAAT reveals that beingness (personhood or character) is based on the fact that "the order of all things, physical and spiritual, whether created or manifested, should be established at the beginning (of becoming) and remain for all time (throughout Beingness)." As the metaphysical meaning of being, MAAT reveals that beingness (personhood or character) is based on the belief that 1.) a just and proper relationship characterizes everything including the relationship of the rulers and the ruled, the victors and the vanquished, directors and the directed, and the teachers and the taught; and 2.) that something is true not only because it is susceptible to testing and validation, but because its beingness is recognized as being in its true and proper place in a divinely ruled universe.

It is important to remind ourselves that when Africa was invaded and our people were murdered, tortured, raped, stolen, and kidnapped, we did not give up, loan, sell, denounce, lose, or throw away our membership in the African family. Starting with ancient Kemet (Egypt), African American people have ancestral rights and spiritual connections to African peoples living in the Senegambia (Bantu, Wolof, Mandingo, Malinka, Bambara, Fulani, Papel,

Limba, Bola, Balante, etc.), the Sierra Leone Coast (Temne, Mende, etc.), the Liberian Coast (Vai, De, Gola, Kisa, Bassa, Crabo, etc.), the Gold Coast (Yoruba, Nupe, Benin, Fon, Ewe, Ga, Pop, Edo-Bini, Asante-Fante, etc.), the Niger-Delta (Efik-Ibibio, Ijan, Ibani, Igbos, etc.), Central Africa (Bakongo, Malimbo, Bambo, Ndungo, Balimbe, Badongo, Luba, Loango, Ovimbundu, etc.) and, of course, the ancient Nile valley (cf. Holloway, 1991). We are no less African than the Africans left behind in Africa and made victims of European colonialism and Christian and Islamic religious conversion.

MAAT, and all the best traditions of our ancestors, require that we, as elder brothers in the Academy, help younger brothers and sisters understand their just and proper relationship to everything in a divinely ruled universe. We, in effect, must become the African Jegnoch.

Jegna: The Responsibility of Elder Brothers

Language via words, concepts, and meanings reflect and/or represent phenomena within a particular culture. Every language, therefore, reflects and represents some particular people's culture. Language reflects and represents a people. When African people utilize nonAfrican concepts (i.e., Greek, Roman, Anglo Saxon, etc), we unknowingly, incorporate the psychological energy associated with these people via the words, meanings, and concepts represented in their language. Consequently we need to or should carefully explore the deeper implications of blindly adopting nonAfrican terms, roles, practices, and beliefs.

For example one of the roles and responsibilities given to elder brothers in higher education is to serve as "mentors" to younger African faculty, staff, and students. I would like to caution us, however, in the use of the term, *mentor*. Note, if you will, that in the Greek Odyssey, Mentor was a friend of April who wanted to go off to the Trojan Wars where the Greeks plundered, raped, and destroyed. Given the human expectations of this culture, April knew he could not leave his family alone for fear that someone else would attack in his absence and destroy his home, rape his wife, and demean and dominate his children and household servants. April, therefore, asked his friend Mentor to stay and protect his family and to care for and educate his son, Telemachus, in his absence. April made this request of Mentor because they were living in a culture that supported disloyalty, evil, and destruction. Living in such a time, one could not leave one's family alone because someone would come and destroy it. History has it that Mentor did this (protected April's son and family) with faith and loyalty. In actuality, Mentor should mean someone who is an accomplice to rape, murder, and destruction. However, "Mentor" has undeservedly come to mean a wise, loyal, advisor and trusted counselor. Without the help of Mentor, the cruelty and destructive behavior of his friend might not have happened.

The terms we use can have psychological transformative power in that the words, concepts, and ideas reinforce or reject the cultural moorings or foundation of a cultural community. Africans should, at every opportunity, use African concepts to describe and give meaning to African phenomena.

Jegna (Jegnoch, plural form) are those special people who have (1) been tested in struggle or battle, (2) demonstrated extraordinary and unusual fearlessness, (3) shown determination and courage in protecting his/her people, land, and culture, (4) shown diligence and dedication to our people, (5) produced exceptionally high quality work, and (6) dedicated themselves to the protection, defense, nurturance, and development of our young by advancing our people, place, and culture. The easiest and foremost interpretation of the Jegna is one whose central focus is on the culture and character of one's people. The Jegnoch cherish and love their people. In classical Ethiopian history there are several directions leading to the creation of the Jegna person[1]. First and foremost is the respect for one's mother and one's wife and, through the union of husband and wife, the sacredness of children. Underlying each of these (mother, wife, children) is a fundamental character of protection and nurturance, which is essential to the calling to be a Jegna. A second essential character is the desire for right governance. The Jegnoch are devoted to defending "the right."

In order to become a Jegna one has to make a life and death decision. That is, the Jegna must be willing to put everything (career, reputation, status, and even their life) on the line for what they believe. If a foreign enemy is in the territory of the country, the Jegna is the first to organize for war. Since their aim is non political ambition the choice of a Jegna is based solely on good character. The Jegnoch sometimes break all the rules of their class status because the Jegna could be born from the peasants as well as the aristocracy.

It is also important to point out that there are women Jegnoch. In Ethiopian history there were many women Jegnoch. It is well known that without their contributions the victory of the Ethiopians over the Italians would not have been realized. Exemplary of the character of the Jegna was Archbishop Petros, whose marble statue stands in the center of Addis Ababa. When the Italians succeeded in invading the interior of Ethiopia, Jegna Petros

---

[1] I wish to thank Professor Taddele Hiwot of U.C. Berkeley's Department of African American Studies for personally providing me with invaluable insights about the history and practice of the Jegna in Ethiopia.

organized the people and led the fight against the Italians. He was captured and killed by firing squad, however, before he died he spoke to his people who were forced to witness his death. With his last breath he cursed his people to become dogs if they ever accepted the rule of the foreign enemy. Another Jegna was named Belay Zeleqe, who after the war was given the title of "Dejazmatch" from Emporor Haile Selassie. He refused to take the title and said, "My mother has given me what is beyond all, when she gave me the name 'Belay'." Belay Zeleke was hanged in the city of Addis Ababa for confronting the Emperor. The point of both men's lives was their undying spirit, sensitivity, courage, and willingness to give their lives in response to any attack (internal or external), denigration, or harm directed at one's mother (culture), people, or identity. The real Jegna is one whose purpose and goal are not directed by financial reward or rank and privilege. The cause that creates a Jegna is the spirit of peoplehood that is buried deep down in the very nature of the person.

As elder brothers in the academy we must accept our responsibility to become the special people who have (1) been tested in struggle or battle, (2) demonstrated extraordinary and unusual fearlessness, (3) shown determination and courage in protecting our people, land, and culture, (4) shown diligence and dedication to our people, (5) produced exceptionally high quality work, and (6) dedicated ourselves to the protection, defense, nurturance, and development of our young by advancing our people, place, and culture. We must, I believe, function as Jegnoch.

The Role of Elder Brothers in Higher Education

With increasing years of longevity, one's status and value in the community rises. Living to a very old age is considered a blessing. It is thought to be an honor to be in the presence of an elder. In fact, to have elders live with you, and for you to have available their daily guidance, is considered a great blessing and advantage. Eldership takes decades of experiential learning and refinement. It is, however, more than mere aging. It requires increasing generosity, wisdom, integrity, and gratefulness with advancing years. In the Yoruba tradition, the transition from adult to elder involves a significant shift in personal and collective responsibilities. Generally, it is the responsibility of adult men to protect and defend the community, while adult women's responsibility is to nurture and educate the community. Accordingly, adult men are often consumed with the purpose and task of obtaining and providing those resources that sustain life for themselves and their families. Similarly, adult women's time and interest are devoted to securing and establishing an environment or area that is conducive to the growth and development of life.

When men enter the community of elders, however, they take on the role of "Baba Agba," which means senior father, or more correctly, "nurturing father." When women enter the community of elders they take on the role of "Iya Agba," which means senior mother or "warrior mother." It is the Iya Agba who have the primary role as the spiritual protector of the community. With the status of eldership, women are devoted to protecting and defending (warrior mother) the spiritual balance of the community, while men are dedicated to securing and establishing (nurturing father) the spiritual harmony in the community. Although there appears to be a reversal in the male-female roles and energy at the onset of eldership, the balance and complementarity of the male principle and the female principle is inviolate and always present.

As elders, both men and women devote themselves to the higher responsibility of utilizing the collective spirit to guide and direct the permanent ascension of the community and to channel its vital life force. The utilization and understanding of the natural spiritual power of the community is, in fact, perceived as the "wisdom of eldership." This is an all-consuming task. In order to do this, elders are generally not involved in the survival struggles of life (i.e., wage-dependent work). They are generally "retired" and can devote themselves to the full-time pursuit of wisdom and the understanding of the high values and traditions of the community. In effect, the elder's "work" is to synthesize wisdom from long life experience and to formulate this into a legacy for future generations.

Elders are responsible for continually contemplating the good and the right. Because of their eldership status, they are not—or should not be—driven by personal interest or individual reward. They cannot be tempted or influenced by appeals to favoritism or personal desires. The status of eldership places them above the needs of "getting over" or from asking, "What's in it for me personally?" Although male and female elders have distinct responsibilities in traditional life, in general, as elders they share in the responsibility for correcting imbalances, maintaining peace, and revitalizing community life. Their singular goal is to guide and guarantee the cooperative good and collective advancement. The elder knows the traditions, history, values, beliefs, and cultural laws that are inviolate. The judgments and decisions of the elders are always consistent with their community's cultural integrity and are directed toward truth and justice. Accordingly, the community knows that submitting to the direction and governance of the elders is not an abdication of individual rights or personal freedom. It is, in fact, a relationship that results in a deep sense of psychological security and collective homeostasis.

For brothers to be accorded the status of elder, we must be "nurturing fathers" whose singular goal, as an elder, is to guide and guarantee the cooperative good and collective advancement and security of the African family in the Academy. In addition to our university duties and academic responsibilities, we must also create time and space to provide us with opportunities to constantly and continually pursue wisdom and under-standing of our own (African) high values, beliefs, and traditions. It is our responsibility to know our (African) traditions, history, values, beliefs, and cultural laws that are inviolate and requisite to the success of African peo-ple now and in the future. The African family in the Academy should expect that we, elder brothers, have and are synthesizing the experience of African people in such a way that we are able to formulate our heritage of struggle and achievement into a legacy for future generations. For instance, one syn-thesis of traditional African relationships concerns the respect for elders. Another recognizes that all elder women are to be treated like one's mother and all elder men like one's father. In fact, in many instances one refers to all elder women as mother (Iya) and all elder men as father (Baba). Accord-ingly, one doesn't really have, for example, cousins because your mother's or father's sister's or brother's (technically aunts or uncles) children are con-sidered your brothers and sisters. One legacy of this convention in the African American community is the use of the term "brother" or "sister" as salutation ("what's up brotha" or "how you doin sista") to all Black peo-ple. As elders in the Academy, a synthesis of this traditional African system of relating could be used to help our male children (students and younger faculty and staff) to understand that every woman should be related to as a mother, sister, daughter, or wife and that every female student (faculty or staff) should relate to every male as either father, brother, son, or husband. With the greater understanding of the deeper duties, responsibilities, expec-tations, rights, and privileges of each of these familial relationships, such a synthesis would result in the realization that our male—female relationships should and must be governed by "respect" and "responsibility." Hence issues ranging from casual sex to date rape to sexual exploitation all come under the judgement of being extremely inappropriate and absolutely anti-thetical to how one relates to one's mother/father, sister/brother, daughter/ son, or husband/wife. Guidance from such a synthesis would help us as eld-ers guide student and faculty/staff conduct by redirecting that all our rela-tionships are familial relations and must, therefore, be driven by high regard, deep respect, and mutual responsibility.

In the African tradition of eldership, elder brothers in the Academy, as Jegnoch, must, I believe, utilize the collective spirit of the African family to guide, develop, and direct programs, projects, systems, initiatives, and policies that insure the permanent advancement of our colleagues, staff, and students.

The Council of Jegnoch (Elders) in Higher Education

In terms of negotiating the Academy, more than anyone else, elder brothers (and sisters), the Jegnoch, need to represent and reflect "normality" in our personal and collective behaviors. In traditional African healing, it was often "normal" for the doctor to take the medicine she or he prepared for the patient. There are many reasons for this practice. One is to establish a symbiotic bond with the patient. Another is for the doctor to experience the effects of the treatment. Another is to eliminate incompetent physicians.

For many of us the reclamation of our traditional cultural practices is a requisite part of our collective healing. Accordingly we need to take the medicine we are prescribing to our students. By reclaiming the tradition of eldership, we, in fact, are re-aligning ourselves to a universal field of energy that recognizes the law of progeny and stimulates a vibration that constitutes the residue of an original form or process. In addition to serving as advisors to students and younger colleagues, for the purpose of providing wisdom and guidance and conducting formal rituals and ceremonies, the Jegnoch will be responsible for providing clarification, interpretation, or judgment regarding our traditions, beliefs, positions, and ethics. Our elder brothers should therefore actively help the members of their campus community to determine what cultural laws, beliefs, and traditions are inviolate in the African community in America. In cases of disagreement or during moments of confusion, the campus community should defer or look to the elders for opinion, clarification, direction, and, ultimately, a decision. In this regard, and upon thorough deliberation and discussion, the Jegnoch should give the community further direction or make an irrevocable decision relative to our deeper spiritual essence and the higher good. In this capacity, the elder brothers should take the responsibility for guiding the family in the campus community and directing its path to higher levels of right living and functioning.

Traditionally, it is said that "the elders have said" or "the elders have spoken," which means that this is how it will be and we accept their decision with a "good heart" (with no remorse or resentment). Once the elders have spoken on an issue, they will have taken the issue and us to a higher level of understanding and functioning. We, the community or family, should, in turn, welcome the directive to move to a higher level of right thinking and right being. However, the elder brothers in the academy cannot correct imbalance, maintain peace and harmony, and reinforce our standards of rightness if we, ourselves, are not righteous and the family membership is not willing to accept the elders' role and the corollary role of acceptance and submission. Both our newly established council of elders and the family at large will need to respect and be obedient to the institution of eldership as we practice this traditional relationship.

As "Baba Agba," (nurturing fathers) and "Iya Agba" (warrior mothers), the elder brothers (and sisters), the Jegnoch can be one of the most important structures created by Black people in the Academy. Its creation signals and simultaneously guides our continual movement toward the greater capacity of Black people to be African and excellent. It will allow us to construct campus experiences for Black people that benefit from the "force" of the African family and "mixes" the college life with our own essence.

Finally, as a last word in this short discussion, I would ask that the would-be Jegnoch, the Black elder brothers and sisters in the Academy, seriously contemplate the Fanonian questions of identity and existence; "Who am I?," "Am I really who I am?;" and, "Am I all I ought to be?" From the location of "Na Ezaleli," elders must and should recognize that being Black in the Academy like in America requires an ongoing and constant struggle with social structures and conventions that attempt to make our quest for human authenticity futile and irrelevant. In fact, to raise the question of Blackness becomes almost embarrassing if not silly or in the political correctness of today, equals the childish or unfair "playing of the race card." As Jegnoch, we must not fall victim to the attempt to neuter or make mute our authentic claim to an African (Black) existence. In our work in the academy, whether constructing instructional information, chairing University governance committees, or advising younger faculty/staff and/or students, we can and should speak from "Na Ezaleli," from being with our own African (Black) essence. As Jegnoch, we must constantly raise and be driven by the questions of agency, location, identity, authenticity, and liberation for African (Black) people living in a decidedly anti-African reality. We must, for ourselves, our ancestors, and those yet-to-be-born be with our own essence (Na Ezaleli) and stand on our own ground. In so doing, a system or council of Jegnoch will and can, in effect, make life in higher education for the African family, at all levels, Na Ezaleli, and therefore better.

References

Ani, M. (1994). *Yurugu: An African-centered critique of European cultural thought and behavior.* New Jersey. African World Press.

DuBois, W.E.B. (1982). *The souls of Black folk.* New York: New American Library. (Original work published 1903.)

Equiano, O. (1996). *The interesting narrative of the life of Olaudah Equiano.* Vincent Caretta (ed.), Penguin Books.Fu-Kiau (1991). *Self healing power and therapy-old teachings from Africa.* New York. Vantage Press.

Fu-Kiau (1991). *Self healing power and therapy—Old teachings from Africa.* NewYork: Vantage Press.

Holloway, J.E. (ed.) (1991). *Africanisms in American culture.* Bloomington: Indiana University Press.

Karenga, M. (ed.) (1990). *Reconstructing kemetic culture: Papers, perspectives, projects.* Los Angeles: University of Sankore Press.

Nobles, W.W. (1994). *A national agenda.* Washington D.C.: Association of Black Psychologist Address, Psych Discourse.

Nobles, W.W. (1997). *To be African or not to be:* The question of identity or authenticity—Some preliminary thoughts, In Jones, R. (ed), *African American identity development: Theory, research and intervention.*

Charlie Nelms

Charlie Nelms assumed his position as vice president for Student Development and Diversity for the Indiana University system and vice chancellor of the Bloomington campus in January 1998. Nelms is also a tenured professor in the Department of Educational Leadership and Policy Studies, where he teaches courses in higher education administration. Prior to his current appointment, Dr. Nelms served with distinction as chancellor at two universities: the University of Michigan at Flint and Indiana University at Richmond. During his 30-year career in higher education, he has also held teaching and administrative positions at Earlham College (IN), Indiana University Northwest (IN), Lehman College (NY), Sinclair Community College (OH), and the University of Arkansas at Pine Bluff (AR). Nelms has worked in the areas of academic affairs, student development, and enrollment management.

The focus of his scholarly and research activities includes college access and degree attainment for African Americans and other underrepresented groups. He has made numerous presentations at professional conferences throughout the United States and abroad. In addition to his many articles, he was a contributor to the book *Grass Roots and Glass Ceilings: African American Administrators in Predominately White Universities,* which was published by the State University of New York in 1999. With a major grant from the Mott Foundation in 1999, Dr. Nelms established the Interracial Communications Project at four urban universities.

Dr. Nelms' service activities have included chair of the Leadership Commission of the American Council on Education; co-founder of the Millennium Initiative—a program designed to identify and mentor the next generation of minority college presidents and chancellors; and as a member of the Editorial Board of the *Negro Educational Review.* He currently serves as chair of the board of trustees of the NCA Higher Learning Commission, which is the largest regional accrediting body in the United States. Dr. Nelms' work in quality improvement in higher education and accreditation has taken him to South Africa, Japan, the United Arab Emirates, and the United Kingdom.

15

THE PREREQUISITES FOR ACADEMIC LEADERSHIP

Charlie Nelms

The end of education is to know God and the laws and purposes of His universe, and to reconcile one's life with these laws. The first aim of a good college is not to teach books, but the meaning and purpose of life. Hard study and the learning of books are only means to this end. We develop power and courage and determination and we go out to achieve Truth, Wisdom and Justice. If we do not come to this, the cost of schooling is wasted.
—John Brown Watson, First President, Arkansas AM&N College

Growing up in the delta region of Arkansas, an area characterized by suffocating segregation, racism, poverty, and despair, made an indelible impression on me. The impact of this experience was so profound that I made a vow as a young child to devote my life to bringing hope to the hopeless and help to the helpless. Exactly how that vow was to be fulfilled was not clear, but Reverend George Mitchell, the pastor of Shiloh Missionary Baptist Church, a little, nondescript edifice where my family and I worshiped every Sunday, had me convinced that I could make a difference. And, there was mama and papa, two poorly educated but exceedingly wise people, who convinced my ten siblings and me that we could be anything we wanted to be. Anything!

As I progressed through high school and had the opportunity to study Negro History—as it was then known—I gained a deeper appreciation for the genesis of this unrelenting faith in education as the primary pathway to freedom. This faith was proclaimed by preachers, possessed by parents, and reinforced by teachers. Whether one was a proponent of W.E.B. Dubois or Booker T. Washington, Benjamin Mays or Carter G. Woodson, Howard Thurmen or Samuel Proctor, history is clear that these intellectual giants espoused a philosophy and a theology designed to liberate people who suffered the negative physical, psychological, and spiritual effects of slavery. Education was and continues to be viewed as the cornerstone and the centerpiece—the foundation—upon which freedom and opportunity for African Americans rest.

When taught by my parents nearly forty years ago to believe that I could be anything that I wished to be, I was too young to fully appreciate what that all meant. In retrospect, I must acknowledge that being "anything" I wished to be did not include, in my mind, being chancellor at two universities or vice president of a multi-campus university system with nearly one hundred thousand students—all predominantly Caucasian. My faith during my formative years was so influenced by segregation and racism during the 1950s and the 1960s that I limited my early thoughts of "anything" to include things that related to African Americans only.

My more systematic analysis of the conditions of African Americans during college and my involvement in the civil rights movement of the 1960s freed me of limiting my aspirations to opportunities that had been shaped by slavery and reinforced by racism and segregation. I came to appreciate more fully what Gandhi meant when he proclaimed that "we must be the change that we wish to see in the world." I came to more fully appreciate why Governors Orval Faubus and George Wallace took such a passionate and fervent stance against integration at the K–12 and the university levels. They realized that education—quality education—wherever it is delivered is a liberator of people and that it prepares them for opportunities not otherwise possible. It was this recognition that propelled me along the path of becoming an academic leader.

What follows are what I view as the prerequisites for succeeding as an academic leader in higher education. These observations are based on more than three decades of work as an administrator, mentor, protégé, and teacher. The true beneficiaries of successful leadership in the Academy are students and communities of color wherever they are found.

Establishing a goal: Success in becoming an academic leader, as distinguished from one who aspires to be a manager in higher education, begins with a clear response to several basic questions, "Why do I want to lead? What do I wish to accomplish? What strategies can I employ to maximize my chances of becoming a leader and my success upon achieving my goal?" Each of these questions speaks to the importance of career development and planning. To illustrate the importance of planning and the necessity for a plan, consider this advice from someone who once observed, "if you don't know where you are going any road will get you there." One's responses to the aforementioned questions are what establish the framework for preparing for academic leadership.

Preparation: Clearly the most significant requirement for effective leadership is preparation. The preparation of which I speak must occur on at least three levels. The first of these entails obtaining the academic credentials that will enable one to engage in the basic activities of the academy—namely teaching, scholarship, and service. The area in which one obtains his/her degree is less important than where these credentials are obtained. Some might naively argue that a terminal degree from a regionally accredited university is all that matters. Quite the contrary. Anyone who aspires to teach or lead in a Research I university, for example, would be well advised to obtain a terminal degree from such a university. While there are always exceptions, being screened "out of consideration" because of where one obtained a degree is an all too common phenomena to be ignored. In addition to earning one's graduate credentials from a nationally recognized university, it is important to have excelled academically.

The second critical element of preparation is experience—experience as a teacher and as a scholar. Those with the best opportunity for academic leadership are those who have distinguished themselves first as teachers and second as scholars whose record reflects a productive pattern of research and professional development. A pattern of scholarship includes authoring books, publishing articles, presenting at conferences, and engaging in professional service and relevant consultation. Similarly, those whose portfolio reflects creativity and success in designing, implementing, and assessing a wide array of programs and services that help the institution achieve its mission and vision are more likely to succeed in securing leadership positions than those who have pursued a less adventuresome route. While one should always seek to avoid being perceived as a "job-hopper," as a rule, one's opportunity for leadership in higher education is significantly enhanced if he/she can point to a record of achievement at more than one institution and in more than one program or department.

To master the scholarship and experience components of preparation requires self-discipline, focus, and an investment in one's own development. Having been a campus chief executive officer for many years, I know from experience that few institutions can afford to fully fund a program of professional development for their faculty and staff. In fact, what most universities provide is but a penance in relation to what is needed. With careful planning, pooling resources with colleagues, and securing grants, funding for an active professional development plan can be sustained.

The third and final element of preparation for academic leadership pertains to crafting for oneself a rationale for pursuing such work. To succeed long-term as an academic leader, it is my contention that one must be propelled by more than money, power, and the trappings that are often associated with leadership. True academic leaders are those who have committed themselves to being vessels of change, opportunity, and excellence.

Mentoring: A conversation with a broad sample of successful leaders would no doubt reveal a great deal about their motivations for choosing to pursue a career as an academic leader, as well as the strategies they used to achieve that goal. The common denominator for nearly every leader that I have known was the presence and active involvement of a mentor. As for me, my mentors have come in all sizes, ages, races, and genders, however, they were all committed to my success as a person, as a student, and as a leader. They told me what I needed to hear but did not particularly want to hear—complimentary and non-complimentary. They encouraged and challenged me when I preferred they remain silent. Above all, they advocated for me even in my absence. My advice to all who aspire to become academic leaders is twofold: get yourself a mentor and be the ideal protégé. In doing so, you will discover just how much there is to learn from those who have experienced the many dimensions of success.

Persistence: By persistence, I mean not being deterred from pursuing your dreams and objectives no matter what the odds-makers say about your chances for success. By persistence, I mean being so tenacious and focused that not even your own fears and doubts can survive the strength and the force of your faith for more than a fragment of a moment.

To get you through the rough spots, and help you overcome the barriers, I would strongly encourage you to memorize some poetry for your soul. Not only memorize it, but internalize it and to have it become the fuel source for those dark days when members of the academic establishment attempt to derail you. Memorize a stanza or two that lets you put your challenges in perspective by reminding you of what life was like for the people who cleared the path for you to travel. I call your attention to Langston Hughes' poem,

Mother to Son
Well, son, I'll tell you:
Life for me ain't been no crystal stair.

It's had tacks in it,
And splinters,
And boards torn up,
And places with no carpet on the floor—
Bare.
But all the time
I'se been a-climbin' on,
And reachin' landin's,
And turnin' corners,
And sometimes goin' in the dark
Where there ain't been no light.
So boy, don't you turn back.
Don't you set down on the steps
'Cause you finds it's kinder hard.
Don't you fall now—
For I'se still goin', honey,
I'se still climbin',
And life for me ain't been no crystal stair.

—Langston Hughes

Vision, faith and focus: The founding of Harvard College in 1636 along with the founding of the first Historically Black College more than two hundred years later was based on a confluence of precepts that have had a profound impact on the Academy. Today those who aspire to be educational leaders must be guided by the vision that higher education can be a vehicle for transforming individual lives and for reforming society. They must have the focus to direct their energy toward creating the change they envision. And, they must have the faith that they can create an Academy where equity, excellence, and diversity define the essence of the higher education enterprise.

Passion: During my tenure in higher education I have had the opportunity to meet many people in educational leadership positions. Nearly all of these have been intelligent and articulate, but few seem to possess the passion to galvanize the support, internally or externally, to successfully transform their institution from being good to being excellent. If the Academy is to become more responsive to societal needs generally, and to the needs of people of color in particular, it must be led by people who inspire confidence, instill hope, and educate students who are committed to truth, wisdom and justice.

To lead with passion requires knowledge, commitment, faith, and the belief that one can be the change they wish to see in the world.

INDEX

Note: A *t* following a page number denotes a table.

Academic imperialism, 103
Academic leadership prerequisites, 189–193
  establishing a goal, 190–191
  mentoring, 192
  passion, 193
  persistence, 192–193
  preparation, 191–192
  vision, faith, and focus, 193
Academicians, definitions and titles of, 33
Academies, ancient African, 49
Academy, African American men in, xi–xii
Accepting, 166–167
Access and success framework, 161–170
Achievement gap, 74, 76
"Acting white," 91
Actualizing, 166–167
Adopting, 166–167
Affective knowing, 150, 156–157
Affirmative action, 16, 164–165
African American Electronic Culture
  (iAACE), 157–158
African American females
  degree attainment compared to African
    American males, 21–23
  and relationships with African American
    men, 64
African American men
  and Afrocentricity, 141–146
  as athletes, 69
  corporal punishment and, 5–6
  cultural discontinuity of, 4–5
  educational deficits, 3
  elders in the Academy, 176–177, 182–186
  entrance and exit patterns in colleges and
    universities, 16, 18, 20, 17*t*–20*t*

  gaining access to American Academy,
    xi–xii
  history of in America, 1
  homicide rates, 2
  and Ph.Ds, 73–77
  and the pitfalls of higher education, 68–69
  poor achievement studies, 6–8
  prison statistics, 2
  school suspensions, 6
  suicide rates, 2–3
  teacher expectations of, 3–4, 70, 163
African de-spiritualization
  (de-Africanization), 175
African Diaspora, 49
African family
  in the Academy, 184–186
  tradition of, 178–180
African intellectual tradition, 51–54
African traditions, 46–54
  common views of, 52
Africans in America (BBC documentary),
  175–176
Afrikan Americans, 80
Afrocentric curriculum, 142
Afrocentric Idea, The (Asante), 142
Afrocentricity
  and African American male college
    students, 141–146
  father of, xvii
Afrocentricity (Asante), 142
Afrocentrism, defined, 8
Akbar, Na'im, xvi, 30–41, 85, 138
  Community of Self, The, 134
  Psychology and Human Transformation, 134
Akbar, Na'im Consultants, 30